THE ADVANCE OF ENGLISH POETRY
IN THE TWENTIETH CENTURY

THE
ADVANCE OF ENGLISH POETRY
IN THE TWENTIETH CENTURY

BY

WILLIAM LYON PHELPS

O! 't is an easy thing
To write and sing;
But to write true, unfeigned verse
Is very hard!
      —HENRY VAUGHAN, 1655

KENNIKAT PRESS
Port Washington, N. Y./London

THE ADVANCE OF ENGLISH POETRY
IN THE TWENTIETH CENTURY

First published in 1918
Reissued in 1970 by Kennikat Press
Library of Congress Catalog Card No: 72-111314
SBN 8046-0934-9

Manufactured by Taylor Publishing Company   Dallas, Texas

ESSAY AND GENERAL LITERATURE INDEX REPRINT SERIES

ACKNOWLEDGMENT

The publishers of the works of the poets from whom illustrative passages are cited in this volume, have courteously and generously given permission, and I take this opportunity of expressing my thanks to The Macmillan Company, who publish the poems of Thomas Hardy, William Watson, John Masefield, W. W. Gibson, Ralph Hodgson, W. B. Yeats, "A. E.," James Stephens, E. A. Robinson, Vachel Lindsay, Amy Lowell, Edgar Lee Masters, Sara Teasdale, J. C. Underwood, Fannie Stearns Davis; to Henry Holt and Company, who publish the poems of Walter De La Mare, Edward Thomas, Padraic Colum, Robert Frost, Louis Untermeyer, Sarah N. Cleghorn, Margaret Widdemer, Carl Sandburg, and the two poems by Henry A. Beers quoted in this book, which appeared in *The Ways of Yale;* to Charles Scribner's Sons, publishers of the poems of George Santayana, Henry Van Dyke, Corinne Roosevelt Robinson, Alan Seeger; to Houghton, Mifflin and Company, publishers of the poems of Josephine Peabody, Anna Hempstead Branch, and W. A. Bradley's *Old Christmas;* to The John Lane Company, publishers of the poems of Stephen Phillips, Rupert Brooke, Benjamin R. C. Low; to the Frederick A. Stokes Company, publishers of the poems of Alfred Noyes, Robert Nichols, Thomas MacDonagh, Witter Bynner; to the Yale University Press, publishers of the poems of W. A. Percy, Brian Hooker, W. R. Benét, C. M. Lewis, E. B. Reed, F. E. Pierce, R. B. Glaenzer, L. W. Dodd; to the Oxford University Press, publishers of the poems of Robert Bridges; to Alfred A. Knopf, publisher of the poems of W. H. Davies; to John W. Luce and Company, publishers of the poems of John M. Synge; to Harper and Brothers, publishers of William Watson's *The Man Who Saw;* to Longmans, Green and Company, publishers of the poems of Willoughby Weaving; to Double-day, Page and Company, publishers of the poems of James Elroy Flecker; to the Bobbs-Merrill Company, publishers of the poems of W. D. Foulke; to Thomas B. Mosher, publisher of the poems of W. A. Bradley, W. E. Henley; to James T. White and Company, publishers of William Griffiths; Francis Thompson's *In No Strange Land* appeared in the *Athenæum* and *Lilium Regis* in the *Dublin Review;* the poem by Scudder Middleton appeared in *Contemporary Verse,* that by Allan Updegraff in the *Forum,* and that by D. H. Lawrence in *Georgian Poetry* 1913–15, published by The Poetry Bookshop, London.

The titles of the several volumes of poems with dates of publication are given in my text.

I am grateful to the Yale University Librarians for help on bibliographical matters, and to Professor Charles Bennett and Byrne Hackett, Esquire, for giving some facts about the Irish poets.

W. L. P.

PREFACE

The material in this volume originally appeared in *The Bookman,* 1917–1918. It is now published with much addition and revision.

The Great War has had a stimulating effect on the production of poetry. Professional poets have been spokesmen for the inarticulate, and a host of hitherto unknown writers have acquired reputation. An immense amount of verse has been written by soldiers in active service. The Allies are fighting for human liberty, and this Idea is an inspiration. It is comforting to know that some who have made the supreme sacrifice will be remembered through their printed poems, and it is a pleasure to aid in giving them public recognition.

Furthermore, the war, undertaken by Germany to dominate the world by crushing the power of Great Britain, has united all English-speaking people as nothing else could have done. In this book, all poetry written in the English language is considered as belonging to English literature.

It should be apparent that I am not a sectarian in art, but am thankful for poetry wherever I find it. I have endeavored to make clear the artistic, intellectual, and spiritual significance of many of our contemporary English-writing poets. The difficulties of such an undertaking are obvious; but there are two standards of measure. One is the literature of the past, the other is the life of today. I judge every new poet by these two tests. The fashion in poetry is always swinging from Spenser to Donne, and back again; from Tennyson to Thompson, and back again. At this moment the influence of John Donne is wider than at any time since the mid-seventeenth century. Our latest extras in flesh and spirit can hardly surpass his candour or his ecstasy. Meanwhile, amid the winds of doctrine and the gusts of sentiment, the old tunes are heard. With reference to the life and thought of today, many of our poets may be called reflectors and interpreters.

I have given some biographical detail, because it is important and not always easy to find.

W. L. P.

Yale University,
Tuesday, 4 June 1918.

CONTENTS

CHAPTER   PAGE

I   SOME CONTRASTS—HENLEY, THOMPSON, HARDY, KIPLING   1

II   PHILLIPS, WATSON, NOYES, HOUSMAN   35

III   JOHN MASEFIELD   71

IV   GIBSON AND HODGSON   98

V   BROOKE, FLECKER, DE LA MARE, AND OTHERS . .   124

VI   THE IRISH POETS   157

VII   AMERICAN VETERANS AND FORERUNNERS . . .   194

VIII   VACHEL LINDSAY AND ROBERT FROST   213

IX   AMY LOWELL, ANNA BRANCH, EDGAR LEE MASTERS, LOUIS UNTERMEYER   245

X   SARA TEASDALE, ALAN SEEGER, AND OTHERS . .   277

XI   A GROUP OF YALE POETS   312

APPENDIX   335

INDEX   339

THE ADVANCE OF ENGLISH POETRY
IN THE TWENTIETH CENTURY

THE ADVANCE OF ENGLISH POETRY
IN THE TWENTIETH CENTURY

CHAPTER I

SOME CONTRASTS—HENLEY, THOMPSON, HARDY, KIPLING

Meaning of the word "advance"—the present widespread interest in poetry—the spiritual warfare—Henley and Thompson —Thomas Hardy a prophet in literature—*The Dynasts*—his atheism—his lyrical power—Kipling the Victorian—his future possibilities—Robert Bridges—Robert W. Service.

Although English poetry of the twentieth century seems inferior to the poetry of the Victorian epoch, for in England there is no one equal to Tennyson or Browning, and in America no one equal to Poe, Emerson, or Whitman, still it may fairly be said that we can discern an advance in English poetry not wholly to be measured either by the calendar and the clock, or by sheer beauty of expression. I should not like to say that Joseph Conrad is a greater writer than Walter Scott; and yet in *The Nigger of the Narcissus* there is an intellectual sincerity, a profound psychological analysis, a resolute intention to discover and to reveal the final truth concerning the children of the sea, that one would hardly expect to find in the works of the wonderful Wizard. Shakespeare was surely a

1

greater poet than Wordsworth; but the man of the Lakes, with the rich inheritance of two centuries, had a capital of thought unpossessed by the great dramatist, which, invested by his own genius, enabled him to draw returns from nature undreamed of by his mighty predecessor. Wordsworth was not great enough to have written *King Lear;* and Shakespeare was not late enough to have written *Tintern Abbey.* Every poet lives in his own time, has a share in its scientific and philosophical advance, and his individuality is coloured by his experience. Even if he take a Greek myth for a subject, he will regard it and treat it in the light of the day when he sits down at his desk, and addresses himself to the task of composition. It is absurd to call the Victorians old-fashioned or out of date; they were as intensely modern as we, only their modernity is naturally not ours.

A great work of art is never old-fashioned; because it expresses in final form some truth about human nature, and human nature never changes—in comparison with its primal elements, the mountains are ephemeral. A drama dealing with the impalpable human soul is more likely to stay true than a treatise on geology. This is the notable advantage that works of art have over works of science, the advantage of being and remaining true. No matter how important the contribution of scientific books, they are alloyed with inevitable error, and after the death of their authors must be constantly revised by lesser men, improved by smaller minds; whereas the masterpieces of poetry, drama and fiction cannot be revised, because they are always true. The latest edition of a work of science is the most valuable; of literature, the earliest.

Apart from the natural and inevitable advance in poetry that every year witnesses, we are living in an age characterized both in England and in America by a remarkable advance in poetry as a vital influence. Earth's oldest inhabitants probably cannot remember a time when there were so many poets in activity, when so many books of poems were not only read, but bought and sold, when poets were held in such high esteem, when so much was written and published about poetry, when the mere forms of verse were the theme of such hot debate. There are thousands of minor poets, but poetry has ceased to be a minor subject. Any one mentally alive cannot escape it. Poetry is in the air, and everybody is catching it. Some American magazines are exclusively devoted to the printing of contemporary poems; anthologies are multiplying, not "Keepsakes" and "Books of Gems," but thick volumes representing the bumper crop of the year. Many poets are reciting their poems to big, eager, enthusiastic audiences, and the atmosphere is charged with the melodies of ubiquitous minstrelsy.

The time is ripe for the appearance of a great poet. A vast audience is gazing expectantly at a stage crowded with subordinate actors, waiting for the Master to appear. The Greek dramatists were sure of their public; so were the Russian novelists; so were the German musicians. The "conditions" for poetry are intensified by reason of the Great War. We have got everything except the Genius. And the paradox is that although the Genius may arise out of right conditions, he may not; he may come like a thief in the night. The contrast between public interest in poetry in 1918 and in 1830, for an illustration, is unescapable. At that time the critics and the magazine writers assured the world that "poetry is dead." Ambitious young authors were gravely advised not to attempt anything in verse—as though youth ever listened to advice! Many critics went so far as to insist that the temper of the age was not "adapted" to poetry, that not only was there no interest in it, but that even if the Man should appear, he would find it impossible to sing in such a time and to such a coldly indifferent audience. And yet at that precise moment, Tennyson launched his "chiefly lyrical" volume, and Browning was speedily to follow.

Man is ever made humble by the facts of life; and even literary critics cannot altogether ignore them. Let us not then make the mistake of being too sure of the immediate future; nor the mistake of overestimating our contemporary poets; nor the mistake of despising the giant Victorians. Let us devoutly thank God that poetry has come into its own; that the modern poet, in public estimation, is a Hero; that no one has to apologize either for reading or for writing verse. An age that loves poetry with the passion characteristic of the twentieth century is not a flat or materialistic age. We are not disobedient unto the heavenly vision.

In the world of thought and spirit this is essentially a fighting age. The old battle between the body and the soul, between Paganism and Christianity, was never so hot as now, and those who take refuge in neutrality receive contempt. Pan and Jesus Christ have never had so many enthusiastic followers. We Christians believe our Leader rose from the dead, and the followers of Pan say their god never died at all. It is significant that at the beginning of the twentieth century two English poets wrote side by side, each of whom unconsciously waged an irreconcilable conflict with the other, and each of whom speaks from the grave today to a concourse of followers. These two poets did not "flourish" in the twentieth century, because the disciple of the bodily Pan was a cripple, and the disciple of the spiritual Christ was a gutter-snipe; but they both lived, lived abundantly, and wrote real poetry. I refer to William Ernest Henley, who died in 1903, and to Francis Thompson, who died in 1907.

Both Henley and Thompson loved the crowded streets of London, but they saw different visions there. Henley felt in the dust and din of the city the irresistible urge of spring, the invasion of the smell of distant meadows; the hurly-burly bearing witness to the annual conquest of Pan.

> Here in this radiant and immortal street
> Lavishly and omnipotently as ever
> In the open hills, the undissembling dales,
> The laughing-places of the juvenile earth.
> For lo! the wills of man and woman meet,
> Meet and are moved, each unto each endeared
> As once in Eden's prodigal bowers befel,
> To share his shameless, elemental mirth
> In one great act of faith, while deep and strong,
> Incomparably nerved and cheered,
> The enormous heart of London joys to beat
> To the measures of his rough, majestic song:
> The lewd, perennial, overmastering spell
> That keeps the rolling universe ensphered
> And life and all for which life lives to long
> Wanton and wondrous and for ever well.

The *London Voluntaries* of Henley, from which the above is a fair example, may have suggested something to Vachel Lindsay both in their irregular singing quality and in the direction, borrowed from notation, which accompanies each one, *Andante con moto, Scherzando, Largo e mesto, Allegro maestoso*. Henley's Pagan resistance to Puritan morality and convention, constantly exhibited positively in his verse, and negatively in his defiant Introduction to the Works of Burns and in the famous paper on R. L. S., is the main characteristic of his mind and temperament. He was by nature a rebel—a rebel against the Anglican God and against English social conventions. He loved all fighting rebels, and one of his most spirited poems deals affectionately with our Southern Confederate soldiers, in the last days of their hopeless struggle. His most famous lyric is an assertion of the indomitable human will in the presence of adverse destiny. This trumpet blast has awakened sympathetic echoes from all sorts and conditions of men, although that creedless Christian, James Whitcomb Riley, regarded it with genial contempt, thinking that the philosophy it represented was not only futile, but dangerous, in that it ignored the deepest facts of human life. He once asked to have the poem read aloud to him, as he had forgotten its exact words, and when the reader finished impressively

> I am the Master of my fate:
> I am the Captain of my soul—

"The *hell* you are," said Riley with a laugh.

Henley is, of course, interesting not merely because of his paganism, and robust worldliness; he had the poet's imagination and gift of expression. He loved to take a familiar idea fixed in a familiar phrase, and write a lovely musical variation on the theme. I do not think he ever wrote anything more beautiful than his setting of the phrase "Over the hills and far away," which appealed to his memory much as the three words "Far-far-away" affected Tennyson. No one can read this little masterpiece without that wonderful sense of melody lingering in the mind after the voice of the singer is silent.

Where forlorn sunsets flare and fade
  On desolate sea and lonely sand,
Out of the silence and the shade
  What is the voice of strange command
Calling you still, as friend calls friend
  With love that cannot brook delay,
To rise and follow the ways that wend
  Over the hills and far away?

Hark in the city, street on street
  A roaring reach of death and life,
Of vortices that clash and fleet
  And ruin in appointed strife,
Hark to it calling, calling clear,
  Calling until you cannot stay
From dearer things than your own most dear
  Over the hills and far away.

Out of the sound of ebb and flow,
  Out of the sight of lamp and star,
It calls you where the good winds blc *ʀ*,
  And the unchanging meadows are:
From faded hopes and hopes agleam,
  It calls you, calls you night and day
Beyond the dark into the dream
  Over the hills and far away.

In temperament Henley was an Elizabethan.
Ben Jonson might have irritated him, but he would
have got along very well with Kit Marlowe. He
was an Elizabethan in the spaciousness of his
mind, in his robust salt-water breeziness, in his
hearty, spontaneous singing, and in his deification
of the human will. The English novelist, Miss
Willcocks, a child of the twentieth century, has
remarked, "It is by their will that we recognize
the Elizabethans, by the will that drove them over

the seas of passion, as well as over the seas that ebb and flow with the salt tides. . . . For, from a sensitive correspondence with environment our race has passed into another stage; it is marked now by a passionate desire for the mastery of life —a desire, spiritualized in the highest lives, materialized in the lowest, so to mould environment that the lives to come may be shaped to our will. It is this which accounts for the curious likeness in our today with that of the Elizabethans.''

As Henley was an Elizabethan, so his brilliant contemporary, Francis Thompson, was a ''metaphysical,'' a man of the seventeenth century. Like Emerson, he is closer in both form and spirit to the mystical poets that followed the age of Shakespeare than he is to any other group or school. One has only to read Donne, Crashaw, and Vaughan to recognize the kinship. Like these three men of genius, Thompson was not only profoundly spiritual—he was aflame with religious passion. He was exalted in a mystical ecstasy, all a wonder and a wild desire. He was an inspired poet, careless of method, careless of form, careless of thought-sequences. The zeal for God's house had eaten him up. His poetry is like the burning bush, revealing God in the fire. His strange figures of speech, the molten metal of his language, the sincerity of his faith, have given to his poems a persuasive influence which is beginning to be felt far and wide, and which, I believe, will never die. One critic complains that the young men of Oxford and Cambridge have forsaken Tennyson, and now read only Francis Thompson. He need not be alarmed; these young men will all come back to Tennyson, for sooner or later, everybody comes back to Tennyson. It is rather a matter of joy that Thompson's religious poetry can make the hearts of young men burn within them. Young men are right in hating conventional, empty phrases, words that have lost all hitting power, hollow forms and bloodless ceremonies. Thompson's lips were touched with a live coal from the altar.

Francis Thompson walked with God. Instead of seeking God, as so many high-minded folk have done in vain, Thompson had the real and overpowering sensation that God was seeking him. The Hound of Heaven was everlastingly after him, pursuing him with the certainty of capture. In trying to escape, he found torment; in surrender, the peace that passes all understanding. That extraordinary poem, which thrillingly describes the eager, searching love of God, like a father looking for a lost child and determined to find him, might be taken as a modern version of the one hundred and thirty-ninth psalm, perhaps the most marvellous of all religious masterpieces.

Thou compassest my path and my lying down, and art acquainted with all my ways.
Thou hast beset me behind and before, and laid thine hand upon me.
Whither shall I go from thy spirit? or whither shall I flee from thy presence?

If I ascend up into heaven, thou art there; if I make my bed
in hell, behold, thou art there.
If I take the wings of the morning, and dwell in the uttermost
parts of the sea;
Even there shall thy hand lead me, and thy right hand shall
hold me.

The highest spiritual poetry is not that which
portrays soul-hunger, the bitterness of the weary
search for God; it is that which reveals an intense consciousness of the all-enveloping Divine
Presence.   Children do not seek the love of their
parents; they can not escape its searching, eager,
protecting power.   We know how Dr. Johnson
was affected by the lines

> Quærens me sedisti lassus
> Redemisti crucem passus
> Tantus labor non sit passus.

Francis Thompson's long walks by day and by
night had magnificent company.   In the country,
in the streets of London, he was attended by sera-
phim and cherubim.   The heavenly visions were
more real to him than London Bridge.   Just as
when we travel far from those we love, we are
brightly aware of their presence, and know that
their affection is a greater reality than the scenery from the train window, so Thompson would
have it that the angels were all about us.   They do
not live in some distant Paradise, the only gate
to which is death—they are here now, and their
element is the familiar atmosphere of earth.

Shortly after he died, there was found among

his papers a bit of manuscript verse, called "In No Strange Land." Whether it was a first draft which he meant to revise, or whether he intended it for publication, we cannot tell; but despite the roughnesses of rhythm—which take us back to some of Donne's shaggy and splendid verse—the thought is complete. It is one of the great poems of the twentieth century, and expresses the essence of Thompson's religion.

"IN NO STRANGE LAND"

O world invisible, we view thee:
   O world intangible, we touch thee:
O world unknowable, we know thee:
   Inapprehensible, we clutch thee!

Does the fish soar to find the ocean,
   The eagle plunge to find the air,
That we ask of the stars in motion
   If they have rumour of thee there?

Not where the wheeling systems darken,
   And our benumbed conceiving soars:
The drift of pinions, would we harken,
   Beats at our own clay-shuttered doors.

The angels keep their ancient places—
   Turn but a stone, and start a wing!
'Tis ye, 'tis your estrangèd faces
   That miss the many-splendoured thing.

But (when so sad thou canst not sadder)
   Cry; and upon thy so sore loss
Shall shine the traffic of Jacob's ladder
   Pitched betwixt Heaven and Charing Cross.

Yea, in the night, my Soul, my daughter,
  Cry, clinging heaven by the hems:
And lo, Christ walking on the water,
  Not of Gennesareth, but Thames!

Thompson planned a series of Ecclesiastical
Ballads, of which he completed only two—*Lilium
Regis* and *The Veteran of Heaven*. These were
found among his papers, and were published in
the January-April 1910 number of the *Dublin Review*. Both are great poems; but *Lilium Regis*
is made doubly impressive by the present war.
With the clairvoyance of approaching death,
Thompson foresaw the world-struggle, the temporary eclipse of the Christian Church, and its ultimate triumph. The Lily of the King is Christ's
Holy Church. I do not see how any one can read
this poem without a thrill.

LILIUM REGIS

O Lily of the King! low lies thy silver wing,
And long has been the hour of thine unqueening;
And thy scent of Paradise on the night-wind spills its sighs,
Nor any take the secrets of its meaning.
O Lily of the King! I speak a heavy thing,
O patience, most sorrowful of daughters!
Lo, the hour is at hand for the troubling of the land,
And red shall be the breaking of the waters.

Sit fast upon thy stalk, when the blast shall with thee talk,
With the mercies of the king for thine awning;
And the just understand that thine hour is at hand,
Thine hour at hand with power in the dawning.
When the nations lie in blood, and their kings a broken brood,
Look up, O most sorrowful of daughters!

Lift up thy head and hark what sounds are in the dark,
For His feet are coming to thee on the waters!

O Lily of the King! I shall not see, that sing,
I shall not see the hour of thy queening!
But my song shall see, and wake, like a flower that dawn-winds
    shake,
And sigh with joy the odours of its meaning.
O Lily of the King, remember then the thing
That this dead mouth sang; and thy daughters,
As they dance before His way, sing there on the Day,
What I sang when the Night was on the waters!

There is a man of genius living in England today who has been writing verse for sixty years,
but who received no public recognition as a poet
until the twentieth century. This man is Thomas
Hardy. He has the double distinction of being
one of the great Victorian novelists, and one of
the most notable poets of the twentieth century.
At nearly eighty years of age, he is in full intellectual vigour, enjoys a creative power in verse
that we more often associate with youth, and
writes poetry that in matter and manner belongs
distinctly to our time. He could not possibly be
omitted from any survey of contemporary production.

As is so commonly the case with distinguished
novelists, Thomas Hardy practised verse before
prose. From 1860 to 1870 he wrote many poems,
some of which appear among the Love Lyrics in
Time's Laughingstocks, 1909. Then he began a
career in prose fiction which has left him today
without a living rival in the world. In 1898, with

the volume called *Wessex Poems,* embellished with illustrations from his own hand, he challenged criticism as a professional poet. The moderate but definite success of this collection emboldened him to produce in 1901, *Poems of the Past and Present.* In 1904, 1906, 1908, were issued successively the three parts of *The Dynasts,* a thoroughly original and greatly-planned epical drama of the Napoleonic wars. This was followed by three books of verse, *Time's Laughingstocks* in 1909, *Satires of Circumstance,* 1914, and *Moments of Vision,* 1917; and he is a familiar and welcome guest in contemporary magazines.

Is it possible that when, at the close of the nineteenth century, Thomas Hardy formally abandoned prose for verse, he was either consciously or subconsciously aware of the coming renaissance of poetry? Certainly his change in expression had more significance than an individual caprice. It is a notable fact that the present poetic revival, wherein are enlisted so many enthusiastic youthful volunteers, should have had as one of its prophets and leaders a veteran of such power and fame. Perhaps Mr. Hardy would regard his own personal choice as no factor; the Immanent and Unconscious Will had been busy in his mind, for reasons unknown to him, unknown to man, least of all known to Itself. Leslie Stephen once remarked, ''The deepest thinker is not really—though we often use the phrase—in advance of his day so much as in the line along which advance takes place.''

Looking backward from the year 1918, we may see some new meaning in the spectacle of two modern leaders in fiction, Hardy and Meredith, each preferring as a means of expression poetry to prose, each thinking his own verse better than his novels, and each writing verse that in substance and manner belongs more to the twentieth than to the nineteenth century. Meredith always said that fiction was his kitchen wench; poetry was his Muse.

The publication of poems written when he was about twenty-five is interesting to students of Mr. Hardy's temperament, for they show that he was then as complete, though perhaps not so philosophical a pessimist, as he is now. The present world-war may seem to him a vindication of his despair, and therefore proof of the blind folly of those who pray to Our Father in Heaven. He is, though I think not avowedly so, an adherent of the philosophy of Schopenhauer and von Hartmann. The primal force, from which all things proceed, is the Immanent Will. The Will is unconscious and omnipotent. It is superhuman only in power, lacking intelligence, foresight, and any sense of ethical values. In *The Dynasts*, Mr. Hardy has written an epic illustration of the doctrines of pessimism.

Supernatural machinery and celestial inspiration have always been more or less conventional in

the Epic. Ancient writers invoked the Muse.
When Milton began his great task, he wished to
produce something classic in form and Christian
in spirit. He found an admirable solution of his
problem in a double invocation—first of the Heavenly Muse of Mount Sinai, second, of the Holy
Spirit. In the composition of *In Memoriam,*
Tennyson knew that an invocation of the Muse
would give an intolerable air of artificiality to
the poem; he therefore, in the introductory
stanzas, offered up a prayer to the Son of God.
Now it was impossible for Mr. Hardy to make
use of Greek Deities, or of Jehovah, or of any
revelation of God in Christ; to his mind all three
equally belonged to the lumber-room of discredited
and discarded myth. He believes that any conception of the Primal Force as a Personality is
not only obsolete among thinking men and women,
but that it is unworthy of modern thought. It is
perhaps easy to mistake our own world of thought
for the thought of the world.

In his Preface, written with assurance and
dignity, Mr. Hardy says: "The wide prevalence
of the Monistic theory of the Universe forbade, in
this twentieth century, the importation of Divine
personages from any antique Mythology as ready-
made sources or channels of Causation, even in
verse, and excluded the celestial machinery of, say,
Paradise Lost, as peremptorily as that of the
Iliad or the *Eddas.* And the abandonment of the
masculine pronoun in allusions to the First or

Fundamental Energy seemed a necessary and logical consequence of the long abandonment by thinkers of the anthropomorphic conception of the same.'' Accordingly he arranged a group of Phantom Intelligences that supply adequately a Chorus and a philosophical basis for his world-drama.

Like Browning in the original preface to *Paracelsus,* our author expressly disclaims any intention of writing a play for the stage. It is ''intended simply for mental performance,'' and ''Whether mental performance alone may not eventually be the fate of all drama other than that of contemporary or frivolous life, is a kindred question not without interest.'' The question has been since answered in another way than that implied, not merely by the success of community drama, but by the actual production of *The Dynasts* on the London stage under the direction of the brilliant and audacious Granville Barker. I would give much to have witnessed this experiment, which Mr. Barker insists was successful.

Whether *The Dynasts* will finally take a place among the world's masterpieces of literature or not, must of course be left to future generations to decide. Two things are clear. The publication of the second and third parts distinctly raised public opinion of the work as a whole, and now that it is ten years old, we know that no man on earth except Mr. Hardy could have written it.

To produce this particular epic required a poet, a prose master, a dramatist, a philosopher, and an architect. Mr. Hardy is each and all of the five, and by no means least an architect. The plan of the whole thing, in one hundred and thirty scenes, which seemed at first confused, now appears in retrospect orderly; and the projection of the various geographical scenes is thoroughly architectonic.

If the work fails to survive, it will be because of its low elevation on the purely literary side. In spite of occasional powerful phrases, as

> What corpse is curious on the longitude
> And situation of his cemetery!

the verse as a whole wants beauty of tone and felicity of diction. It is more like a map than a painting. One has only to recall the extraordinary charm of the Elizabethans to understand why so many pages in *The Dynasts* arouse only an intellectual interest. But no one can read the whole drama without an immense respect for the range and the grasp of the author's mind. Furthermore, every one of its former admirers ought to reread it in 1918. The present world-war gives to this Napoleonic epic an acute and prophetic interest nothing short of astounding.

A considerable number of Mr. Hardy's poems are concerned with the idea of God, apparently never far from the author's mind. I suppose he thinks of God every day. Yet his faith is the opposite of that expressed in the *Hound of Heaven* —in few words, it seems to be, "Resist the Lord, and He will flee from you." Mr. Hardy is not content with banishing God from the realm of modern thought; he is not content merely with killing Him; he means to give Him a decent burial, with fitting obsequies. And there is a long procession of mourners, some of whom are both worthy and distinguished. In the interesting poem, *God's Funeral,* written in 1908–1910, which begins

> I saw a slowly stepping train—
> Lined on the brows, scoop-eyed and bent and hoar—
> Following in files across a twilit plain
> A strange and mystic form the foremost bore

the development of the conception of God through human history is presented with skill in concision. He was man-like at first, then an amorphous cloud, then endowed with mighty wings, then jealous, fierce, yet long-suffering and full of mercy.

> And, tricked by our own early dream
> And need of solace, we grew self-deceived,
> Our making soon our maker did we dream,
> And what we had imagined we believed.

> Till, in Time's stayless stealthy swing,
> Uncompromising rude reality
> Mangled the Monarch of our fashioning,
> Who quavered, sank; and now has ceased to be.

Among the mourners is no less a person than the poet himself, for in former years—perhaps as a boy—he, too, had worshipped, and therefore he has no touch of contempt for those who still believe.

> I could not prop their faith: and yet
> Many I had known: with all I sympathized;
> And though struck speechless, I did not forget
> That what was mourned for, I, too, once had prized.

In the next stanza, the poet's oft-expressed belief in the wholesome, antiseptic power of pessimism is reiterated, together with a hint, that when we have once and for all put God in His grave, some better way of bearing life's burden will be found, because the new way will be based upon hard fact.

> Still, how to bear such loss I deemed
> The insistent question for each animate mind,
> And gazing, to my growing sight there seemed
> A pale yet positive gleam low down behind,
>
> Whereof, to lift the general night,
> A certain few who stood aloof had said,
> "See you upon the horizon that small light—
> Swelling somewhat?" Each mourner shook his head.
>
> And they composed a crowd of whom
> Some were right good, and many nigh the best. . . .
> Thus dazed and puzzled 'twixt the gleam and gloom
> Mechanically I followed with the rest.

This pale gleam takes on a more vivid hue in a poem written shortly after *God's Funeral*, called *A Plaint to Man*, where God remonstrates with man for having created Him at all, since His life was to be so short and so futile:

And tomorrow the whole of me disappears,
The truth should be told, and the fact be faced
That had best been faced in earlier years:

The fact of life with dependence placed
On the human heart's resource alone,
In brotherhood bonded close and graced

With loving-kindness fully blown,
And visioned help unsought, unknown.

Other poems that express what is and what ought to be the attitude of man toward God are *New Year's Eve*, *To Sincerity*, and the beautiful lyric, *Let Me Enjoy*, where Mr. Hardy has been more than usually successful in fashioning both language and rhythm into a garment worthy of the thought. No one can read *The Impercipient* without recognizing that Mr. Hardy's atheism is as honest and as sincere as the religious faith of others, and that no one regrets the blankness of his universe more than he. He would believe if he could.

Pessimism is the basis of all his verse, as it is of his prose. It is expressed not merely philosophically in poems of ideas, but over and over again concretely in poems of incident. He is a pessimist both in fancy and in fact, and after reading some of our sugary "glad" books, I find his bitter taste rather refreshing. The titles of his recent collections, *Time's Laughingstocks* and *Satires of Circumstance*, sufficiently indicate the ill fortune awaiting his personages. At his best, his lyrics written in the minor key have a noble, solemn adagio movement. At his worst—for like all poets, he is sometimes at his worst—the truth of life seems rather obstinately warped. Why should legitimate love necessarily bring misery, and illegitimate passion produce permanent happiness? And in the piece, "Ah, are you digging on my grave?" pessimism approaches a *reductio ad absurdum*.

Dramatic power, which is one of its author's greatest gifts, is frequently finely revealed. After reading *A Tramp-woman's Tragedy*, one unhesitatingly accords Mr. Hardy a place among the English writers of ballads. For this is a genuine ballad, in story, in diction, and in vigour.

Yet as a whole, and in spite of Mr. Hardy's love of the dance and of dance music, his poetry lacks grace and movement. His war poem, *Men Who March Away*, is singularly halting and awkward. His complete poetical works are interesting because they proceed from an interesting mind. His range of thought, both in reminiscence and in speculation, is immensely wide; his power of concentration recalls that of Browning.

> I have thought sometimes, and thought long and hard.
> I have stood before, gone round a serious thing,
> Tasked my whole mind to touch and clasp it close,
> As I stretch forth my arm to touch this bar.
> God and man, and what duty I owe both,—
> I dare to say I have confronted these
> In thought: but no such faculty helped here.

No such faculty alone could help Mr. Hardy to the highest peaks of poetry, any more than it

served Caponsacchi in his spiritual crisis. He
thinks interesting thoughts, because he has an original mind.   It is possible to be a great poet without possessing much intellectual wealth; just as it
is possible to be a great singer, and yet be both
shallow and dull.   The divine gift of poetry seems
sometimes as accidental as the formation of the
throat.   I do not believe that Tennyson was either
shallow or dull; but I do not think he had so rich
a mind as Thomas Hardy's, a mind so quaint, so
humorous, so sharp.   Yet Tennyson was incom-
parably a greater poet.

The greatest poetry always transports us, and
although I read and reread the Wessex poet with
never-lagging attention—I find even the drawings
in *Wessex Poems* so fascinating that I wish he
had illustrated all his books—I am always con-
scious of the time and the place.   I never get the
unmistakable spinal chill.   He has too thorough
a command of his thoughts; they never possess
him, and they never soar away with him.   Prose
may be controlled, but poetry is a possession.   Mr.
Hardy is too keenly aware of what he is about.
In spite of the fact that he has written verse all
his life, he seldom writes unwrinkled song.   He
is, in the last analysis, a master of prose who has
learned the technique of verse, and who now
chooses to express his thoughts and his observa-
tions in rime and rhythm.

The title of Mr. Hardy's latest volume of poems,
Moments of Vision, leads one to expect rifts in

the clouds—and one is not disappointed. It is perhaps characteristic of the independence of our author, that steadily preaching pessimism when the world was peaceful, he should now not be perhaps quite so sure of his creed when a larger proportion of the world's inhabitants are in pain than ever before. One of the fallacies of pessimism consists in the fact that its advocates often call a witness to the stand whose testimony counts against them. Nobody really loves life, loves this world, like your pessimist; nobody is more reluctant to leave it. He therefore, to support his argument that life is evil, calls up evidence which proves that it is brief and transitory. But if life is evil, one of its few redeeming features should be its brevity; the pessimist should look forward to death as a man in prison looks toward the day of his release. Yet this attitude toward death is almost never taken by the atheists or the pessimists, while it is the burden of many of the triumphant hymns of the Christian Church. Now, as our spokesman for pessimism approaches the end—which I fervently hope may be afar off —life seems sweet.

"FOR LIFE I HAD NEVER CARED GREATLY"

For Life I had never cared greatly,
  As worth a man's while;
  Peradventures unsought,
  Peradventures that finished in nought,
Had kept me from youth and through manhood till lately
  Unwon by its style.

In earliest years—why I know not—
I viewed it askance;
Conditions of doubt,
Conditions that slowly leaked out,
May haply have bent me to stand and to show not
Much zest for its dance.

With symphonies soft and sweet colour
It courted me then,
Till evasions seemed wrong,
Till evasions gave in to its song,
And I warmed, till living aloofly loomed duller
Than life among men.

Anew I found nought to set eyes on,
When, lifting its hand,
It uncloaked a star,
Uncloaked it from fog-damps afar,
And showed its beams burning from pole to horizon
As bright as a brand.

And so, the rough highway forgetting,
I pace hill and dale,
Regarding the sky,
Regarding the vision on high,
And thus re-illumed have no humour for letting
My pilgrimage fail.

No one of course can judge of another's happiness; but it is difficult to imagine any man on earth who has had a happier life than Mr. Hardy. He has had his own genius for company all his days; he has been successful in literary art beyond the wildest dreams of his youth; his acute perception has made the beauty of nature a million times more beautiful to him than to most of the children of men; his eye is not dim, nor his natural force abated.   He has that which should accompany old age—honour, love, obedience, troops of friends.

The last poem in *Moments of Vision* blesses rather than curses life.

AFTERWARDS

When the Present has latched its postern behind my tremu-
    lous stay
  And the May month flaps its glad green leaves like wings,
Delicate-filmed as new-spun silk, will the people say
  "He was a man who used to notice such things"?

If it be in the dusk when, like an eyelid's soundless blink,
  The dewfall-hawk comes crossing the shades to alight
Upon the wind-warped upland thorn, will a gazer think,
  "To him this must have been a familiar sight"?

If I pass during some nocturnal blackness, mothy and warm,
  When the hedgehog travels furtively over the lawn,
Will they say, "He strove that such innocent creatures should
    come to no harm,
  But he could do little for them; and now he is gone"?

If, when hearing that I have been stilled at last, they stand at
    the door,
  Watching the full-starred heavens that winter sees,
Will this thought rise on those who will meet my face no more,
  "He was one who had an eye for such mysteries"?

And will any say when my bell of quittance is heard in the
    gloom,
  And a crossing breeze cuts a pause in its outrollings,
Till they rise again, as they were a new bell's boom,
  "He hears it not now, but he used to notice such things"?

Should Mr. Hardy ever resort to prayer—which I suppose is unlikely—his prayers ought to be the best in the world. According to Coleridge, he prayeth well who loveth well both man and bird and beast; a beautiful characteristic of our great writer is his tenderness for every living thing. He will be missed by men, women, children, and by the humblest animals; and if trees have any self-consciousness, they will miss him too.

Rudyard Kipling is a Victorian poet, as Thomas Hardy is a Victorian novelist. When Tennyson died in 1892, the world, with approximate unanimity, chose the young man from the East as his successor, and for twenty-five years he has been the Laureate of the British Empire in everything but the title. In the eighteenth century, when Gray regarded the offer of the Laureateship as an insult, Mr. Alfred Austin might properly have been appointed; but after the fame of Southey, and the mighty genius of Wordsworth and of Tennyson, it was cruel to put Alfred the Little in the chair of Alfred the Great. It was not an insult to Austin, but an insult to Poetry. With the elevation of the learned and amiable Dr. Bridges in 1913, the public ceased to care who holds the office. This eminently respectable appointment silenced both opposition and applause. We can only echo the language of Gray's letter to Mason, 19 December, 1757: "I interest myself a little in the history of it, and rather wish somebody may accept it that will retrieve the credit of the thing, if it be retrievable, or ever had any credit. . . . The office itself has always humbled the professor hitherto (even in an age when kings were somebody), if he were a poor writer by making him more conspicuous, and if he were a good one by setting him at war with the little fry of his own profession, for there are poets little enough to envy even a poet-laureat." Mason was willing.

Rudyard Kipling had the double qualification of poetic. genius and of convinced Imperialism. He had received a formal accolade from the aged Tennyson, and could have carried on the tradition of British verse and British arms. Nor has any Laureate, in the history of the office, risen more magnificently to an occasion than did Mr. Kipling at the sixtieth anniversary of the reign of the Queen. Each poet made his little speech in verse, and then at the close of the ceremony, came the thrilling *Recessional,* which received as instant applause from the world as if it had been spoken to an audience. In its scriptural phraseology, in its combination of haughty pride and deep contrition, in its "holy hope and high humility," it expressed with austere majesty the genius of the English race. The soul of a great poet entered immediately into the hearts of men, there to abide for ever.

It is interesting to reflect that not the author of the *Recessional,* but the author of *Regina Cara* was duly chosen for the Laureateship. This poem by Robert Bridges appeared on the same occasion as that immortalized by Kipling, and was subsequently included in the volume of the writ-

er's poetical works, published in 1912. It shows
irreproachable reverence for Queen Victoria.
Apparently its poetical quality was satisfactory
to those who appoint Laureates.

REGINA CARA

Jubilee-Song, for music, 1897

Hark! the world is full of thy praise,
England's Queen of many days;
Who, knowing how to rule the free,
Hast given a crown to monarchy.

Honour, Truth, and growing Peace
Follow Britannia's wide increase,
And Nature yield her strength unknown
To the wisdom born beneath thy throne!

In wisdom and love firm is thy fame:
Enemies bow to revere thy name:
The world shall never tire to tell
Praise of the queen that reignèd well.

O Felix anima, Domina praeclara,
Amore semper coronabere
Regina Cara.

Rudyard Kipling's poetry is as familiar to us
as the air we breathe. He is the spokesman for
the Anglo-Saxon breed. His gospel of orderly
energy is the inspiration of thousands of business
offices; his sententious maxims are parts of current speech: the victrola has carried his singing
lyrics even farther than the banjo penetrates, of
which latter democratic instrument his wonderful
poem is the apotheosis. And we have the word of

a distinguished British major-general to prove
that Mr. Kipling has wrought a miracle of transformation with Tommy Atkins. General Sir
George Younghusband, in a recent book, *A Soldier's Memories,* says, "I had never heard the
words or expressions that Rudyard Kipling's soldiers used. Many a time did I ask my brother
officers whether they had ever heard them. No,
never. But, sure enough, a few years after the
soldiers thought, and talked, and expressed themselves exactly as Rudyard Kipling had taught
them in his stories. Rudyard Kipling made the
modern soldier. Other writers have gone on with
the good work, and they have between them manufactured the cheery, devil-may-care, lovable person enshrined in our hearts as Thomas Atkins.
Before he had learned from reading stories about
himself that he, as an individual, also possessed
the above attributes, he was mostly ignorant of
the fact. My early recollections of the British
soldier are of a bluff, rather surly person, never
the least jocose or light-hearted except perhaps
when he had too much beer."

This is extraordinary testimony to the power
of literature—from a first-class fighting man. It
is as though John Sargent should paint an inac-
curate but idealized portrait, and the original
should make it accurate by imitation. The soldiers were transformed by the renewing of their
minds. Beholding with open face as in a glass a
certain image, they were changed into the same

image, by the spirit of the poet. This is certainly a greater achievement than correct reporting. It is quite possible, too, that the *officers'* attitude toward Tommy Atkins had been altered by the *Barrack-Room Ballads,* and this new attitude produced results in character.

I give General Younghusband's testimony for what it is worth. It is important if true. But it is only fair to add that it has been contradicted by another military officer, who affirms that Kipling reported the soldier as he was. Readers may take their choice. At all events the transformation of character by discipline, cleanliness, hard work, and danger is the ever-present moral in Mr. Kipling's verse. He loves to take the raw recruit or the boyish, self-conscious, awkward subaltern, and show how he may become an efficient man, happy in the happiness that accompanies success. It is a Philistine goal, but one that has the advantage of being attainable. The reach of this particular poet seldom exceeds his grasp. And although thus far in his career—he is only fifty-two, and we may hope as well as remember—his best poetry belongs to the nineteenth century rather than the twentieth, so universally popular a homily as *If* indicates that he has by no means lost the power of preaching in verse. With the exception of some sad lapses, his latter poems have come nearer the earlier level of production than his stories. For that matter, from the beginning I have thought that the genius of Rudyard Kipling had more authentic expression in poetry than in prose. I therefore hope that after the war he will become one of the leaders in the advance of English poetry in the twentieth century, as he will remain one of the imperishable monuments of Victorian literature. The verse published in his latest volume of stories, *A Diversity of Creatures*, 1917, has the stamp of his original mind, and *Macdonough's Song* is impressive. And in a poem which does not appear in this collection, but which was written at the outbreak of hostilities, Mr. Kipling was, I believe, the first to use the name *Hun*—an appellation of considerable adhesive power. Do roses stick like burrs?

His influence on other poets has of course been powerful. As Eden Phillpotts is to Thomas Hardy, so is Robert Service to Rudyard Kipling. Like Bret Harte in California, Mr. Service found gold in the Klondike. But it is not merely in his interpretation of the life of a distant country that the new poet reminds one of his prototype; both in matter and in manner he may justly be called the Kipling of the North. His verse has an extraordinary popularity among American college undergraduates, the reasons for which are evident. They read, discuss him, and quote him with joy, and he might well be proud of the adoration of so many of our eager, adventurous, high-hearted youth. Yet, while Mr. Service is undoubtedly a real poet, his work as a whole seems a clear echo, rather than a new song. It is good, but it is reminiscent of his reading, not merely of Mr. Kipling, but of poetry in general. In *The Land God Forgot,* a fine poem, beginning

> The lonely sunsets flare forlorn
>   Down valleys dreadly desolate;
> The lordly mountains soar in scorn
>   As still as death, as stern as fate,

the opening line infallibly brings to mind Henley's

> Where forlorn sunsets flare and fade.

The poetry of Mr. Service has the merits and the faults of the "red blood" school in fiction, illustrated by the late Jack London and the lively Rex Beach. It is not the highest form of art. It insists on being heard, but it smells of mortality. You cannot give permanence to a book by printing it in italic type.

It is indeed difficult to express in pure artistic form great primitive experiences, even with long years of intimate first-hand knowledge. No one doubts Mr. Service's accuracy or sincerity. But many men have had abundance of material, rich and new, only to find it unmanageable. Bret Harte, Mark Twain, Rudyard Kipling succeeded where thousands have failed. Think of the possibilities of Australia! And from that vast region only one great artist has spoken—Percy Grainger.

CHAPTER II

Stephen Phillips—his immediate success—influence of Stratford-on-Avon—his plays—a traditional poet—his realism—
William Watson—his unpromising start—his lament on the
coldness of the age toward poetry—his Epigrams—*Wordsworth's Grave*—his eminence as a critic in verse—his anti-
imperialism—his Song of Hate—his Byronic wit—his contempt for the "new" poetry—Alfred Noyes—both literary and
rhetorical—an orthodox poet—a singer—his democracy—his
childlike imagination—his sea-poems—*Drake*—his optimism—
his religious faith—A. E. Housman—his paganism and pessimism—his modernity—his originality—his lyrical power—
war poems—Ludlow.

The genius of Stephen Phillips was immediately
recognized by London critics. When the thin
volume, *Poems,* containing *Marpessa, Christ in
Hades,* and some lyrical pieces, appeared in 1897,
it was greeted by a loud chorus of approval, cere-
moniously ratified by the bestowal of the First
Prize from the British Academy. Some of the
more distinguished among his admirers asserted
that the nobility, splendour, and beauty of his
verse merited the adjective Miltonic. I remember
that we Americans thought that the English critics
had lost their heads, and we queried what they
would say if we praised a new poet in the United
States in any such fashion. But that was before
we had seen the book; when we had once read

it for ourselves, we felt no alarm for the safety of
Milton, but we knew that English Literature had
been enriched. Stephen Phillips is among the
English poets.

His career extended over the space of twenty-
five years, from the first publication of *Marpessa*
in 1890 to his death on the ninth of December,
1915. He was born near the city of Oxford, on the
twenty-eighth of July, 1868. His father, the Rev.
Dr. Stephen Phillips, still living, is Precentor of
Peterborough Cathedral; his mother was related
to Wordsworth. He was exposed to poetry germs
at the age of eight, for in 1876 his father became
Chaplain and Sub-Vicar at Stratford-on-Avon,
and the boy attended the Grammar School. Later
he spent a year at Queens' College, Cambridge,
enough to give him the right to be enrolled in the
long list of Cambridge poets. He went on the
stage as a member of Frank Benson's company,
and in his time played many parts, receiving on
one occasion a curtain call as the Ghost in *Hamlet*.
This experience—with the early Stratford inspiration—probably fired his ambition to become a
dramatist. The late Sir George Alexander produced *Paolo and Francesca; Herod* was acted in
London by Beerbohm Tree, and in America by
William Faversham. Neither of these plays was
a failure, but it is regrettable that he wrote for
the stage at all. His genius was not adapted for
drama, and the quality of his verse was not improved by the experiment, although all of his half-

dozen pieces have occasional passages of rare loveliness. His best play, *Paolo and Francesca,* suf-
fers when compared either with Boker's or D'An-
nunzio's treatment of the old story. It lacks the
stage-craft of the former, and the virility of the
latter.

Phillips was no pioneer: he followed the great
tradition of English poetry, and must be counted
among the legitimate heirs. At his best, he resembles Keats most of all; and none but a real
poet could ever make us think of Keats. If he
be condemned for not breaking new paths, we
may remember the words of a wise man—"It is
easier to differ from the great poets than it is to
resemble them." He loved to employ the standard five-foot measure that has done so much of
the best work of English poetry. In *The Woman
with the Dead Soul,* he showed once more the
musical possibilities latent in the heroic couplet,
which Pope had used with such monotonous bril-
liance. In *Marpessa,* he gave us blank verse of
noble artistry. But he was far more than a mere
technician. He fairly meets the test set by John
Davidson. "In the poet the whole assembly of his
being is harmonious; no organ is master; a diapa-
son extends throughout the entire scale; his whole
body, his whole soul is rapt into the making of
his poetry. . . . Poetry is the product of originality, of a first-hand experience and observation of
life, of a direct communion with men and women,
with the seasons of the year, with day and night.

The critic will therefore be well-advised, if he have the good fortune to find something that seems to him poetry, to lay it out in the daylight and the moonlight, to take it into the street and the fields, to set against it his own experience and observation of life."

One of the most severe tests of poetry that I know of is to read it aloud on the shore of an angry sea. Homer, Shakespeare, Milton gain in splendour with this accompaniment.

With the words of John Davidson in mind, let us take two passages from *Marpessa,* and measure one against the atmosphere of day and night, and the other against homely human experience. Although Mr. Davidson was not thinking of Phillips, I believe he would have admitted the validity of this verse.

> From the dark
> The floating smell of flowers invisible,
> The mystic yearning of the garden wet,
> The moonless-passing night—into his brain
> Wandered, until he rose and outward leaned
> In the dim summer; 'twas the moment deep
> When we are conscious of the secret dawn,
> Amid the darkness that we feel is green. . . .
> When the long day that glideth without cloud,
> The summer day, was at her deep blue hour
> Of lilies musical with busy bliss,
> Whose very light trembled as with excess,
> And heat was frail, and every bush and flower
> Was drooping in the glory overcome;

Any poet knows how to speak in authentic tones of the wild passion of insurgent hearts; but not

every poet possesses the rarer gift of setting the
mellower years to harmonious music, as in the
following gracious words:

> But if I live with Idas, then we two
> On the low earth shall prosper hand in hand
> In odours of the open field, and live
> In peaceful noises of the farm, and watch
> The pastoral fields burned by the setting sun. . . .
> And though the first sweet sting of love be past,
> The sweet that almost venom is; though youth,
> With tender and extravagant delight,
> The first and secret kiss by twilight hedge,
> The insane farewell repeated o'er and o'er,
> Pass off; there shall succeed a faithful peace;
> Beautiful friendship tried by sun and wind,
> Durable from the daily dust of life.
> And though with sadder, still with kinder eyes,
> We shall behold all frailties, we shall haste
> To pardon, and with mellowing minds to bless.
> Then though we must grow old, we shall grow old
> Together, and he shall not greatly miss
> My bloom faded, and waning light of eyes,
> Too deeply gazed in ever to seem dim;
> Nor shall we murmur at, nor much regret
> The years that gently bend us to the ground,
> And gradually incline our face; that we
> Leisurely stooping, and with each slow step,
> May curiously inspect our lasting home.
> But we shall sit with luminous holy smiles,
> Endeared by many griefs, by many a jest,
> And custom sweet of living side by side;
> And full of memories not unkindly glance
> Upon each other. Last, we shall descend
> Into the natural ground—not without tears—
> One must go first, ah God! one must go first;
> After so long one blow for both were good;
> Still like old friends, glad to have met, and leave
> Behind a wholesome memory on the earth.

Although *Marpessa* and *Christ in Hades* are subjects naturally adapted for poetic treatment, Phillips did not hesitate to try his art on material less malleable. In some of his poems we find a realism as honest and clear-sighted as that of Crabbe or Masefield. In *The Woman with the Dead Soul* and *The Wife* we have naturalism elevated into poetry. He could make a London night as mystical as a moonlit meadow. And in a brief couplet he has given to one of the most familiar of metropolitan spectacles a pretty touch of imagination. The traffic policeman becomes a musician.

> The constable with lifted hand
> Conducting the orchestral Strand.

Stephen Phillips's second volume of collected verse, *New Poems* (1907), came ten years after the first, and was to me an agreeable surprise. His devotion to the drama made me fear that he had burned himself out in the *Poems* of 1897; but the later book is as unmistakably the work of a poet as was the earlier. The mystical communion with nature is expressed with authority in such poems as *After Rain, Thoughts at Sunrise, Thoughts at Noon*. Indeed the first-named distinctly harks back to that transcendental mystic of the seventeenth century, Henry Vaughan. The greatest triumph in the whole volume comes where we should least expect it, in the eulogy on Gladstone. Even the most sure-footed bards often miss their path in the Dark Valley. Yet in these

seven stanzas on the Old Parliamentary Hand
there is not a single weak line, not a single false
note; word placed on word grows steadily into a
column of majestic beauty.

This poem is all the more refreshing because
admiration for Gladstone had become unfashion-
able; his work was belittled, his motives befouled,
his clear mentality discounted by thousands of
pygmy politicians and journalistic gnats. The
poet, with a poet's love for mountains, turns the
powerful light of his genius on the old giant; the
mists disappear; and we see again a form vener-
able and august.

> The saint and poet dwell apart; but thou
> Wast holy in the furious press of men,
> And choral in the central rush of life.
> Yet didst thou love old branches and a book,
> And Roman verses on an English lawn. . . .
>
> Yet not for all thy breathing charm remote,
> Nor breach tremendous in the forts of Hell,
> Not for these things we praise thee, though these things
> Are much; but more, because thou didst discern
> In temporal policy the eternal will;
>
> Thou gav'st to party strife the epic note,
> And to debate the thunder of the Lord;
> To meanest issues fire of the Most High.

William Watson, a Yorkshireman by birth and
ancestry, was born on the second of August, 1858.
His first volume, *The Prince's Quest,* appeared in
1880. Seldom has a true poet made a more unpromising start, or given so little indication, not

only of the flame of genius, but of the power of thought. No twentieth century English poet has a stronger personality than William Watson. There is not the slightest tang of it in *The Prince's Quest*. This long, rambling romance, in ten sections, is as devoid of flavour as a five-finger exercise. It is more than objective; it is somnambulistic. It contains hardly any notable lines, and hardly any bad lines. Although quite dull, it never deviates into prose—it is always somehow poetical without ever becoming poetry. It is written in the heroic couplet, written with a fatal fluency; not good enough and not bad enough to be interesting. It is like the student's theme, which was returned to him without corrections, yet with a low mark; and in reply to the student's resentful question, "Why did you not correct my faults, if you thought meanly of my work?" the teacher replied wearily, "Your theme has no faults; it is distinguished by a lack of merit."

In *The Prince's Quest* Mr. Watson exhibited a rather remarkable command of a barren technique. He had neither thoughts that breathe, nor words that burn. He had one or two unusual words— his only indication of immaturity in style—like "wox" and "himseemed." (Why is it that when "herseemed" as used by Rossetti, is so beautiful, "himseemed" should be so irritating?) But aside from a few specimens, the poem is as free from affectations as it is from passion. When we remember the faults and the splendours of

Pauline, it seems incredible that a young poet could write so many pages without stumbling and without soaring; that he could produce a finished work of mediocrity. I suppose that those who read the poem in 1880 felt quite sure that its author would never scale the heights; and they were wrong; because William Watson really has the divine gift, and is one of the most deservedly eminent among living poets.

It is only fair to add, that in the edition of his works in 1898, *The Prince's Quest* did not appear; he was persuaded, however, to include it in the two-volume edition of 1905, where it enjoys considerable revision, "wox" becoming normal, and "himseemed" becoming dissyllabic. For my part, I am glad that it has now been definitely retained. It is important in the study of a poet's development. It would seem that the William Watson of the last twenty-five years, a fiery, eager, sensitive man, with a burning passion to express himself on moral and political ideas, learned the mastery of his art before he had anything to say.

Perhaps, being a thoroughly honest craftsman, he felt that he ought to keep his thoughts to himself, until he knew how to express them. After proving it on an impersonal romance, he was then ready to speak his mind. No poet has spoken his mind more plainly.

In an interesting address, delivered in various cities in the United States, and published in 1913, called *The Poet's Place in the Scheme of Life,*

Mr. Watson said, "Since my arrival on these shores I have been told that here also the public interest in poetry is visibly on the wane." Now whoever told him that was mistaken. The public interest in poetry and in poets has visibly *wox,* to use Mr. Watson's word. It is always true that an original genius, like Browning, like Ibsen, like Wagner, must wait some time for public recognition, although these three all lived long enough to receive not only appreciation, but idolatry; but the "reading public" has no difficulty in recognizing immediately first-rate work, when it is produced in the familiar forms of art. In the Preface that preceded his printed lecture, Mr. Watson complained with some natural resentment, though with no petulance, that his poem, *King Alfred,* starred as it was from the old armories of literature, received scarcely any critical comment, and attracted no attention. But the reason is plain enough— *King Alfred,* as a whole, is a dull poem, and is therefore not provocative of eager discussion. The critics and the public rose in reverence before *Wordsworth's Grave,* because it is a noble work of art. Its author did not have to tell us of its beauty—it was as clear as a cathedral.

I do not agree with Mr. Watson or with Mr. Mackaye, that real poets are speaking to deaf ears, or that they should be stimulated by forced attention. I once heard Percy Mackaye make an eloquent and high-minded address, where, if my memory serves me rightly, he advocated something like a stipend for young poets. A distinguished old man in the audience, now with God, whispered audibly, "What most of them need is hanging!" I do not think they should be rewarded either by cash or the gallows. Let them make their way, and if they have genius, the public will find it out. If all they have is talent, and no means to support it, poetry had better become their avocation.

Mr. Watson has expressly disclaimed that in his lecture he was lamenting merely "the insufficient praise bestowed upon living poets." It is certainly true that most poets cannot live by the sale of their works. Is this especially the fault of our age? is it the fault of our poets? is it a fault in human nature? Mr. Watson said, "Yet I am bound to admit that this need for the poet is felt by but few persons in our day. With one exception there is not a single living English poet, the sales of whose poems would not have been thought contemptible by Scott and Byron. The exception is, of course, that apostle of British imperialism—that vehement and voluble glorifier of Britannic ideals, whom I dare say you will readily identify from my brief, and, I hope, not disparaging description of him. With that one brilliant and salient exception, England's living singers succeed in reaching only a pitifully small audience." In commenting on this passage, we ought to remember that Scott and Byron were colossal figures, so big that no eye could miss them; and that the reason why Kipling has enjoyed substantial rewards is not because of his political views, nor because of his glorification of the British Empire, but simply because of his literary genius. He is a brilliant and salient exception to the common run of poets, not merely in royalties, but in creative power. Furthermore, shortly after this lecture was delivered, Alfred Noyes and then John Masefield passed from city to city in America in a march of triumph. Mr. Gibson and Mr. De La Mare received homage everywhere; "Riley day" is now a legal holiday in Indiana; Rupert Brooke has been canonized.

Mr. Watson is surely mistaken when he offers "his poetical contemporaries in England" his "most sincere condolences on the hard fate which condemned them to be born there at all in the latter part of the nineteenth century." But he is not mistaken in wishing that more people everywhere were appreciative of true poetry. I wish this with all my heart, not so much for the poet's sake, as for that of the people. But the chosen spirits are not rarer in our time than formerly. The fault is in human nature. Material blessings are instantly appreciated by every man, woman, and child, and by all the animals. For one person who knows the joys of listening to music, or looking at pictures, or reading poetry, there are a hundred thousand who know only the joys of food, clothing, shelter. Spiritual delights are not so immediately apparent as the gratification of physical desires. Perhaps if they were, man's growth would stop. As Browning says,

> While were it so with the soul,—this gift of truth
> Once grasped, were this our soul's gain safe, and sure
> To prosper as the body's gain is wont,—
> Why, man's probation would conclude, his earth
> Crumble; for he both reasons and decides,
> Weighs first, then chooses: will he give up fire
> For gold or purple once he knows its worth?
> Could he give Christ up were his worth as plain?
> Therefore, I say, to test man, the proofs shift,
> Nor may he grasp that fact like other fact,
> And straightway in his life acknowledge it,
> As, say, the indubitable bliss of fire.

One of the functions of the poet is to awaken men and women to the knowledge of the delights of the mind, to give them life instead of existence. As Mr. Watson nobly expresses it, the aim of the poet "is to keep fresh within us our often flagging sense of life's greatness and grandeur." We can exist on food; but we cannot live without our poets, who lift us to higher planes of thought and feeling. The poetry of William Watson has done this service for us again and again.

In 1884 appeared *Epigrams of Art, Life, and Nature*. I do not think these have been sufficiently admired. As an epigrammatist Mr. Watson has no rival in Victorian or in contemporary verse. The epigram is a quite definite form of art, especially cultivated by the poets in the first half of the seventeenth century. Their formula was the terse expression of obscene thoughts.

Mr. Watson excels the best of them in wit, concision, and grace; it is needless to say he makes no attempt to rival them as a garbage-collector. Of the large number of epigrams that he has contributed to English literature, I find the majority not only interesting, but richly stimulating. This one ought to please Mr. H. G. Wells:

> When whelmed are altar, priest, and creed;
>   When all the faiths have passed;
> Perhaps, from darkening incense freed,
>   God may emerge at last.

This one, despite its subject, is far above doggerel:

> His friends he loved. His direst earthly foes—
>   Cats—I believe he did but feign to hate.
> My hand will miss the insinuated nose,
>   Mine eyes the tail that wagg'd contempt at fate.

But his best epigrams are on purely literary themes:

> Your Marlowe's page I close, my Shakespeare's ope.
>   How welcome—after gong and cymbal's din—
> The continuity, the long slow slope
>   And vast curves of the gradual violin!

With the publication in 1890 of his masterpiece, *Wordsworth's Grave*, William Watson came into his own. This is worthy of the man it honours, and what higher praise could be given? It is superior, both in penetration and in beauty, to Matthew Arnold's famous *Memorial Verses*. Indeed, in the art of writing subtle literary criticism

in rhythmical language that is itself high and pure
poetry, Mr. Watson is unapproachable by any of
his contemporaries, and I do not know of any
poet in English literature who has surpassed him.
This is his specialty, this is his clearest title to
permanent fame. And although his criticism is
so valuable, when employed on a sympathetic
theme, that he must be ranked among our modern
interpreters of literature, his style in expressing
it could not possibly be translated into prose, sure
test of its poetical greatness. In his *Apologia*, he
says

> I have full oft
> In singers' selves found me a theme of song,
> Holding these also to be very part
> Of Nature's greatness, and accounting not
> Their descants least heroical of deeds.

The poem *Wordsworth's Grave* not only expresses, as no one else has expressed, the quality
of Wordsworth's genius, but in single lines as-
signed to each, the same service is done for Milton,
Shakespeare, Shelley, Coleridge, and Byron.
This is a matchless illustration of the kind of
criticism that is in itself genius; for we may
quarrel with Mr. Spingarn as much as we please
on his general dogmatic principle of the identity
of genius and taste; here we have so admirable
an example of what he means by creative criticism,
that it is a pity he did not think of it himself.
"For it still remains true," says Mr. Spingarn,
"that the æsthetic critic, in his moments of high-

est power, rises to heights where he is at one with the creator whom he is interpreting. At that moment criticism and 'creation' are one."

All great poets have the power of noble indignation, a divine wrath against wickedness in high places. The poets, like the prophets of old, pour out their irrepressible fury against what they believe to be cruelty and oppression. Milton's magnificent Piedmont sonnet is a glorious roar of righteous rage; and since his time the poets have ever been the spokesmen for the insulted and injured. Robert Burns, more than most statesmen, helped to make the world safe for democracy. I do not know what humanity would do without its poets—they are the champions of the individual against the tyranny of power, the cruel selfishness of kings, and the artificial conventions of society. We may or may not agree with Mr. Watson's anti-imperialistic sentiments as expressed in the early days of our century; he himself, like most of us, has changed his mind on many subjects since the outbreak of the world-war, and unless he ceases to develop, will probably change it many times in the future. But whatever our opinions, we cannot help admiring lines like these, published in 1897:

HOW WEARY IS OUR HEART

Of kings and courts; of kingly, courtly ways
In which the life of man is bought and sold;
How weary is our heart these many days!

Of ceremonious embassies that hold
Parley with Hell in fine and silken phrase,
How weary is our heart these many days!

Of wavering counsellors neither hot nor cold,
Whom from His mouth God speweth, be it told
How weary is our heart these many days!

Yea, for the ravelled night is round the lands,
And sick are we of all the imperial story.
The tramp of Power, and its long trail of pain;
The mighty brows in meanest arts grown hoary;
The mighty hands,
That in the dear, affronted name of Peace
Bind down a people to be racked and slain;
The emulous armies waxing without cease,
All-puissant all in vain;
The pacts and leagues to murder by delays,
And the dumb throngs that on the deaf thrones gaze;
The common loveless lust of territory;
The lips that only babble of their mart,
While to the night the shrieking hamlets blaze;
The bought allegiance, and the purchased praise,
False honour, and shameful glory;—
Of all the evil whereof this is part,
How weary is our heart,
How weary is our heart these many days!

Another poem I cite in full, not for its power and beauty, but as a curiosity. I do not think it has been remembered that in the *New Poems* of 1909 Mr. Watson published a poem of Hate some years before the Teutonic hymn became famous. It is worth reading again, because it so exactly expresses the cold reserve of the Anglo-Saxon, in contrast with the sentimentality of the German. There is, of course, no indication that its author had Germany in mind.

HATE

(To certain foreign detractors)

Sirs, if the truth must needs be told,
We love not you that rail and scold;
And, yet, my masters, you may wait
Till the Greek Calends for our hate.

No spendthrifts of our hate are we;
Our hate is used with husbandry.
We hold our hate too choice a thing
For light and careless lavishing.

We cannot, dare not, make it cheap!
For holy uses will we keep
A thing so pure, a thing so great
As Heaven's benignant gift of hate.

Is there no ancient, sceptred Wrong?
No torturing Power, endured too long?
Yea; and for these our hatred shall
Be cloistered and kept virginal.

He found occasion to draw from his cold storage
of hate much sooner than he had anticipated. Being a convinced anti-imperialist, and having not
a spark of antagonism to Germany, the early days
of August, 1914, shocked no one in the world more
than him. But after the first maze of bewilder-
ment and horror, he drew his pen against the
Kaiser in holy wrath. Most of his war poems
have been collected in the little volume *The Man
Who Saw*, published in the summer of 1917. He
has now at all events one satisfaction, that of being
in absolute harmony with the national sentiment.
In his Preface, after commenting on the pain he

had suffered in times past at finding himself in
opposition to the majority of his countrymen, he
manfully says, ''During the present war, with all
its agonies and horrors, he has had at any rate
the one private satisfaction of feeling not even
the most momentary doubt or misgiving as to
the perfect righteousness of his country's cause.
There is nothing on earth of which he is more certain than that this Empire, throughout this supreme ordeal, has shaped her course by the light
of purest duty.'' The volume opens with a fine
tribute to Mr. Lloyd George, ''the man who
saw,'' and *The Kaiser's Dirge* is a savage male-
diction. The poems in this book—of decidedly
unequal merit—have the fire of indignation if not
always the flame of inspiration. Taken as a
whole, they are more interesting psychologically
than as a contribution to English verse. I sympathize with the author's feelings, and admire his
sincerity; but his reputation as a poet is not
heightened overmuch. Perhaps the best poem in
the collection is *The Yellow Pansy,* accompanied
with Shakespeare's line, ''There's pansies—that's
for thoughts.''

> Winter had swooped, a lean and hungry hawk;
> It seemed an age since summer was entombed;
> Yet in our garden, on its frozen stalk,
> A yellow pansy bloomed.
>
> 'Twas Nature saying by trope and metaphor:
> "Behold, when empire against empire strives,
> Though all else perish, ground 'neath iron war,
> The golden thought survives."

Although, with the exception of his marriage
and travels in America, Mr. Watson's verse tells
us little of the facts of his life, few poets have
ever revealed more of the history of their mind.
What manner of man he is we know without waiting for the publication of his intimate correspondence. It is fortunate for his temperament that,
combined with an almost morbid sensitiveness, he
has something of Byron's power of hitting back.
His numerous volumes contain many verses scor-
ing off adverse critics, upon whom he exercises a
sword of satire not always to be found among a
poet's weapons; which exercise seems to give
him both relief and delight. Apart from these
thrusts edged with personal bitterness, William
Watson possesses a rarely used vein of ironical
wit that immediately recalls Byron, who might
himself have written some of the stanzas in *The
Eloping Angels*. Faust requests Mephisto to pro-
cure for them both admission into heaven for half-
an-hour:

To whom Mephisto: "Ah, you underrate
    The hazards and the dangers, my good Sir.
Peter is stony as his name; the gate,
    Excepting to invited guests, won't stir.
'Tis long since he and I were intimate;
    We differed;—but to bygones why refer?
Still, there are windows; if a peep through these
Would serve your turn, we'll start whene'er you please. . . ."

So Faust and his companion entered, by
    The window, the abodes where seraphs dwell.
"Already morning quickens in the sky,
    And soon will sound the heavenly matin bell;

Our time is short," Mephisto said, "for I
  Have an appointment about noon in hell.
Dear, dear! why, heaven has hardly changed one bit
Since the old days before the historic split."

The excellent conventional technique displayed
in *The Prince's Quest* has characterized nearly
every page of Mr. Watson's works. He is not
only content to walk in the ways of traditional
poesy, he glories in it. He has a contempt for
heretics and experimenters, which he has expressed frequently not only in prose, but in verse.
It is natural that he should worship Tennyson;
natural (and unfortunate for him) that he can see
little in Browning. And if he is blind to Browning, what he thinks of contemporary "new" poets
may easily be imagined. With or without inspiration, he believes that hard work is necessary, and
that good workmanship ought to be rated more
highly. This idea has become an obsession; Mr.
Watson writes too much about the sweat of his
brow, and vents his spleen on "modern" poets too
often. In his latest volume, *Retrogression,* published in 1917, thirty-two of the fifty-two poems
are devoted to the defence of standards of poetic
art and of purity of speech. They are all interesting and contain some truth; but if the "new"
poetry and the "new" criticism are really balder-
dash, they should not require so much attention
from one of the most eminent of contemporary
writers. I think Mr. Watson is rather stiff-
necked and obstinate, like an honest, hearty coun-

try squire, in his sturdy following of tradition.
Smooth technique is a fine thing in art; but I do
not care whether a poem is written in conventional
metre or in free verse, so long as it is unmistakably poetry. And no garments yet invented or
the lack of them can conceal true poetry. Perhaps
the Traditionalist might reply that uninspired
verse gracefully written is better than uninspired
verse abominably written. So it is; but why
bother about either? He might once more insist
that inspired poetry gracefully written is better
than inspired poetry ungracefully written. And
I should reply that it depended altogether on the
subject. I should not like to see Whitman's
Spirit that formed this Scene turned into a Spen-
serian stanza. I cannot forget that David Mallet
tried to smoothen Hamlet's soliloquy by jamming
it into the heroic couplet. Mr. Watson thinks that
the great John Donne is dead. On the contrary,
he is audibly alive; and the only time he really ap-
proached dissolution was when Pope "versified"
him.

Stephen Phillips, William Watson, Alfred
Noyes—each published his first volume of poems
at the age of twenty-two, additional evidence of
the old truth that poets are born, not made. Alfred Noyes is a Staffordshire man, though his report of the county differs from that of Arnold
Bennett as poetry differs from prose. They did
not see the same things in Staffordshire, and if
they had, they would not have been the same

things, anyhow. Mr. Noyes was born on the sixteenth of September, 1880, and made his first departure from the traditions of English poetry in
going to Oxford. There he was an excellent illustration of *mens sana in corpore sano,* writing
verses and rowing on his college crew. He is married to an American wife, is a professor at Princeton, and understands the spirit of America better
than most visitors who write clever books about
us. He has the wholesome, modest, cheerful temperament of the American college undergraduate,
and the Princeton students are fortunate, not only
in hearing his lectures, but in the opportunity of
fellowship with such a man.

Mr. Noyes is one of the few poets who can read
his own verses effectively, the reason being that
his mind is by nature both literary and rhetorical
—a rare union. The purely literary temperament
is usually marked by a certain shyness which un-
fits its owner for the public platform. I have
heard poets read passionate poetry in a muffled
sing-song, something like a child learning to "recite." The works of Alfred Noyes gain distinctly
by his oral interpretation of them.

He is prolific. Although still a young man, he
has a long list of books to his credit; and it is
rather surprising that in such a profusion of literary experiments, the general level should be so
high. He writes blank verse, octosyllabics, terza-
rima, sonnets, and is particularly fond of long
rolling lines that have in them the music of the

sea. His ideas require no enlargement of the orchestra, and he generally avoids by-paths, or unbeaten tracks, content to go lustily singing along the highway. Perhaps it shows more courage to compete with standard poets in standard measures, than to elude dangerous comparisons by making or adopting a new fashion. Mr. Noyes openly challenges the masters on their own field and with their own weapons. Yet he shows nothing of the schoolmasterish contempt for the "new" poetry so characteristic of Mr. Watson. He actually admires Blake, who was in spirit a twentieth century poet, and he has written a fine poem *On the Death of Francis Thompson*, though he has nothing of Thompson in him except religious faith.

In the time-worn but useful classification of versemakers under the labels *Vates* and *Poeta*, Alfred Noyes belongs clearly to the latter group. He is not without ideas, but he is primarily an artist, a singer. He is one of the most melodious of modern writers, with a witchery in words that at its best is irresistible. He has an extraordinary command of the resources of language and rhythm. Were this all he possessed, he would be nothing but a graceful musician. But he has the imagination of the inspired poet, giving him creative power to reveal anew the majesty of the untamed sea, and the mystery of the stars. With this clairvoyance—essential in poetry—he has a hearty, charming, uncondescending sympathy with "common" people, common flowers, common music. One of his most original and most captivating poems is *The Tramp Transfigured, an Episode in the Life of a Corn-flower Millionaire.* This contains a character worthy of Dickens, a faery touch of fantasy, a rippling, singing melody, with delightful audacities of rime.

Tick, tack, tick, tack, I couldn't wait no longer!
Up I gets and bows polite and pleasant as a toff—
"Arternoon," I says, "I'm glad your boots are going stronger;
Only thing I'm dreading is your feet 'ull both come off."
Tick, tack, tick, tack, she didn't stop to answer,
"Arternoon," she says, and sort o' chokes a little cough,
"I must get to Piddinghoe tomorrow if I can, sir!"
"Demme, my good woman! Haw! Don't think I mean to
    loff,"
  Says I, like a toff,
"Where d'you mean to sleep tonight? God made this grass
    for go'ff."

His masterpiece, *The Barrel-Organ,* has something of Kipling's rollicking music, with less noise and more refinement. Out of the mechanical grinding of the hand organ, with the accompaniment of city omnibuses, we get the very breath of spring in almost intolerable sweetness. This poem affects the head, the heart, and the feet. I defy any man or woman to read it without surrendering to the magic of the lilacs, the magic of old memories, the magic of the poet. Nor has any one ever read this poem without going imme-

diately back to the first line, and reading it all over
again, so susceptible are we to the romantic pleasure of melancholy.

> Mon coeur est un luth suspendu:
> Sitôt qu'on le touche, il résonne.

Alfred Noyes understands the heart of the
child; as is proved by his *Flower of Old Japan,*
and *Forest of Wild Thyme,* a kind of singing Al-
ice-in-Wonderland. These are the veritable stuff
of dreams—wholly apart from the law of causation—one vision fading into another. It is our
fault, and not that of the poet, that Mr. Noyes
had to explain them: "It is no new wisdom to
regard these things through the eyes of little children; and I know—however insignificant they
may be to others—these two tales contain as deep
and true things as I, personally, have the power
to express. I hope, therefore, that I may be
pardoned, in these hurried days, for pointing out
that the two poems are not to be taken merely
as fairy-tales, but as an attempt to follow the
careless and happy feet of children back into
the kingdom of those dreams which, as we said
above, are the sole reality worth living and dying for; those beautiful dreams, or those fantastic jests—if any care to call them so—for which
mankind has endured so many triumphant mar-
tyrdoms that even amidst the rush and roar of
modern materialism they cannot be quite forgotten." Mr. William J. Locke says he would rather

give up clean linen and tobacco than give up his dreams.

Nearly all English poetry smells of the sea; the waves rule Britannia. Alfred Noyes loves the ocean, and loves the old sea-dogs of Devonshire. He is not a literary poet, like William Watson, and has seldom given indication of possessing the insight or the interpretative power of his contemporary in dealing with pure literature. He has the blessed gift of admiration, and his poems on Swinburne, Meredith, and other masters show a high reverence; but they are without subtlety, and lack the discriminating phrase. He is, however, deeply read in Elizabethan verse and prose, as his *Tales of the Mermaid Tavern,* one of his longest, most painstaking, and least successful works, proves; and of all the Elizabethan men of action, Drake is his hero. The English lovers of the sea, and the German lovers of efficiency, have both done honour to Drake. I remember years ago, being in the town of Offenburg in Germany, and seeing at a distance a colossal statue, feeling some surprise when I discovered that the monument was erected to Sir Francis Drake, "in recognition of his having introduced the potato into Europe." Here was where eulogy became almost too specific, and I felt that their Drake was not my Drake.

Mr. Noyes called *Drake,* published in 1908, an English Epic. It is not really an epic—it is a historical romance in verse, as *Aurora Leigh* is a novel. It is interesting from beginning to end, more interesting as narrative than as poetry. It is big rather than great, rhetorical rather than literary, declamatory rather than passionate. And while many descriptive passages are fine, the pictures of the terrible storm near Cape Horn are surely less vivid than those in *Dauber*. Had Mr. Noyes written *Drake* without the songs, and written nothing else, I should not feel certain that he was a poet; I should regard him as an extremely fluent versifier, with remarkable skill in telling a rattling good story. But the *Songs*, especially the one beginning, "Now the purple night is past," could have been written only by a poet. In *Forty Singing Seamen* there is displayed an imagination quite superior to anything in *Drake;* and I would not trade *The Admiral's Ghost* for the whole "epic."

As a specific illustration of his lyrical power, the following poem may be cited.

THE MAY-TREE

The May-tree on the hill
   Stands in the night
So fragrant and so still,
   So dusky white.

That, stealing from the wood,
   In that sweet air,
You'd think Diana stood
   Before you there.

If it be so, her bloom
   Trembles with bliss.
She waits across the gloom
   Her shepherd's kiss.

Touch her.   A bird will start
From those pure snows,—
The dark and fluttering heart
Endymion knows.

Alfred Noyes is "among the English poets."
His position is secure.   But because he has never
identified himself with the "new" poetry—either
in choice of material or in free verse and polyphonic prose—it would be a mistake to suppose
that he is afraid to make metrical experiments.
The fact of the matter is, that after he had mastered the technique of conventional rime and
rhythm, as shown in many of his lyrical pieces, he
began playing new tunes on the old instrument.
In *The Tramp Transfigured*, to which I find myself always returning in a consideration of his
work, because it displays some of the highest
qualities of pure poetry, there are new metrical
effects.   The same is true of the Prelude to the
Forest of Wild Thyme, and of *The Burial of a
Queen;* there are new metres used in *Rank and
File* and in *Mount Ida*.   The poem *Astrid*, included in the volume *The Lord of Misrule* (1915),
is an experiment in *initial* rhymes.   Try reading
it aloud.

White-armed Astrid,—ah, but she was beautiful!—
Nightly wandered weeping thro' the ferns in the moon,
Slowly, weaving her strange garland in the forest,
Crowned with white violets,
Gowned in green.
Holy was that glen where she glided,
Making her wild garland as Merlin had bidden her,

Breaking off the milk-white horns of the honeysuckle,
Sweetly dripped the new upon her small white
Feet.

The English national poetry of Mr. Noyes worthily expresses the spirit of the British people, and indeed of the Anglo-Saxon race. We are no lovers of war; military ambition or the glory of conquest is not sufficient motive to call either Great Britain or America to arms; but if the gun-drunken Germans really believed that the English and Americans would not fight to save the world from an unspeakable despotism, they made the mistake of their lives. There must be a Cause, there must be an Idea, to draw out the full fighting strength of the Anglo-Saxons. Alfred Noyes made a correct diagnosis and a correct prophecy in 1911, when he published *The Sword of England.*

She sheds no blood to that vain god of strife
  Whom tyrants call "renown";
She knows that only they who reverence life
  Can nobly lay it down;

And these will ride from child and home and love,
  Through death and hell that day;
But O, her faith, her flag, must burn above,
  Her soul must lead the way!

I think none the worse of the mental force exhibited in the poetry of Alfred Noyes because he is an optimist. It is a common error to suppose that cheerfulness is a sign of a superficial mind, and melancholy the mark of deep thinking. Pessimism in itself is no proof of intellectual greatness. Every honest man must report the world as he sees it, both in its external manifestations and in the equally salient fact of human emotion. Mr. Noyes has always loved life, and rejoiced in it; he loves the beauty of the world and believes that history proves progress. In an unashamed testimony to the happiness of living he is simply telling truths of his own experience. Happiness is not necessarily thoughtlessness; many men and women have gone through pessimism and come out on serener heights.

Alfred Noyes proves, as Browning proved, that it is possible to be an inspired poet and in every other respect to remain normal. He is healthy-minded, without a trace of affectation or decadence. He follows the Tennysonian tradition in seeing that "Beauty, Good, and Knowledge are three sisters." He is religious. A clear-headed, pure-hearted Englishman is Alfred Noyes.

Although *A Shropshire Lad* was published in 1896, there is nothing of the nineteenth century in it except the date, and nothing Victorian except the allusions to the Queen. A double puzzle confronts the reader: how could a University Professor of Latin write this kind of poetry, and how, after having published it, could he refrain from writing more? Since the date of its appearance, he has published an edition of *Manilius,* Book I, followed nine years later by Book II; also an edition of *Juvenal,* and many papers representing the result of original research. Possibly

> Chill Pedantry repressed his noble rage,
> And froze the genial current of his soul.

Alfred Edward Housman was born on the twenty-sixth of March, 1859, was graduated from Oxford, was Professor of Latin at University College, London, from 1892 to 1911, and since then has been Professor of Latin at Cambridge. Few poets have made a deeper impression on the literature of the time than he; and the sixty-three short lyrics in one small volume form a slender wedge for so powerful an impact. This poetry, except in finished workmanship, follows no English tradition; it is as unorthodox as Samuel Butler; it is thoroughly "modern" in tone, in temper, and in emphasis. Although entirely original, it reminds one in many ways of the verse of Thomas Hardy. It has his paganism, his pessimism, his human sympathy, his austere pride in the tragedy of frustration, his curt refusal to pipe a merry tune, to make one of a holiday crowd.

> Therefore, since the world has still
> Much good, but much less good than ill,
> And while the sun and moon endure
> Luck's a chance, but trouble's sure,
> I'd face it as a wise man would,
> And train for ill and not for good.
> 'Tis true, the stuff I bring for sale
> Is not so brisk a brew as ale:
> Out of a stem that scored the hand
> I wrung it in a weary land.
> But take it: if the smack is sour,
> The better for the embittered hour;

> It should do good to heart and head
> When your soul is in my soul's stead;
> And I will friend you, if I may,
> In the dark and cloudy day.

Those lines might have been written by Thomas Hardy. They express not merely his view of life, but his faith in the healing power of the bitter herb of pessimism. But we should remember that *A Shropshire Lad* was published before the first volume of Mr. Hardy's verse appeared, and that the lyrical element displayed is natural rather than acquired.

Though at the time of its publication the author was thirty-six years old, many of the poems must have been written in the twenties. The style is mature, but the constant dwelling on death and the grave is a mark of youth. Young poets love to write about death, because its contrast to their present condition forms a romantic tragedy, sharply dramatic and yet instinctively felt to be remote. Tennyson's first volume is full of the details of dissolution, the falling jaw, the eye-balls fixing, the sharp-headed worm. Aged poets do not usually write in this manner, because death seems more realistic than romantic. It is a fact rather than an idea. When a young poet is obsessed with the idea of death, it is a sign, not of morbidity, but of normality.

The originality in this book consists not in the contrast between love and the grave, but in the

acute self-consciousness of youth, in the pagan
determination to enjoy nature without waiting till
life's summer is past.

> Loveliest of trees, the cherry now
> Is hung with bloom along the bough,
> And stands about the woodland ride
> Wearing white for Eastertide.
>
> Now, of my threescore years and ten,
> Twenty will not come again,
> And take from seventy springs a score,
> It only leaves me fifty more.
>
> And since to look at things in bloom
> Fifty springs are little room,
> About the woodlands I will go
> To see the cherry hung with snow.

The death of the body is not the greatest tragedy
in this volume, for suicide, a thought that youth
loves to play with, is twice glorified. The death
of love is often treated with an ironical bitterness
that makes one think of *Time's Laughingstocks*.

> Is my friend hearty,
>   Now I am thin and pine,
> And has he found to sleep in
>   A better bed than mine?
>
> Yes, lad, I lie easy,
>   I lie as lads would choose;
> I cheer a dead man's sweetheart,
>   Never ask me whose.

The point of view expressed in *The Carpenter's
Son* is singularly detached not only from conventional religious belief, but from conventional

reverence. But the originality in *A Shropshire Lad,* while more strikingly displayed in some poems than in others, leaves its mark on them all. It is the originality of a man who thinks his own thoughts with shy obstinacy, makes up his mind in secret meditation, quite unaffected by current opinion. It is not the poetry of a rebel; it is the poetry of an independent man, too indifferent to the crowd even to fight them. And now and then we find a lyric of flawless beauty, that lingers in the mind like the glow of a sunset.

> Into my heart an air that kills
>   From yon far country blows:
> What are those blue remembered hills,
>   What spires, what farms are those?
>
> That is the land of lost content,
>   I see it shining plain,
> The happy highways where I went,
>   And cannot come again.

Mr. Housman's poems are nearer to the twentieth century in spirit than the work of the late Victorians, and many of them are curiously prophetic of the dark days of the present war. What strange vision made him write such poems as *The Recruit, The Street Sounds to the Soldiers' Tread, The Day of Battle,* and *On the Idle Hill of Summer?* Change the colour of the uniforms, and these four poems would fit today's tragedy accurately. They are indeed superior to most of the war poems written by the professional poets since 1914.

Ludlow, for ever associated with Milton's *Comus,* is now and will be for many years to come also significant in the minds of men as the home of a Shropshire lad.

CHAPTER III

JOHN MASEFIELD

John Masefield—new wine in old bottles—back to Chaucer—the self-conscious adventurer—early education and experiences—*Dauber*—Mr. Masefield's remarks on Wordsworth—Wordsworth's famous Preface and its application to the poetry of Mr. Masefield—*The Everlasting Mercy*—*The Widow in the Bye Street* and its Chaucerian manner—his masterpiece—*The Daffodil Fields*—similarities to Wordsworth—the part played by the flowers—comparison of *The Daffodil Fields* with *Enoch Arden*—the war poem, *August 1914*—the lyrics—the sonnets—the novels—his object in writing—his contribution to the advance of poetry.

Poets are the Great Exceptions. Poets are for ever performing the impossible. "No man putteth new wine into old bottles . . . new wine must be put into new bottles." But putting new wine into old bottles has been the steady professional occupation of John Masefield. While many of our contemporary vers librists and other experimentalists have been on the hunt for new bottles, sometimes, perhaps, more interested in the bottle than in the wine, John Masefield has been constantly pouring his heady drink into receptacles five hundred years old. In subject-matter and in language he is not in the least "traditional," not at all Victorian; he is wholly modern, new, contemporary. Yet while he draws his themes and his heroes from his own experience, his

71

inspiration as a poet comes directly from Chaucer, who died in 1400. He is, indeed, the Chaucer of today; the most closely akin to Chaucer—not only in temperament, but in literary manner—of all the writers of the twentieth century. The beautiful metrical form that Chaucer invented—rime royal—ideally adapted for narrative poetry, as shown in *Troilus and Criseyde,* is the metre chosen by John Masefield for *The Widow in the Bye Street* and for *Dauber;* the only divergence in *The Daffodil Fields* consisting in the lengthening of the seventh line of the stanza, for which he had plenty of precedents. Mr. Masefield owes more to Chaucer than to any other poet.

Various are the roads to poetic achievement. Browning became a great poet at the age of twenty, with practically no experience of life outside of books. He had never travelled, he had never "seen the world," but was brought up in a library; and was so deeply read in the Greek poets and dramatists that a sunrise on the Ægean Sea was more real to him than a London fog. He never saw Greece with his natural eyes. In the last year of his life, being asked by an American if he had been much in Athens, he replied contritely, "Thou stick'st a dagger in me." He belied Goethe's famous dictum.

John Masefield was born at Ledbury, in western England, in 1874. He ran away from home, shipped as cabin boy on a sailing vessel, spent some years before the mast, tramped on foot through various countries, turned up in New York, worked in the old Columbia Hotel in Greenwich Avenue, and had plenty of opportunity to study human nature in the bar-room. Then he entered a carpet factory in the Bronx. But he was the last man in the world to become a carpet knight. He bought a copy of Chaucer's poems, stayed up till dawn reading it, and for the first time was sure of his future occupation.

John Masefield is the real man-of-war-bird imagined by Walt Whitman. He is the bird self-conscious, the wild bird plus the soul of the poet.

To cope with heaven and earth and sea and hurricane,
Thou ship of air that never furl'st thy sails,
Days, even weeks untired and onward, through spaces, realms
    gyrating,
At dusk that look'st on Senegal, at morn America,
That sport'st amid the lightning-flash and thunder-cloud,
In them, in thy experiences, had'st thou my soul,
What joys! what joys were thine!

They that go down to the sea in ships, that do business in great waters, these see the works of the Lord, and His wonders in the deep. They do indeed; they see them as the bird sees them, with no spiritual vision, with no self-consciousness, with no power to refer or to interpret. It is sad that so many of those who have marvellous experiences have nothing else; while those who are sensitive and imaginative live circumscribed. What does the middle watch mean to an average seaman? But occasionally the sailor is a Joseph Conrad or a John Masefield. Then the visions of splendour and the glorious voices of nature are seen and heard not only by the eye and the ear, but by the spirit.

Although Chaucer took Mr. Masefield out of the carpet factory even as Spenser released Keats, it would be a mistake to suppose (as many do) that the Ledbury boy was an uncouth vagabond, who, without reading, without education, and without training, suddenly became a poet. He had a good school education before going to sea; and from earliest childhood he longed to write. Even as a little boy he felt the impulse to put his dreams on paper; he read everything he could lay his hands on, and during all the years of bodily toil, afloat and ashore, he had the mind and the aspiration of a man of letters. Never, I suppose, was there a greater contrast between an individual's outer and inner life. He mingled with rough, brutal, decivilized creatures; his ears were assaulted by obscene language, spoken as to an equal; he saw the ugliest side of humanity, and the blackest phases of savagery. Yet through it all, sharing these experiences with no trace of condescension, his soul was like a lily.

He descended into hell again and again, coming out with his inmost spirit unblurred and shining, even as the rough diver brings from the depths the perfect pearl. For every poem that he has written reveals two things: a knowledge of the harshness of life, with a nature of extraordinary purity, delicacy, and grace. To find a parallel to this, we must recall the figure of Dostoevski in the Siberian prison.

Many men of natural good taste and good breeding have succumbed to a coarse environment. What saved our poet, and made his experiences actually minister to his spiritual flame, rather than burn him up? It was perhaps that final miracle of humanity, acute self-consciousness, stronger in some men than in others, strongest of all in the creative artist. Even at the age of twenty, Browning felt it more than he felt anything else, and his words would apply to John Masefield, and explain in some measure his thirst for sensation and his control of it.

> I am made up of an intensest life,
> Of a most clear idea of consciousness
> Of self, distinct from all its qualities,
> From all affections, passions, feelings, powers;
> And thus far it exists, if tracked, in all:
> But linked, in me, to self-supremacy,
> Existing as a centre to all things,
> Most potent to create and rule and call
> Upon all things to minister to it;
> And to a principle of restlessness
> Which would be all, have, see, know, taste, feel, all—
> This is myself.

Although the poem *Dauber* is a true story—for there was such a man, who suffered both horrible fear within and brutal ridicule without, who finally conquered both, and who, in the first sweets of victory, as he was about to enter upon his true career, lost his life by falling from the yardarm—

I cannot help thinking that Mr. Masefield put a good deal of himself into this strange hero. The adoration of beauty, which is the lodestar of the poet, lifted Dauber into a different world from the life of the ship. He had an ungovernable desire to paint the constantly changing phases of beauty in the action of the vessel and in the wonders of the sea and sky. In this passion his shy, sensitive nature was stronger than all the brute strength enjoyed by his shipmates; they could destroy his paintings, they could hurt his body, they could torture his heart. But they could not prevent him from following his ideal. Dauber died, and his pictures are lost. But in the poem describing his aims and his sufferings, Mr. Masefield has accomplished with his pen what Dauber failed to do with his brush; the beauty of the ship, the beauty of dawn and of midnight, the majesty of the storm are revealed to us in a series of unforgettable pictures. And one of Edison's ambitions is here realized. At the same moment we *see* the frightful white-capped ocean mountains, and we *hear* the roar of the gale.

> Water and sky were devils' brews which boiled,
>
> Boiled, shrieked, and glowered; but the ship was saved.
> Snugged safely down, though fourteen sails were split.
> Out of the dark a fiercer fury raved.
> The grey-backs died and mounted, each crest lit
> With a white toppling gleam that hissed from it
> And slid, or leaped, or ran with whirls of cloud,
> Mad with inhuman life that shrieked aloud.

Mr. Masefield is a better poet than critic. In the New York *Tribune* for 23 January 1916, he spoke with modesty and candour of his own work and his own aims, and no one can read what he said without an increased admiration for him. But it is difficult to forgive him for talking as he did about Wordsworth, who "wrote six poems and then fell asleep." And among the six are not *Tintern Abbey* or the *Intimations of Immortality*. Meditative poetry is not Mr. Masefield's strongest claim to fame, and we do not go to poets for illuminating literary criticism. Swinburne was so violent in his "appreciations" that his essays in criticism are adjectival volcanoes. Every man with him was God or Devil. It is rare that a creative poet has the power of interpretation of literature possessed by William Watson. Mr. Masefield does not denounce Wordsworth, as Swinburne denounced Byron; he is simply blind to the finest qualities of the Lake poet. Yet, although he carries Wordsworth's famous theory of poetry to an extreme that would have shocked the author of it—if Mr. Masefield does not like *Tintern Abbey*, we can only imagine Wordsworth's horror at *The Everlasting Mercy*—the philosophy of poetry underlying both *The Everlasting Mercy, The Widow in the Bye Street,* and other works is essentially that of William Wordsworth. Keeping *The Everlasting Mercy* steadily in mind, it is interesting, instructive, and even amusing to read an extract from Wordsworth's famous Preface of 1800.

"The principal object, then, proposed in these Poems was to choose incidents and situations from common life, and to relate or describe them, throughout, as far as was possible in a selection of language really used by men, and, at the same time, to throw over them a certain colouring of imagination, whereby ordinary things should be presented to the mind in an unusual aspect; and, further, and above all, to make these incidents and situations interesting by tracing in them, truly though not ostentatiously, the primary laws of our nature; chiefly, as far as regards the manner in which we associate ideas in a state of excitement. Humble and rustic life was generally chosen, because, in that condition, the essential passions of the heart find a better soil in which they can attain their maturity, are less under restraint, and speak a plainer and more emphatic language; because in that condition of life our elementary feelings co-exist in a state of greater simplicity, and, consequently, may be more accurately contemplated, and more forcibly communicated; because the manners of rural life germinate from those elementary feelings, and, from the necessary character of rural occupations, are more easily comprehended, and are more durable; and, lastly, because in that condition the passions of men are incorporated with the beautiful and permanent forms of nature."

When Wordsworth wrote these dicta, he followed them up with some explicit reservations, and made many more implicit ones. Mr. Masefield, in the true manner of the twentieth century makes none at all. Taking the language of Wordsworth exactly as it stands in the passage quoted above, it applies with precision to the method employed by Mr. Masefield in the poems that have given him widest recognition. And in carrying this theory of poetry to its farthest extreme in *The Everlasting Mercy,* not only did its author break with tradition, the tradition of nineteenth-century poetry, as Wordsworth broke with that of the eighteenth, he succeeded in shocking some of his contemporaries, who refused to grant him a place among English poets. It was in the *English Review* for October, 1911, that *The Everlasting Mercy* first appeared. It made a sensation. In 1912 the Academic Committee of the Royal Society of Literature awarded him the Edmond de Polignac prize of five hundred dollars. This aroused the wrath of the orthodox poet Stephen Phillips, who publicly protested, not with any animosity toward the recipient, but with the conviction that true standards of literature were endangered.

It is unfortunate for an artist or critic to belong to any "school" whatsoever. Belonging to a school circumscribes a man's sympathies. It shuts him away from outside sources of enjoyment, and makes him incapable of appreciating many new works of art, because he has prejudged them even before they were written. Poetry is

greater than any definition of it. There is no
doubt that *Marpessa* is a real poem; and there is
no doubt that the same description is true of *The
Everlasting Mercy*.

In *The Everlasting Mercy*, the prize-fight, given
in detail, by rounds, is followed by an orgy of
drunkenness rising to a scale almost Homeric.
The man, crazy with alcohol, runs amuck, and
things begin to happen. The village is turned up-
side down. Two powerful contrasts are dramati-
cally introduced, one as an interlude between violent phases of the debauch, the other as a conclusion. The first is the contrast between the insane
buffoon and the calm splendour of the night.

> I opened window wide and leaned
> Out of that pigstye of the fiend
> And felt a cool wind go like grace
> About the sleeping market-place.
> The clock struck three, and sweetly, slowly,
> The bells chimed Holy, Holy, Holy;
> And in a second's pause there fell
> The cold note of the chapel bell,
> And then a cock crew, flapping wings,
> And summat made me think of things.
> How long those ticking clocks had gone
> From church and chapel, on and on,
> Ticking the time out, ticking slow
> To men and girls who'd come and go.

These thoughts suddenly become intolerable.
A second fit of madness, wilder than the first,
drives the man about the town like a tornado.
Finally and impressively comes the contrast between the drunkard's horrible mirth and the sud-

den calm in his mind when the tall pale Quakeress
hypnotizes him with conviction of sin. She drives
out the devils from his breast with quiet authority,
and the peace of God enters into his soul.

From the first word of the poem to the last the
man's own attitude toward fighting, drink, and
religion is logically sustained. It is perfect
drama, with never a false note. The hero is one
of the "twice-born men," and the work may fairly
be taken as one more footnote to the varieties of
religious experience.

I have been told on good authority that of all his
writings Mr. Masefield prefers *Nan, The Widow
in the Bye Street,* and *The Everlasting Mercy.* I
think he is right. In these productions he has no
real competitors. They are his most original,
most vivid, most powerful pieces. He is at his
best when he has a story to tell, and can tell it
freely in his own unhampered way, a combination
of drama and narrative. In *The Everlasting
Mercy,* written in octosyllabics, the metre of
Christmas Eve, he is unflinchingly realistic, as
Browning was in describing the chapel. The
Athenæum thought Browning ought not to write
about the mysteries of the Christian faith in doggerel. But *Christmas Eve* is not doggerel. It
is simply the application of the rules of realism
to a discussion of religion. It may lack the dignity of the *Essay on Man,* but it is more interesting because it is more definite, more concrete, more
real. In *The Everlasting Mercy* we have beauti-

ful passages of description, sharply exciting narration, while the dramatic element is furnished by conversation—and what conversation! It differs from ordinary poetry as the sermons of an evangelist differ from the sermons of Bishops. Mr. Masefield is a natural-born dramatist. He is never content to describe his characters; he makes them talk, and talk their own language, and you will never go far in his longer poems without seeing the characters rise from the page, spring into life, and immediately you hear their voices raised in angry altercation. It is as though he felt the reality of his men and women so keenly that he cannot keep them down. They refuse to remain quiet. They insist on taking the poem into their own hands, and running away with it.

When we are reading *The Widow in the Bye Street* we realize that Mr. Masefield has studied with some profit the art of narrative verse as displayed by Chaucer. The story begins directly, and many necessary facts are revealed in the first stanza, in a manner so simple that for the moment we forget that this apparent simplicity is artistic excellence. The *Nun's Priest's Tale* is a model of attack.

> A poure wydwe, somdel stope in age,
> Was whilom dwellynge in a narwe cottage,
> Beside a grove, stondynge in a dale.
> This wydwe, of which I telle yow my tale,
> Syn thilke day that she was last a wyf,
> In pacience ladde a ful symple lyf,
> For litel was hir catel and hir rente.

Now if I could have only one of Mr. Masefield's books, I would take *The Widow in the Bye Street*. Its opening lines have the much-in-little so characteristic of Chaucer.

> Down Bye Street, in a little Shropshire town,
> There lived a widow with her only son:
> She had no wealth nor title to renown,
> Nor any joyous hours, never one.
> She rose from ragged mattress before sun
> And stitched all day until her eyes were red,
> And had to stitch, because her man was dead.

This is one of the best narrative poems in modern literature. It rises from calm to the fiercest and most tumultuous passions that usurp the throne of reason. Love, jealousy, hate, revenge, murder, succeed in cumulative force. Then the calm of unmitigated and hopeless woe returns, and we leave the widow in a solitude peopled only with memories. It is melodrama elevated into poetry. The mastery of the artist is shown in the skill with which he avoids the quagmire of sentimentality. We can easily imagine what form this story would take under the treatment of many popular writers. But although constantly approaching the verge, Mr. Masefield never falls in. He has known so much sentimentality, not merely in books and plays, but in human beings, that he understands how to avoid it. Furthermore, he is steadied by seeing so plainly the weaknesses of his characters, just as a great nervous specialist gains in poise by observing his patients. And perhaps our author feels the sorrows of the widow too deeply to talk about them with any conventional affectation.

I should like to find some one who, without much familiarity with the fixed stars in English literature, had read *The Daffodil Fields,* and then ask him to guess who wrote the following stanzas:

> A gentle answer did the old Man make,
> In courteous speech which forth he slowly drew;
> And him with further words I thus bespake,
> "What occupation do you there pursue?
> This is a lonesome place for one like you."
> Ere he replied, a flash of mild surprise
> Broke from the sable orbs of his yet-vivid eyes.
>
> "This will break Michael's heart," he said at length.
> "Poor Michael," she replied; "they wasted hours.
> He loved his father so.   God give him strength.
> This is a cruel thing this life of ours."
> The windy woodland glimmered with shut flowers,
> White wood anemones that the wind blew down.
> The valley opened wide beyond the starry town.

And I think he would reply with some confidence, "John Masefield." He would be right concerning the second stanza; but the first is, as every one ought to know and does not, from *Resolution and Independence,* by William Wordsworth. It is significant that this is one of the six poems excepted by Mr. Masefield from the mass of Wordsworthian mediocrity. It is, of course, a great poem, although when it was published (1807, written in 1802), it seemed by conventional standards no poem at all. Shortly after its appearance, some one read it aloud to an intelligent woman; she sobbed unrestrainedly; then, recovering herself, said shamefacedly, "After all, it isn't poetry." The reason, I suppose, why she thought it could not be poetry was because it was so much nearer life than "art." The simplicity of the scene; the naturalness of the dialogue; the homeliness of the old leech-gatherer; these all seemed to be outside the realm of the heroic, the elevated, the sublime,—the particular business of poetry, as she mistakenly thought. The reason why John Masefield admires this poem is because of its vitality, its naturalness, its easy dialogue—main characteristics of his own work. In writing *The Daffodil Fields,* he consciously or unconsciously selected the same metre, introduced plenty of conversation, as he loves to do in all his narrative poetry, and set his tragedy on a rural stage.

It is important here to repeat the last few phrases already quoted from Wordsworth's famous Preface: "The manners of rural life germinate from those elementary feelings, and, from the necessary character of rural occupations, are more easily comprehended, and are more durable; and, lastly, because in that condition the passions of men are incorporated with the beautiful and permanent forms of nature." If Mr. Masefield had written this preface for *The Daffodil Fields,* he could not have more accurately expressed both the artistic aim of his poem and its natural atmosphere. "The passions of men are incorporated with the beautiful and permanent forms of nature.'' In this work, each one of the seven sections ends with the daffodils; so that no matter how base and truculent are the revealed passions of man, the final impression at the close of each stage is the unchanging loveliness of the delicate golden flowers. Indeed, the daffodils not only fill the whole poem with their fluttering beauty, they play the part of the old Greek chorus. At the end of each act in this steadily growing tragedy, they comment in their own incomparable way on the sorrows of man.

> So the night passed; the noisy wind went down;
> The half-burnt moon her starry trackway rode.
> Then the first fire was lighted in the town,
> And the first carter stacked his early load.
> Upon the farm's drawn blinds the morning glowed;
> And down the valley, with little clucks and rills,
> The dancing waters danced by dancing daffodils.

But if, consciously or unconsciously, Mr. Mase-field in the composition of *The Daffodil Fields* followed the metre and the manner of Words-worth in *Resolution and Independence,* in the story itself he challenges Tennyson's *Enoch Arden.* Whether he meant to challenge it, I do not know; but the comparison is unescapable. Tennyson did not invent the story, and any poet has the right to use the material in his own fashion. Knowing Mr. Masefield from *The Everlasting Mercy* and *The Widow in the Bye Street,* it would have been safe to prophesy in advance that his own Enoch

would not show the self-restraint practised by the
Tennysonian hero. Reserve and restraint were
the trump cards of the Typical Victorian, just as
the annihilation of all reserve is a characteristic
of the twentieth-century artist. In the *Idylls of
the King*, the parting of Guinevere and Arthur was
what interested Tennyson; the poets of today
would of course centre attention on the parting of
Guinevere and Lancelot, and like so many "advances," they would in truth be only going back
to old Malory.

"Neither in the design nor in the telling did,
or could, *Enoch Arden* come near the artistic
truth of *The Daffodil Fields*," says Professor
Quiller-Couch, of Cambridge. I am not entirely
sure of the truth of this very positive statement.
Each is a rural poem; the characters are simple;
the poetic accompaniment supplied by the daffodils in one poem is supplied in the other by the
sea. And yet, despite this latter fact, if one reads
Enoch Arden immediately after *The Daffodil
Fields*, it seems to be without salt. It lacks
flavour, and is almost tasteless compared with the
biting condiments of the other poem, prepared as
it was for the sharper demands of twentieth-century palates. We like, as Browning thought
Macready would like "stabbing, drabbing, *et
autres gentillesses*," and Mr. Masefield knows how
to supply them. Yet I am not sure that the self-
denial of Enoch and the timid patience of Philip
do not both indicate a certain strength absent in

Mr. Masefield's wildly exciting tale. Of course Tennyson's trio are all "good" people, and he meant to make them so. In the other work Michael is a selfish scoundrel, Lion is a murderer, and Mary an adulteress; and we are meant to sympathize with all three, as Mr. Galsworthy wishes us to sympathize with those who follow their instincts rather than their consciences. One poem celebrates the strength of character, the other the strength of passion. But there can be no doubt that Enoch (and perhaps Philip) loved Annie more than either Michael or Lion loved Mary—which is perhaps creditable; for Mary is more attractive.

One should remember also that in these two poems—so interesting to compare in so many different ways—Tennyson tried to elevate a homely theme into "poetry"; whereas Mr. Masefield finds the truest poetry in the bare facts of life and feeling. Tennyson is at his best outside of drama, wherever he has an opportunity to adorn and embellish; Mr. Masefield is at his best in the fierce conflict of human wills. Thus *Enoch Arden* is not one of Tennyson's best poems, and the best parts of it are the purely descriptive passages; whereas in *The Daffodil Fields* Mr. Masefield has a subject made to his hand, and can let himself go with impressive power. In the introduction of conversation into a poem—a special gift with Mr. Masefield—Tennyson is usually weak, which ought to have taught him never to venture into

drama. Nothing is worse in *Enoch Arden* than
passages like these:

> "Annie, this voyage by the grace of God
> Will bring fair weather yet to all of us.
> Keep a clean hearth and a clear fire for me,
> For I'll be back, my girl, before you know it."
> Then lightly rocking baby's cradle, "and he,
> This pretty, puny, weakly little one,—
> Nay—for I love him all the better for it—
> God bless him, he shall sit upon my knees
> And I will tell him tales of foreign parts,
> And make him merry, when I come home again.
> Come, Annie, come, cheer up before I go."

One of the reasons why twentieth-century readers are so impatient with *Enoch Arden,* is because
Tennyson refused to satisfy the all but universal
love of a fight. The conditions for a terrific
"mix-up" were all there, and just when the spectator is looking for an explosion of wrath and
blood, the poet turns away into the more heroic
but less thrilling scene of self-conquest. Mr.
Masefield may be trusted never to disappoint his
readers in such fashion. It might be urged that
whereas Tennyson gave a picture of man as he
ought to be, Mr. Masefield painted him as he really
is.

But *The Daffodil Fields* is not melodrama. It
is a poem of extraordinary beauty. Every time
I read it I see in it some "stray beauty-beam"
that I missed before. It would be impossible to
translate it into prose; it would lose half its interest, and all of its charm. It would be easier

to translate Tennyson's *Dora* into prose than *The Daffodil Fields*. In fact, I have often thought that if the story of *Dora* were told in concise prose, in the manner of Guy de Maupassant, it would distinctly gain in force.

No poet, with any claim to the name, can be accurately labelled by an adjective or a phrase. You may think you know his "manner," and he suddenly develops a different one; this you call his "later" manner, and he disconcerts you by harking back to the "earlier," or trying something, that if you must have labels, you are forced to call his "latest," knowing now that it is subject to change without notice. Mr. Masefield published *The Everlasting Mercy* in 1911; *The Widow in the Bye Street* in 1912; *Dauber* in 1912; *The Daffodil Fields* in 1913. We had him classified. He was a writer of sustained narrative, unscrupulous in the use of language, bursting with vitality, sacrificing anything and everything that stood in the way of his effect. This was "red blood" verse raised to poetry by sheer inspiration, backed by remarkable skill in the use of rime. We looked for more of the same thing from him, knowing that in this particular field he had no rival.

Then came the war. As every soldier drew his sword, every poet drew his pen. And of all the poems published in the early days of the struggle, none equalled in high excellence *August 1914*, by John Masefield. And its tone was precisely the opposite of what his most famous efforts had led

us to expect. It was not a lurid picture of wholesale murder, nor a bottle of vitriol thrown in the
face of the Kaiser. After the thunder and the
lightning, came the still small voice. It is a poem
in the metre and manner of Gray, with the same
silver tones of twilit peace—heartrending by contrast with the Continental scene.

> How still this quiet cornfield is to-night;
>   By an intenser glow the evening falls,
> Bringing, not darkness, but a deeper light;
>   Among the stooks a partridge covey calls.
>
> The windows glitter on the distant hill;
>   Beyond the hedge the sheep-bells in the fold
> Stumble on sudden music and are still;
>   The forlorn pinewoods droop above the wold.
>
> An endless quiet valley reaches out
>   Past the blue hills into the evening sky;
> Over the stubble, cawing, goes a rout
>   Of rooks from harvest, flagging as they fly.
>
> So beautiful it is I never saw
>   So great a beauty on these English fields
> Touched, by the twilight's coming, into awe,
>   Ripe to the soul and rich with summer's yields.

The fields are inhabited with the ghosts of
ploughmen of old who gave themselves for England, even as the faithful farmers now leave scenes
inexpressibly dear. For the aim of our poet is to
magnify the lives of the humble and the obscure,
whether on land or sea. In the beautiful *Conse-
cration* that he prefixed to *Salt-Water Ballads,* he
expressly turns his back on Commanders, on Rul-

ers, on Princes and Prelates, in order to sing of the stokers and chantymen, yes, even of the dust and scum of the earth. They work, and others get the praise. They are inarticulate, but have found a spokesman and a champion in the poet. His sea-poems in this respect resemble Conrad's sea-novels. This is perhaps one of the chief functions of the man of letters, whether he be poet, novelist or dramatist—never to let us forget the anonymous army of toilers. For, as Clyde Fitch used to say, the great things do not happen to the great writers; the great things happen to the little people they describe.

Although Mr. Masefield's reputation depends mainly on his narrative poems, he has earned a high place among lyrical poets. These poems, at least many of them, are as purely subjective as *The Everlasting Mercy* was purely objective. Rarely does a poem unfurl with more loveliness than this:

> I have seen dawn and sunset on moors and windy hills
>   Coming in solemn beauty like slow old tunes of Spain;
> I have seen the lady April bringing the daffodils,
>   Bringing the springing grass and the soft warm April rain.

In *Tewkesbury Road* and in *Sea Fever* the poet expresses the urge of his own heart. In *Biography* he quite properly adopts a style exactly the opposite of the biographical dictionary. Dates and events are excluded. But the various moments when life was most intense in actual experience, sights of mountains on sea and land, long walks and talks with an intimate friend, the frantically fierce endeavour in the racing cutter, quiet scenes of beauty in the peaceful country-side. "The days that make us happy make us wise."

As Mr. Masefield's narratives take us back to Chaucer, so his *Sonnets* (1916) take us back to the great Elizabethan sequences. Whether or not Shakespeare unlocked his heart in his sonnets is impossible to determine. Wordsworth thought he did, Browning thought quite otherwise. But these sonnets of our poet are undoubtedly subjective; no one without the necessary information would guess them to come from the author of *The Everlasting Mercy*. They reveal what has always been—through moving accidents by flood and field—the master passion of his mind and heart, the worship of Beauty. The entire series illustrates a tribute to Beauty expressed in the first one—"Delight in her made trouble in my mind." This mental disturbance is here the spur to composition. They are experiments in relative, meditative, speculative poetry; and while they contain some memorable lines, and heighten one's respect for the dignity and sincerity of their author's temperament, they are surely not so successful as his other work. They are not clearly articulate. Instead of the perfect expression of perfect thoughts—a gift enjoyed only by Shakespeare—they reveal the extreme difficulty of metrically voicing his "trouble." It is in a way like the music of the *Liebestod*. He is struggling to say what is in his mind, he approaches it, falls away, comes near again, only to be finally baffled.

In 1918 Mr. Masefield returned to battle, murder and sudden death in the romantic poem *Rosas*. This is an exciting tale told in over a hundred stanzas, and it is safe to say that any one who reads the first six lines will read to the end without moving in his chair. Although this is the latest in publication of our poet's works, it sounds as if it were written years ago, before he had attained the mastery so evident in *The Widow in the Bye Street*. It will add little to the author's reputation.

I do not think Mr. Masefield has received sufficient credit for his prose fiction. In 1905 he published *A Mainsail Haul,* which contained a number of short stories and sketches, many of which had appeared in the Manchester *Guardian*. It is interesting to recall his connection with that famous journal. These are the results partly of his experiences, partly of his reading. It is plain that he has turned over hundreds of old volumes of buccaneer lore. And humour is as abundant here as it is absent from his best novels, *Captain Margaret* and *Multitude and Solitude*. These two books, recently republished in America, met with a chilling reception from the critics. For my part, I not only enjoyed reading them, I think every student of Mr. Masefield's poetry might read them with profitable pleasure. They are romances that only a poet could have written. It would be easier to turn them into verse than it would be to turn his verse-narratives into prose, and less would be lost in the transfer. In *Multitude and Solitude,* the author has given us more of the results of his own thinking than can be found in most of the poems. Whole pages are filled with the pith of meditative thought. In *Captain Margaret,* we have a remarkable combination of the love of romance and the romance of love.

In response to a question asked him by the *Tribune* interviewer, as to the guiding motive in his writing, Mr. Masefield replied: "I desire to interpret life both by reflecting it as it appears and by portraying its outcome. Great art must contain these two attributes. Examine any of the dramas of Shakespeare, and you will find that their action is the result of a destruction of balance in the beginning. It is like a cartful of apples which is overturned. All the apples are spilled in the street. But you will notice that Shakespeare piles them up again in his incomparable manner, many bruised, broken, and maybe a few lost." This is certainly an interesting way of putting the doctrine of analysis and synthesis as applied to art.

What has Mr. Masefield done then for the advance of poetry? One of his notable services is to have made it so interesting that thousands look

forward to a new poem from him as readers look
for a new story by a great novelist. He has
helped to take away poetry from its conventional
"elevation" and bring it everywhere poignantly in
contact with throbbing life. Thus he is emphatic-
ally apart from so-called traditional poets who
brilliantly follow the Tennysonian tradition, and
give us another kind of enjoyment. But although
Mr. Masefield is a twentieth century poet, it would
be a mistake to suppose that he has *originated* the
doctrine that the poet should speak in a natural
voice about natural things, and not cultivate a
"diction." Browning spent his whole life fighting for that doctrine, and went to his grave cov-
ered with honourable scars. Wordsworth successfully rebelled against the conventional garments
of the Muse. Chaucer, Shakespeare, and Browning are the poets who took human nature as they
found it; who thought life itself was more interesting than any theory about it; who made language appropriate to the time, the place, and the
man, regardless of the opinion of those who
thought the Muse ought to wear a uniform. The
aim of our best twentieth century poets is not
really to write something new and strange, it is to
get back to those poets who lived up to their conviction that the business of poetry is to chronicle
the stages of all life. This is not the only kind of
poetry, but it is the kind high in favour during
these present years. The fountain-head of poetry
is human nature, and our poets are trying to get

back to it, just as many of the so-called advances in religious thought are really attempts to get back to the Founder of Christianity, before the theologians built their stockade around Him. Mr. Masefield is a mighty force in the renewal of poetry; in the art of dramatic narrative he goes back to the sincerity and catholicity of Chaucer. For his language, he has carried Wordsworth's idea of "naturalness" to its extreme limits. For his material, he finds nothing common or unclean. But all his virility, candour, and sympathy, backed by all his astonishing range of experience, would not have made him a poet, had he not possessed imagination, and the power to express his vision of life, the power, as he puts it, of getting the apples back into the cart.

CHAPTER IV

GIBSON AND HODGSON

Two Northumberland poets—Wilfrid Wilson Gibson—his early failures—his studies of low life—his collected poems—his short dramas of pastoral experiences—*Daily Bread*—lack of melody—uncanny imagination—whimsies—poems of the Great War—their contrast to conventional sentimental ditties—the accusation—his contribution to the advance of poetry.—Ralph Hodgson—his shyness—his slender output—his fastidious self-criticism—his quiet facing of the known facts in nature and in humanity—his love of books—his humour—his respect for wild and tame animals—the high percentage of artistic excellence in his work.—Lascelles Abercrombie.

Wilfrid Wilson Gibson—a horrible mouthful—was born in Hexham, Northumberland, in 1878. Like Walt Whitman's, his early poetry was orthodox, well groomed, and uninteresting. It produced no effect on the public, but it produced upon its author a mental condition of acute discontent—the necessary conviction of sin preceding regeneration. Whether he could ever succeed in bringing his verse down to earth, he did not then know; but so far as he was concerned, he not only got down to earth, but got under it. He made subterranean expeditions with the miners, he followed his nose into slums, he talked long hours with the unclassed, and listened sympathetically to the lamentations of sea-made widows. His nature—extraordinarily delicate and sensitive—

98

received deep wounds, the scars of which appeared
in his subsequent poetry. Now he lives where
John Masefield was born, and like him, speaks for
the inarticulate poor.

In 1917 Mr. Gibson collected his poems in one
thick volume of some five hundred and fifty pages.
This is convenient for reference, but desperately
hard to read, on account of the soggy weight of the
book. Here we have, however, everything that
he has thus far written which he thinks worth pre-
serving. The first piece, *Akra the Slave* (1904),
is a romantic monologue in free verse. Although
rather short, it is much too long, and few persons
will have the courage to read it through. It is
incoherent, spineless, consistent only in dulness.
Possibly it is worth keeping as a curiosity. Then
comes *Stonefolds* (1906), a series of bitter bucolics.
This is pastoral poetry of a new and refreshing
kind—as unlike to the conventional shepherd-
shepherdess mincing, intolerable dialogue as could
well be imagined. For, among all the groups of
verse, in which, for sacred order's sake, we arrange English literature, pastoral poetry easily
takes first place in empty, tinkling artificiality.
In *Stonefolds,* we have six tiny plays, never containing more than four characters, and usually
less, which represent, in a rasping style, the un-
ending daily struggle of generation after generation with the relentless forces of nature. It is surprising to see how, in four or five pages, the author
gives a clear view of the monotonous life of sev-

enty years; in this particular art, Strindberg himself has done no better. The experience of age is contrasted with the hope of youth. Perhaps the most impressive of them all is *The Bridal* where, in the presence of the newly wedded pair, the man's old, bed-ridden mother speaks of the chronic misery of her married life, intimates that the son is just like his dead father, and that therefore the bride has nothing ahead of her but tragedy. Then comes the conclusion, which reminds one somewhat of the close of Ibsen's *Lady from the Sea.* The young husband throws wide the door, and addresses his wife as follows:

> The door is open; you are free to go.
> Why do you tarry? Are you not afraid?
> Go, ere I hate you. I'll not hinder you.
> I would not have you bound to me by fear.
> Don't fear to leave me; rather fear to bide
> With me who am my father's very son.
> Go, lass, while yet I love you!
>
> ESTHER (*closing the door*). I shall bide.
> I have heard all; and yet, I would not go.
> Nor would I have a single word unsaid.
> I loved you, husband; yet, I did not know you
> Until your mother spoke. I know you now;
> And I am not afraid.

The first piece in *Stonefolds* represents the tragic helplessness of those newly born and those very old, a favourite theme with Maeterlinck. A lamb and a child are born on the same night, and both die before dawn. The lamb is a poetic symbol of babyhood. Nicholas, the aged shepherd,

who longs to go out into the night and do his share
of the work that must be done, but who is unable
even to move, thus addresses the dying lamb:

> Poor, bleating beast! We two are much alike,
> At either end of life, though scarce an hour
> You've been in this rough world, and I so long
> That death already has me by the heels;
> For neither of us can stir to help himself,
> But both must bleat for others' aid. This world
> Is rough and bitter to the newly born,
> But far more bitter to the nearly dead.

In *Daily Bread* (1908–09), there are eighteen
brief plays, written not in orthodox blank verse,
like *Stonefolds,* but in irregular, brittle, breathless
metres. Here is where art takes the short cut
to life, sacrificing every grace to gain reality; the
typical goal and method of twentieth-century
poetry. So long as a vivid impression of character and circumstance is produced, the writer apparently cares nothing about style. I say "apparently," because the styleless style is perhaps
the one best adapted to produce the sought-for
effect. There is ever one difference between life
and "art"—between drama and theatre—that Mr.
Gibson has, I suppose, tried to cancel in these
poems of daily bread. In art, the bigger the
drama, the bigger the stage; one could not mount
Götterdämmerung in a village schoolhouse. But
Life does not fit the splendour of the setting to
the grandeur of the struggle. In bleak farm cottages, in dull dwellings in city blocks, in slum tene-

ments, the greatest of life's tragedies and come-
dies are enacted—love, hate, avarice, jealousy,
revenge, birth, death—the most terrific passions
known to human nature are fully presented, without the slightest care for appropriate scenery
from the Master of the show.   Thus our poet leads
us by the hand into sea-girt huts, into hovels at
the mouths of mines, into garrets of noisy cities,
and makes us silent witnesses of elemental woe.
Here Labour, man's greatest blessing, takes on
the aspect of the primal curse, since so many
tragedies spring from the simple root of poverty.
The love of money may be the root of all evil, but
the lack of it is the cause of much pain.

It was a happy inspiration that made Mr. Gibson call these scenes *Daily Bread;* for it is the
struggle, not for comfort, but for existence, that
drives these men from mother, wife, and child
into the thick of the fight.   Many novels and plays
are written nowadays against "big business,"
where, among other real and imagined evils, the
Business itself is represented as the villain in the
home, alienating the husband's affections from
wife and children.   Whatever may be the case
with the private soldiers, the Captain of Industry
does not, and by the nature of things cannot, con-
fine his labours to an eight-hour day—when he
finally comes home, he brings the business with
him, forming a more well-founded cause of jealousy than the one usually selected for conventional
drama.   Mr. Gibson, however, is not interested

in the tragic few, but in the tragic many, and in
his poems the man of the house leaves early and
returns late.   The industrial war caused by social
conditions takes him from home as surely and as
perilously as though he were drafted into an ex-
peditionary force.   The daily parting is poignant,
for every member of the family knows he may
not come back.   Perhaps the most dramatic illustration of this corroding worry is seen in *The
Night-Shift*, where four women with a newly-born
baby spend a night of agonized waiting, only to
have their fears confirmed in the dawn.

The wife, weak from childbirth, sits up in bed,
and speaks:

> Will no one stop that tapping?
> I cannot sleep for it.
> I think that someone is shut in somewhere,
> And trying to get out.
> Will no one let them out,
> And stop the tapping?
> It keeps on tapping, tapping. . . .
> Tap . . . tap . . . tap . . . tap . . .
> And I can scarcely breathe,
> The darkness is so thick.
> It stifles me,
> And weighs so heavily upon me,
> And drips, and drips. . . .
> My hair is wet already;
> There's water all about my knees. . . .
> As though great rocks were hanging overhead!
> And dripping, dripping. . . .
> I cannot lift my feet,
> The water holds them,
> It's creeping . . . creeping . . . creeping. . . .
> My wet hair drags me down.

> Ah, God!
> Will no one stop that tapping. . . .
> I cannot sleep. . . .
> And I would sleep
> Till he comes home. . . .
> Tap . . . tap . . . tap . . . tap . . .

These poems were, of course, composed before the war. In the greater tragedy, some of the lesser ones disappear. For example, Mr. Gibson represents young, able-bodied, healthy and temperate men as unable to find work of any kind; their wives and children starve because of the absence of employment. Surely, since August, 1914, this particular cause of suffering has been removed.

In *Womenkind* (1909), dedicated to Rabbi and Mrs. Wise, we have a real play, not only dramatic in character and situation, but fitted for stage representation without the change of a word. The theme is just the opposite of Middleton's old drama, *Women Beware Women*. Here the two young women, one the mistress-mother, and one the bride, join forces against the man, and walk out of his house on the wedding-day. They feel that the tie between them is stronger than the tie which had united them severally to the man, and depart to live together. The play closes on a note of irony, for Jim, his blind father, and his weary mother repeat in turn—but with quite different emphasis—the accusation that women are a faithless lot.

The long series of poems called *Fires* (1910–11)

differ in matter and manner from the earlier works. The form of drama is abandoned, and in its place we have vivid rimed narrative, mingled with glowing pictures of natural scenery, taken at all hours of the day and night. Each of his poems must be taken as a whole, for each poem strives for a single effect. This effect is often gained by taking some object, animate or inanimate, as a symbol. Thus, in *The Hare,* the hunted animal is the symbol of woman. *The Flute, The Light-house,* and *The Money* mean more than their definition. Mr. Gibson is somewhat kinder to his readers in this collection, for the monotony of woe, that hangs over his work like a cloud, is rifted here and there by a ray of happiness. In *The Shop,* the little boy actually recovers from pneumonia, and our share in the father's delight is heightened by surprise, for whenever any of our poet's characters falls into a sickness, we have learned to expect the worst. Still, the darker side of life remains the author's chosen field of exploration. Two pieces are so uncanny that one might almost think they proceeded from a disordered imagination. The blind boy, who every day has rowed his father back and forth from the fishing-grounds, while the man steered, one day rows cheerfully toward home, unaware that his father is dead. The boy wonders at his father's silence, and laughingly asserts that he has heard him snoring. Then his mirth changes to fear, and fear to horror.

> Though none has ever known
> How he rowed in, alone,
> And never touched a reef.
> Some say they saw the dead man steer—
> The dead man steer the blind man home—
> Though, when they found him dead,
> His hand was cold as lead.

Another strange poem describes how a cripple sits in his room, with a mother eternally stitching for bread, and watches out of the window the giant crane swinging vast weights through the sky. One night, while he is half-dead with fear, the great crane swoops down upon him, clutches his bed, and swings him, bed and all, above the sleeping city, among the blazing stars.

Following Mr. Gibson's development as a poet, year by year, we come to *Thoroughfares* (1908–14). These are short poems more conventional in form than their predecessors, but just as stark and grim as chronicles of life. Every one remembers the torture inflicted on women in the good-old-times, when they were strapped to posts on the flats at low tide, and allowed to watch the cruel slowness of approaching death. The same theme, with an even more terrible termination, is selected by Mr. Gibson in *Solway Ford*, where the carter is pinned by the heavy, overturned wagon on the sands; while the tide gradually brings the water toward his helpless body. He dies a thousand deaths in imagination, but is rescued just as the waves are lapping the wheels. Now he lies in bed, an incurable idiot, smiling as

he sees gold and sapphire fishes swimming in the
water over his head. . . . That rarest of all English metres—which Browning chose for *One Word
More*—is employed by Mr. Gibson in a compound
of tragedy-irony called *The Vindictive Staircase.*
Unfortunately the rhythm is so closely associated
with Browning's love-poem, that these lines sound
like a parody:

> Mrs. Murphy, timidest of spectres,
> You who were the cheeriest of charers,
> With the heart of innocence and only
> Torn between a zest for priest and porter,
> Mrs. Murphy of the ample bosom,—
> Suckler of a score or so of children.

It seems best to leave this measure in the undis-
turbed possession of the poet who used it supremely well. Yet some of the verses in *Thoroughfares* are an advance on Mr. Gibson's previous work. No reader will ever forget *Wheels.*

Passing over *Borderlands* (1912–14) which,
with the exception of *Akra,* is the least successful
of Mr. Gibson's works, we come to his most original contribution to modern poetry, the short
poems included under the heading *Battle*
(1914–15). These verses afford one more bit of
evidence that in order to write unconventional
thoughts, it is not necessary to use unconventional
forms. The ideas expressed here can be found
in no other war-poet; they are idiosyncratic to
the highest degree; yet the verse-forms in which
they are written are stanzaic, as traditional as the

most conservative critic could desire. There is, of course, no reason why any poet should not compose in new and strange rhythms if he prefers to do so; but I have never believed that originality in thought *necessarily* demands metrical measures other than those found in the history of English literature.

These lyrical poems are dramatic monologues. Each one is the testimony of some soldier in the thick of the fight as to what he has seen or heard, or as to what memories are strongest in his mind as he lies in the filth of the trenches. Conventional emotions of enthusiasm, glory, sacrifice, courage, are omitted, not because they do not exist, but simply because they are taken for granted; these boys are aflame with such feelings at the proper time. But Mr. Gibson is more interested in the strange, fantastic thoughts, waifs of memory, that wander across the surface of the mind in the midst of scenes of horror. And we feel that the more fantastic these thoughts are, the more do they reflect the deep truths of experience. Home naturally looms large, and some of the recollections of home take on a grim humour, strangely in contrast with the present environment of the soldier.

HIS FATHER

> I quite forgot to put the spigot in.
>   It's just come over me. . . . And it is queer
> To think he'll not care if we lose or win.
>   And yet be jumping-mad about that beer.

I left it running full. He must have said
A thing or two. I'd give my stripes to hear
What he will say if I'm reported dead
Before he gets me told about that beer!

It would appear that the world has grown up,
or at all events, grown much older, during the
last forty years. It has grown older at a high
rate of speed. The love of country is the same
as ever, because that is a primal human passion,
that will never change, any more than the love of
the sexes; but the expression of battle-poems
seems more mature, more sophisticated, if you
like, in this war than in any preceding conflict.
Most of the verses written in England and in
America are as different as may be from "Just
before the battle, mother," which was so popular
during our Civil War. Never before has the
psychology of the soldier been so acutely studied
by national poets. And instead of representing
the soldier as a man swayed by a few elemental
passions and lush sentiment, he is presented as
an extraordinarily complex individual, with every
part of his brain abnormally alert. Modern
poetry, in this respect, has, I think, followed the
lead of the realistic prose novel. Such books as
Tolstoi's *Sevastopol,* and Zola's *La Débâcle,* have
had a powerful effect in making war poetry more
analytical; while that original story, *The Red
Badge of Courage,* written by an inspired young
American, Stephen Crane, has left its mark on
many a volume of verse that has been produced

since August, 1914. The unabashed realism of
the trenches, together with the psychology of the
soldier, is clearly and significantly reflected in
From the Front (1918), a book of poems written by men in service, edited by Lieut. C. E. Andrews.

What is going to become of us all if the obsession of self-consciousness grows ever stronger?

There is not a trace of cheap sentiment in *Battle*. Even the poems that come nearest to the
emotional surface are saved by some specific
touch, like the sense of smell, which, as every one
knows, is a sharper spur to the memory than any
other sensation.

> Tonight they're sitting by the peat
>   Talking of me, I know—
> Grandfather in the ingle-seat,
>   Mother and Meg and Joe.
>
> I feel a sudden puff of heat
>   That sets my ears aglow,
> And smell the reek of burning peat
>   Across the Belgian snow.

Browning wrote of Shelley, who had been dead
eleven years,

> *The air seems bright with thy past presence yet.*

A similar effect of brightness in life and afterglow in death, seems to have been made on every
one who knew him by Rupert Brooke. No young
poet of the twentieth century has left such a flam-

ing glory as he. The prefatory poem to Mr. Gibson's *Friends* (1915–16), beautifully expresses the common feeling:

> He's gone.
> I do not understand.
> I only know
> That as he turned to go
> And waved his hand
> In his young eyes a sudden glory shone:
> And I was dazzled by a sunset glow,
> And he was gone.

The fine sonnets that follow strengthen the strong colour, and are among the most authentic claims to poetry that their author has set forth. The second one, contrasting the pale glimmer of the London garret with the brilliant apparition of Brooke at the open door, "like sudden April," is poignant in its beauty. The verses in this volume are richer in melody than is customary with Mr. Gibson, yet *The Pessimist* and *The Ice-Cart* show that he is as whimsical as ever. He has no end of fun with his fancy.

Livelihood (1914–16) takes us back to the bitter pessimism of *Stonefolds* and *Daily Bread;* only instead of being dialogues, these stories are given in descriptive form, and for the most part in regular pentameter rime. The best of them is *In the Orchestra,* where the poor fiddler in the band at the cheap music-hall plays mechanically every night for his daily bread, while his heart is torn by the vulture of memory. This poem shows a firm grasp of the material; every word adds something to the total impression.

Mr. Gibson's constantly repeated pictures of the grinding, soul-crushing labour of the poor seem to say *J'accuse!* Yet he nowhere says it explicitly. He never interrupts his narrative with "My Lords and Gentlemen," nor does he comment, like Hood in *The Song of the Shirt.*

Yet the effect of his work is an indictment. Only, whom does he accuse? Is it the government; is it society; is it God?

Mr. Gibson's latest book of poems, *Hill-Tracks* (1918), differs from his previous works in two respects. It is full of pictures of the open fields of Northumberland, the county where he was born; and nearly every piece is an attempt at a singing lyric, something seldom found in his *Collected Poems.* I say an "attempt" with deliberation, for song is not the most natural expression of this realistic writer, and not more than half of the fifty lyrics in this handsome volume are successfully melodious. Some are trivial, and hardly deserve such beauty of type and paper; others, however, will be gladly welcomed by all students of Mr. Gibson's work, because they exhibit the powers of the author in an unusual and charming manner. I should think that those familiar with the topography and with the colloquialisms constantly appearing in this book, would read it with a veritable delight of reminiscence.

NORTHUMBERLAND

Heatherland and bent-land—
Black land and white,
God bring me to Northumberland,
The land of my delight.

Land of singing waters,
And winds from off the sea,
God bring me to Northumberland,
The land where I would be.

Heatherland and bent-land,
And valleys rich with corn,
God bring me to Northumberland,
The land where I was born.

The shadow of the war darkens nearly every page of this volume, and the last poem expresses not the local but the universal sentiment of us who remain in our homes.

We who are left, how shall we look again
Happily on the sun, or feel the rain,
Without remembering how they who went
Ungrudgingly, and spent
Their all for us, loved, too, the sun and rain?

A bird among the rain-wet lilac sings—
But we, how shall we turn to little things
And listen to the birds and winds and streams
Made holy by their dreams,
Nor feel the heart-break in the heart of things?

An interesting feature of the *Collected Poems* is a striking unfinished portrait of the author by Mrs. Wise; but I think it was an error to publish all these verses in one volume. They produce an impression of grey monotony which is hardly fair to the poet. The individuals change their names, but they pass through the same typical woe of childbirth, desertion, loveless old age, incipient insanity, with eternal joyless toil. One will form a higher opinion if one reads the separate volumes as they appeared, and not too much at a time.

His contribution to the advance of English poetry is seen mainly in his grim realism, in his direct, unadorned presentation of what he believes to be the truth, whether it be the facts of environment, or the facts of thought. Conventional war-poetry, excellently represented by Tennyson's *Charge of the Light Brigade,* which itself harks back to Drayton's stirring *Ballad of Agincourt,* has not the slightest echo in these volumes; and ordinary songs of labour are equally remote. Face to face with Life—that is where the poet leads us, and where he leaves us. He is far indeed from possessing the splendid lyrical gift of John Masefield; he has nothing of the literary quality of William Watson. He writes neither of romantic buccaneers nor of golden old books. But he is close to the grimy millions. He writes the short and simple annals of the poor. He is a poet of the people, and seems to have taken a vow that we shall not forget them.

Ralph Hodgson was born somewhere in Northumberland about forty years ago, and successfully eluded the notice of the world until the year

1907. He is by nature such a recluse that I feel
certain he would prefer to attract no attention
whatever were it not for the fact that it is as
necessary for a poet to print his songs as it is
for a bird to sing them. His favourite companions are Shelley, Wordsworth, and a bull terrier,
and he is said to play billiards with "grim earnest-
ness." In 1907 he published a tiny volume called
The Last Blackbird, and in 1917 another and
tinier one called *Poems.* During this decade he
printed in a few paper booklets, which some day
will be valuable curiosities, separate pieces such
as *Eve, The Bull, The Mystery.* These are now
permanently preserved in the 1917 book. This
thin volume, weighing only two or three ounces,
is a real addition to the English poetry of the
twentieth century.

It is impossible to read the verse of Ralph
Hodgson without admiration for the clarity of
his art and respect for the vigour of his mind.
Although many of his works are as aloof from his
own opinions as a well-executed statue, the
strength of his personality is an immanent force.
He writes much and publishes little; he is an intellectual aristocrat. He has the fastidiousness
which was the main characteristic of the temperament of Thomas Gray; and he has as well Gray's
hatred of publicity and much of Gray's lambent
humour, more salty than satiric. His work is decidedly caviare to the general, not because it is
obscure, which it is not, but because it presupposes

much background. Lovers of nature and lovers of books will love these verses, and reread them many times; but they are not for all markets. No contemporary poet is more truly original than he; but his originality is seen in his mental attitude rather than in newness of form or strangeness of language. The standard metres are good enough for him, and so are the words in common use. His subjects are the world-old subjects of poetry —birds, flowers, men and women. Religion is as conspicuously absent as it is in the works of Keats; its place is taken by sympathy for humanity and an extraordinary sympathy for animals. He is as far from the religious passion of Francis Thompson as he is from the sociological inquisitiveness of Mr. Gibson. To him each bird, each flower appears as a form of worship. Men and women appeal to him not because they are poor or downtrodden, but simply because they are men and women. He is neither an optimist nor a pessimist; the world is full of objects both interesting and beautiful, which will pay a rich return to those who observe them accurately. This is as near as he has thus far come to any philosophy or any theology:

THE MYSTERY

He came and took me by the hand
 Up to a red rose tree,
He kept His meaning to Himself
 But gave a rose to me.

I did not pray Him to lay bare
  The mystery to me,
Enough the rose was Heaven to smell,
  And His own face to see.

It is the absolute object that interests this poet,
rather than vague or futile speculation about it.
The flower in the crannied wall he would leave
there. He would never pluck it out, root and all,
wondering about the mystery of the life principle.
No poet is more clean-eyed. His eyes are achro-
matic. He has lost his illusions gladly; every
time he has lost an illusion he has gained a new
idea. The world as it is seems to him more beautiful, more interesting than any false-coloured picture of it or any longing to remould it nearer to
the heart's desire. He faces life with steady composure. But it is not the composure either of
stoicism or of despair. He finds it so wonderful
just as it is that he is thankful that he has eyes
to see its beauty, ears to hear its melodies—
enough for his present mortal state.

AFTER

"How fared you when you mortal were?
  What did you see on my peopled star?"
"Oh, well enough," I answered her,
  "It went for me where mortals are!

"I saw blue flowers and the merlin's flight
  And the rime on the wintry tree,
Blue doves I saw and summer light
  On the wings of the cinnamon bee."

There is in all this a kind of reverent worship without any trace of mysticism. And still less of that modern attitude more popular and surely more fruitless than mysticism—defiance.

There is a quite different side to the poetry of Mr. Hodgson, which one would hardly suspect after reading his outdoor verse. The lamplit silence of the library is as charming to him as the fragrant silence of the woods. He is as much of a recluse among books as he is among flowers. No poet of today seems more self-sufficient. Although a lover of humanity, he seems to require no companionship. He is no more lonely than a cat, and has as many resources as Tabby herself. Now when he talks about books, his poetry becomes intimate, and forsakes all objectivity. His humour, a purely intellectual quality with him, rises unrestrainedly.

MY BOOKS

When the folks have gone to bed,
  And the lamp is burning low,
And the fire burns not so red
  As it burned an hour ago,

Then I turn about my chair
  So that I can dimly see
Into the dark corners where
  Lies my modest library.

Volumes gay and volumes grave,
  Many volumes have I got;
Many volumes though I have,
  Many volumes have I not.

I have not the rare Lucasta,
  London, 1649;
I'm a lean-pursed poetaster,
  Or the book had long been mine. . . .

Near the "Wit's Interpreter"
  (Like an antique Whitaker,
Full of strange etcetera),
  "Areopagitica,"

And the muse of Lycidas,
  Lost in meditation deep,
Give the cut to Hudibras,
  Unaware the knave's asleep. . . .

There lies Coleridge, bound in green,
  Sleepily still wond'ring what
He meant Kubla Khan to mean,
  In that early Wordsworth, Mat.

Arnold knows a faithful prop,—
  Still to subject-matter leans,
Murmurs of the loved hill-top,
  Fyfield tree and Cumnor scenes.

The poem closes with a high tribute to Shelley, "more than all the others mine."

The following trifle is excellent fooling:

THE GREAT AUK'S GHOST

The Great Auk's ghost rose on one leg,
  Sighed thrice and three times winkt,
And turned and poached a phantom egg,
  And muttered, "I'm extinct."

But it is in the love of unextinct animals that Mr. Hodgson's poetic powers find their most effective display. His masterpiece on the old unhappy Bull is surprisingly impressive; surprisingly, because we almost resent being made to feel such ardent sympathy for the poor old Bull, when there are so many other and more important objects to be sorry for. Yet the poet draws us away for the moment from all the other tragedies in God's universe, and absolutely compels our pity for the Bull. The stanzas in this poem swarm with life.

From a certain point of view, poets are justified in calling attention to the sufferings of our animal brothers. For it is the sufferings of animals, even more than the sorrows of man, that check our faith either in the providence or in the love of God. Human suffering may possibly be balanced against the spiritual gain it (sometimes) brings; and at all events, we know that there is no road to greatness of character except through pain. But what can compensate the dumb animals for their physical anguish? It is certainly difficult to see their reward, unless they have immortal souls. That this is no slight obstacle in the way of those who earnestly desire to believe in an ethical universe, may be seen from the fact that it was the sight of a snake swallowing a toad that destroyed once for all the religious beliefs of Turgenev; and I know a man of science in America who became an agnostic simply from observation of a particular Texas fly that bites the cattle. The Founder of Christianity recognized this problem, as He did every other painful

fact in life, when He made the remark about the
sparrow.

Yet even the pessimists ought not to be quite so
sure that God is morally inferior to man. Even
their God may be no more amused by human
anguish then men are amused by the grotesque
floppings of a dying fish.

The villains in the world are those who have
no respect for the personality of birds and beasts.
And their cruelty to animals is not deliberate or
vindictive—it arises from crass stupidity.

STUPIDITY STREET

I saw with open eyes
  Singing birds sweet
Sold in the shops
  For the people to eat,
Sold in the shops of
  Stupidity Street.

I saw in vision
  The worm in the wheat,
And in the shops nothing
  For people to eat;
Nothing for sale in
  Stupidity Street.

The poet's attitude toward the lion in the jun-
gle, the bull in the field, the cat in the yard, the bird
on the tree is not one of affectionate petting, for
love and sympathy are often mingled—consciously
or unconsciously—with condescension. There is
no trace of condescension in the way Mr. Hodgson writes of animals. He treats them with re-

spect, and not only hates to see them hurt, he hates to see their dignity outraged.

THE BELLS OF HEAVEN

'Twould ring the bells of Heaven
The wildest peal for years,
If Parson lost his senses
And people came to theirs,
And he and they together
Knelt down with angry prayers
For tamed and shabby tigers
And dancing dogs and bears,
And wretched, blind pit ponies,
And little hunted hares.

I confess that I have often felt a sense of shame for humanity when I have observed men and women staring through the bars at the splendid African cats in cages, and have also observed that their foolish stare is returned by the lion or tiger with a dull look of infinite boredom. Nor is it pleasant to see small boys pushing sticks through the safe bars, in an endeavour to irritate the royal captives. One remembers Browning's superb lion in *The Glove,* whom the knight was able to approach in safety, because the regal beast was completely lost in thought—he was homesick for the desert, oblivious of the little man-king and his duodecimo court.

Although the total production of Ralph Hodgson is slight in quantity, the percentage of excellence is remarkably high. The reason for this is clear. Instead of printing everything he writes, and leaving the employment of the cream-separator to his readers, he gives to the public only what has passed his own severe scrutiny. He is a true poet, with an original mind.

As for the work of Lascelles Abercrombie, which has been much praised in certain circles, I should prefer to leave the criticism of that to those who enjoy reading it. If I should attempt to "do justice" to his poetry, I should seem to his friends to be doing just the opposite—the opposite of just.

CHAPTER V

BROOKE, FLECKER, DE LA MARE, AND OTHERS

Rupert Brooke—a personality—the spirit of youth—his horror at old age—Henry James's tribute—his education—a genius—his poems of death—his affected cynicism—his nature poems—war sonnets—his supreme sacrifice—his charming humour—his masterpiece, *Grantchester.*—James Elroy Flecker —the editorial work of Mr. Squire—no posthumous puffery— the case of Crashaw—life of Flecker—his fondness for revision—his friendship with Rupert Brooke—his skill as a translator—his austerity—art for art's sake—his "brightness" —love of Greek mythology—steady mental development—his definition of the aim of poetry.—Walter De La Mare—the poet of shadow—Hawthorne's tales—his persistence—his reflective mood—his descriptive style—his Shakespeare characters—his sketches from life.—D. H. Lawrence—his lack of discipline—his subjectivity—absence of reserve—a master of colour—his glaring excesses.—John Drinkwater—the west of England—his healthy spirit.—W. H. Davies—the tramp poet. —Edward Thomas—his death—originality of his work.—Robert Nichols—Willoughby Weaving.—The young Oxford poets.

Rupert Brooke left the world in a chariot of fire. He was something more than either a man or a poet; he was and is a Personality. It was as a Personality that he dazzled his friends. He was overflowing with tremendous, contagious vitality. He was the incarnation of the spirit of youth, wearing the glamour and glory of youth like a shining garment. Despite our loss, it almost seems fitting that he did not live to that old age which he never understood, for which he had such little sympathy, and which he seems to have hated more than death. For he had the splendid insolence of youth. Youth commonly feels high-spirited in an unconscious, instinctive fashion, like a kitten or a puppy; but Rupert Brooke was as self-consciously young as a decrepit pensioner is self-consciously old. He rejoiced in the strength of his youth, and rolled it as a sweet morsel under his tongue. He was so glad to be young, and to know every morning on rising from sleep that he was still young! His passionate love of beauty made him see in old age only ugliness; he could not foresee the joys of the mellow years. All he saw consisted of grey hairs, wrinkles, double chins, paunches. To him all old people were Struldbrugs. We smile at the insolence of youth, because we know it will pass with the beauty and strength that support it. Ogniben says, "Youth, with its beauty and grace, would seem bestowed on us for some such reason as to make us partly endurable till we have time for really becoming so of ourselves, without their aid; when they leave us . . . little by little, he sees fit to forego claim after claim on the world, puts up with a less and less share of its good as his proper portion; and when the octogenarian asks barely a sup of gruel and a fire of dry sticks, and thanks you as for his full allowance and right in the common good of life,—hoping nobody may murder him,—he who began by asking and expecting the whole of us to bow down in worship to him,—why, I say he is advanced.''

Henry James—whose affectionate tribute in the preface to Brooke's *Letters* is impressive testimony—saw in the brilliant youth, besides the accident of genius, a perfect illustration of the highest type of Englishman, bred in the best English way, in the best traditions of English scholarship, and adorned with the good sense, fine temper, and healthy humour of the ideal Anglo-Saxon. He indeed enjoyed every possible advantage; like Milton and Browning, had he been intended for a poet from the cradle, his bringing-up could not have been better adapted to the purpose. He was born at Rugby, on the third of August, 1887, where his father was one of the masters in the famous school. He won a poetry prize there in 1905. The next year he entered King's College, Cambridge; his influence as an undergraduate was notable. He took honours in classics, went abroad to study in Munich, and returned to Grantchester, which he was later to celebrate in his best poem. He had travelled somewhat extensively on the Continent, and in 1913 went on a journey through the United States and Canada to the South Seas. I am glad he saw the Hawaiian Islands, for no one should die before beholding that paradise. At the outbreak of war, he enlisted, went to Antwerp, and later embarked on the expedition to the Dardanelles. He was bitten by a fly, and died of bloodpoisoning on a French hospital ship, the day being Shakespeare's, the twenty-third of April, 1915. He was buried on a Greek island.

Rupert Brooke lived to be nearly twenty-eight years old, a short life to show ability in most of the ways of the world, but long enough to test the quality of a poet, not merely in promise, but in performance. There is no doubt that he had the indefinable but unmistakable touch of genius. Only a portion of his slender production is of high rank, but it is enough to preserve his name. His *Letters,* which have been underestimated, prove that he had mental as well as poetical powers. Had he lived to middle age, it seems certain that his poetry would have been tightly packed with thought. He had an alert and inquisitive mind.

Many have seemed to think that the frequent allusions to death in his poetry are vaguely prophetic. They are, of course—with the exception of the war-poems—nothing of the kind, being merely symptomatic of youth. They form the most conventional side of his work. His cynicism toward the love of the sexes was a youthful affectation, strengthened by his reading. He was deeply read in the seventeenth-century poets, who delighted in imagining themselves passing from one woman to another—swearing "by love's sweetest part, variety." At all events, these poems, of which there are comparatively many, exhibit his least attractive side. The poem addressed to *The One Before the Last,* ends

> Oh! bitter thoughts I had in plenty,
>   But here's the worst of it—
> I shall forget, in Nineteen-twenty,
>   You ever hurt a bit!

He was perhaps, too young to understand two great truths—that real love can exist in the midst of wild passion, and that the best part of it can and often does survive the early flames. Such poems as *Menelaus and Helen, Jealousy*, and others, profess a profound knowledge of life that is really a profound ignorance.

His pictures of nature, while often beautiful, lack the penetrative quality seen so constantly in Wordsworth and Browning; these greater poets saw nature not only with their eyes, but with their minds. Their representations glow with enduring beauty, but they leave in the spectator something even greater than beauty, something that is food for reflection and imagination, the source of quick-coming fancies. Compare the picture of the pines in Brooke's poem *Pine-Trees and the Sky: Evening*, with Browning's treatment of an identical theme in *Paracelsus*, remembering that Browning's lines were written when he was twenty-two years old. Brooke writes,

> Then from the sad west turning wearily,
>   I saw the pines against the white north sky,
> Very beautiful, and still, and bending over
>   Their sharp black heads against a quiet sky.

Browning writes,

The herded pines commune, and have deep thoughts,
A secret they assemble to discuss,
When the sun drops behind their trunks which glare
Like grates of hell.

Both in painting and in imagination the second passage is instantly seen to be superior.

The war sonnets of 1914 receive so much additional poignancy by the death of the author that it is difficult, and perhaps undesirable, to judge them as objective works of art. They are essentially noble and sincere, speaking from the depths of high-hearted self-sacrifice. He poured out his young life freely and generously, knowing what it meant to say good-bye to his fancy. There is always something eternally sublime—something that we rightly call divine—in the spendthrift giving of one's life-blood for a great cause. And Rupert Brooke was intensely aware of the value of what he unhesitatingly gave.

The two "fish" poems exhibit a playful, charming side to Brooke's imagination; but if I could have only one of his pieces, I should assuredly choose *Grantchester*. Nostalgia is the mother of much fine poetry; but seldom has the expression of it been mingled more exquisitely with humour and longing. By the rivers of Babylon he sat down and laughed when he remembered Zion. And his laughter at Babylon is so different from his laughter at Grantchester. A few felicitous adjectives sum up the significant difference between Germany and England. Writing in a Berlin café, he says:

> Here tulips bloom as they are told;
> Unkempt about those hedges blows
> An English unofficial rose;
> And there the unregulated sun
> Slopes down to rest when day is done,
> And wakes a vague unpunctual star,
> A slippered Hesper; and there are
> Meads toward Haslingfield and Coton
> Where *das Betreten's* not *verboten*. . . .
> Oh, is the water sweet and cool,
> Gentle and brown, above the pool?
> And laughs the immortal river still
> Under the mill, under the mill?
> Say, is there Beauty yet to find?
> And Certainty? and Quiet kind?
> Deep meadows yet, for to forget
> The lies, and truths, and pain? . . . oh! yet
> Stands the Church clock at ten to three?
> And is there honey still for tea?

When Hamlet died, he bequeathed his reputation to Horatio, the official custodian of his good name. He could not have made a better choice. Would that all poets who die young were equally fortunate in their posthumous editors! For there are some friends who conceive it to be their duty to print every scrap of written paper the bard left behind him, even if they have to act as scavengers to find the "remains"; and there are others who think affection and admiration for the dead are best shown by adopting the methods and the language of the press-agent. To my mind, the pious memoir of Tennyson is injured by the inclu-

sion of a long list of "testimonials," which assure
us that Alfred Tennyson was a remarkable poet.
Mr. J. C. Squire, under whose auspices the works
of Flecker appear in one handsome volume, is an
admirable editor. His introduction is a model of
its kind, giving the necessary biographical information, explaining the chronology, the origin,
the background of the poems, and showing how
the poet revised his earlier work; the last paragraph ought to serve as an example to those who
may be entrusted with a task of similar delicacy
in the future. "My only object in writing this
necessarily rather disjointed Introduction is to
give some information that may interest the
reader and be useful to the critic; and if a few
personal opinions have slipped in they may con-
veniently be ignored. A vehement 'puff prelim-
inary' is an insolence in a volume of this kind;
it might pardonably be supposed to imply either
doubts about the author or distrust of his readers."

As a contrast to the above, it is interesting to
recall the preface that an anonymous friend contributed to a volume of Crashaw's verse in the
seventeenth century, which, in his own words, "I
have impartially writ of this Learned young
Gent." Fearing that readers might not appreciate his poetry at its true value, the friend writes,
"It were prophane but to mention here in the
Preface those under-headed Poets, Retainers to
seven shares and a halfe; Madrigall fellowes,

whose onely business in verse, is to rime a poore six-penny soule a Suburb sinner into hell;—May such arrogant pretenders to Poetry vanish, with their prodigious issue of tumorous heats, and flashes of their adulterate braines, and for ever after, may this our Poet fill up the better roome of man. Oh! when the generall arraignment of Poets shall be, to give an accompt of their higher soules, with what a triumphant brow shall our divine Poet sit above, and looke downe upon poore Homer, Virgil, Horace, Claudian; &c. who had amongst them the ill lucke to talke out a great part of their gallant Genius, upon Bees, Dung, froggs, and Gnats, &c. and not as himself here, upon Scriptures, divine Graces, Martyrs and Angels." Our prefatory friend set a pace that it is hopeless for modern champions to follow, and they might as well abandon the attempt.

James Elroy Flecker, the eldest child of the Rev. Dr. Flecker, who is Head Master of an English school, was born on the fifth of November, 1884, in London. He spent five years at Trinity College, Oxford, and later studied Oriental languages at Caius College, Cambridge. He went to Constantinople in 1910. In that same year signs of tuberculosis appeared, but after some months at an English sanatorium, he seemed to be absolutely well. In 1911 he was in Constantinople, Smyrna, and finally in Athens, where he was married to Miss Skiadaressi, a Greek. In March the dreaded illness returned, and the rest of his short life was spent in the vain endeavour to recover his health. He died in Switzerland, on the third of January, 1915, at the age of thirty. "I cannot help remembering," says Mr. Squire, "that I first heard the news over the telephone, and that the voice which spoke was Rupert Brooke's."

He had published four books of verse and four books of prose, leaving many poems, essays, short stories, and two plays, in manuscript. All his best poetry is now included in the *Collected Poems* (1916).

Flecker had the Tennysonian habit of continually revising; and in this volume we are permitted to see some of the interesting results of the process. I must say, however, that of the two versions of *Tenebris Interlucentem*, although the second is called a "drastic improvement," I prefer the earlier. Any poet might be proud of either.

Flecker liked the work of Mr. Yeats, of Mr. Housman, of Mr. De La Mare; and Rupert Brooke was an intimate friend, for the two young men were together at Cambridge. He wrote a sonnet on Francis Thompson, though he was never affected by Thompson's literary manner. Indeed, he is singularly free from the influence of any of the modern poets. His ideas and his style are his own; he thought deeply on the art of writing, and was given to eager and passionate discussion of it with those who had his confidence. His originality is the more remarkable when we remember his fondness for translating verse from a

variety of foreign languages, ancient and modern.
He was an excellent translator. His skill in this
art can only be inferred where we know nothing
at first hand of the originals; but his version of
Goethe's immortal lyric is proof of his powers.
The only blemish—an unavoidable one—is "far"
and "father" in the last two lines.

> Knowest thou the land where bloom the lemon trees?
> And darkly gleam the golden oranges?
> A gentle wind blows down from that blue sky;
> Calm stands the myrtle and the laurel high.
> Knowest thou the land?   So far and fair!
> Thou, whom I love, and I will wander there.
>
> Knowest thou the house with all its rooms aglow,
> And shining hall and columned portico?
> The marble statues stand and look at me.
> Alas, poor child, what have they done to thee?
> Knowest thou the land?   So far and fair.
> My Guardian, thou and I will wander there.
>
> Knowest thou the mountain with its bridge of cloud?
> The mule plods warily: the white mists crowd.
> Coiled in their caves the brood of dragons sleep;
> The torrent hurls the rock from steep to steep.
> Knowest thou the land?   So far and fair.
> Father, away!   Our road is over there!

Fletcher was more French than English in his
dislike of romanticism, sentimentalism, intimate,
and confessional poetry; and of course he was
strenuously opposed to contemporary standards
in so far as they put correct psychology above
beauty. Much contemporary verse reads and
sounds like undisciplined thinking out loud, where

each poet feels it imperative to tell the reader in detail not only all his adventures, and passions, but even the most minute whimsies and caprices. When the result of this bosom-cleansing is real poetry, it justifies itself; but the method is the exact opposite of Flecker's. His master was Keats, and in his own words, he wrote "with the single intention of creating beauty." Austerity and objectivity were his ideals.

Strangely enough, he was able to state in a new and more convincing way the doctrine of art for art's sake. "However few poets have written with a clear theory of art for art's sake, it is by that theory alone that their work has been, or can be, judged;—and rightly so if we remember that art embraces all life and all humanity, and sees in the temporary and fleeting doctrines of conservative or revolutionary only the human grandeur or passion that inspires them."

Perhaps the best noun that describes Flecker's verse is *brightness*. He had a consumptive's longing for sunshine, and his sojourns on the Mediterranean shores illuminate his pages. The following poem is decidedly characteristic:

IN PHÆACIA

Had I that haze of streaming blue,
    That sea below, the summer faced,
I'd work and weave a dress for you
    And kneel to clasp it round your waist,
And broider with those burning bright
    Threads of the Sun across the sea,

And bind it with the silver light
That wavers in the olive tree.

Had I the gold that like a river
Pours through our garden, eve by eve,
Our garden that goes on for ever
Out of the world, as we believe;
Had I that glory on the vine
That splendour soft on tower and town,
I'd forge a crown of that sunshine,
And break before your feet the crown.

Through the great pinewood I have been
An hour before the lustre dies,
Nor have such forest-colours seen
As those that glimmer in your eyes.
Ah, misty woodland, down whose deep
And twilight paths I love to stroll
To meadows quieter than sleep
And pools more secret than the soul!

Could I but steal that awful throne
Ablaze with dreams and songs and stars
Where sits Night, a man of stone,
On the frozen mountain spars
I'd cast him down, for he is old,
And set my Lady there to rule,
Gowned with silver, crowned with gold,
And in her eyes the forest pool.

It seems to me improbable that Flecker will be
forgotten; he was a real poet. But a remark
made of Tennyson is still more applicable to
Flecker. "He was an artist before he was a
poet." Even as a small boy, he had astonishing facility, but naturally wrote little worth pre-
serval. The *Collected Poems* show an extraordinary command of his instrument. He had the

orthodox virtues of the orthodox poet—rime and
rhythm, cunning in words, skill in nature-painting,
imagination. The richness of his colouring and
the loveliness of his melodies make his verses a
delight to the senses. His mind was plentifully
stored with classical authors, and he saw nature
alive with old gods and fairies. In one of his
most charming poems, *Oak and Olive,* he declares,

> When I go down the Gloucester lanes
>   My friends are deaf and blind:
> Fast as they turn their foolish eyes
>   The Mænads leap behind,
> And when I hear the fire-winged feet,
>   They only hear the wind.
>
> Have I not chased the fluting Pan,
>   Through Cranham's sober trees?
> Have I not sat on Painswick Hill
>   With a nymph upon my knees,
> And she as rosy as the dawn,
>   And naked as the breeze?

His poetry is composed of sensations rather
than thoughts. What it lacks is intellectual content. A richly packed memory is not the same
thing as original thinking, even when the memories are glorified by the artist's own imagination.
Yet the death of this young man was a cruel loss
to English literature, for his mental development
would eventually have kept pace with his gift of
song. His cheerful Paganism would, I think, have
given place to something deeper and more fruitful. Before he went to Constantinople, he had,
as it is a fashion for some modern Occidentals to

have, a great admiration for Mohammedanism. A friend reports a rather naïve remark of his, "his intercourse with Mohammedans had led him to find more good in Christianity than he had previously suspected." I have sometimes wondered whether a prolonged residence among Mohammedans might not temper the enthusiasm of those who so loudly insist on the superiority of that faith to Christianity. Mr. Santayana speaks somewhere of "the unconquerable mind of the East." Well, my guess is that this unconquerable mind will some day be conquered by the Man of Nazareth, just as I think He will eventually— some centuries ahead—conquer even us.

Flecker died so soon after the opening of the Great War that it is vain to surmise what the effect of that struggle would have been upon his soul. That it would have shaken him to the depths—and perhaps given him the spiritual experience necessary for his further advance—seems not improbable. One of his letters on the subject contains the significant remark, "What a race of deep-eyed and thoughtful men we shall have in Europe—now that all those millions have been baptized in fire!"

The last stanza of his poem *A Sacred Dialogue* reads as follows:

> Then the black cannons of the Lord
>   Shall wake crusading ghosts
> And the Milky Way shall swing like a sword
>   When Jerusalem vomits its horde

> On the Christmas Day preferred of the Lord,
> The Christmas Day of the Hosts!

He appended a footnote in December, 1914, when he was dying: "Originally written for Christmas, 1912, and referring to the first Balkan War, this poem contains in the last speech of Christ words that ring like a prophecy of events that may occur very soon." As I am copying his Note, December, 1917, the English army is entering Jerusalem.

Flecker was essentially noble-minded; and without any trace of conceit, felt the responsibility of his talents. There is not an unworthy page in the *Collected Poems*. In a memorable passage, he stated the goal of poetry. "It is not the poet's business to save man's soul, but to make it worth saving."

Walter De La Mare, a close personal friend of Rupert Brooke, came of Huguenot, English and Scotch ancestry, and was born at Charlton, Kent, on the twenty-fifth of April, 1873. He was educated at St. Paul's Cathedral Choir School. Although known today exclusively as a poet, he has written much miscellaneous prose—critical articles for periodicals, short stories, and a few plays. His first poetry-book, *Songs of Childhood,* appeared in 1902; in 1906, *Poems;* in 1910, *The Return,* which won the Edmond de Polignac prize; *The Listeners,* which gave him a wide reputation, appeared in 1912; *Peacock Pie,* in 1917, and *Motley and Other Poems* in 1918. When, in November, 1916, the Howland Memorial Prize at Yale University was formally awarded to the work of Rupert Brooke, it was officially received in New Haven by Walter De La Mare, who came from England for the purpose.

If Flecker's poems were written in a glare of light, Mr. De La Mare's shy Muse seems to live in shadow. It is not at all the shadow of grief, still less of bitterness, but rather the cool, grateful shade of retirement. I can find no words anywhere that so perfectly express to my mind the atmosphere of these poems as the language used by Hawthorne to explain the lack of excitement that readers would be sure to notice in his tales. "They have the pale tint of flowers that blossom in too retired a shade,—the coolness of a meditative habit, which diffuses itself through the feeling and observation of every sketch. Instead of passion there is sentiment; and, even in what purport to be pictures of actual life, we have allegory, not always so warmly dressed in its habiliments of flesh and blood as to be taken into the reader's mind without a shiver. Whether from lack of power, or an uncontrollable reserve, the author's touches have often an effect of tameness. . . . The book, if you would see anything in it, requires to be read in the clear, brown, twilight atmosphere in which it was written; if opened in the sunshine, it is apt to look exceedingly like a volume of blank pages."

Hawthorne is naturally not popular today with

readers whose sole acquaintance with the art of
the short story is gleaned from magazines that
adorn the stalls at railway-stations; and to those
whose taste in poetry begins and ends with melodrama, who prefer the hoarse cry of animal passion to the still, sad music of humanity, it would
not be advisable to recommend a poem like *The
Listeners,* where the people are ghosts and the
sounds only echoes. Yet there are times when it
would seem that every one must weary of strident
voices, of persons shouting to attract attention,
of poets who capitalize both their moral and literary vices, of hawking advertisers of the latest
verse-novelties; then a poem like *The Listeners*
reminds us of Lindsay's bird, whose simple melody
is not defeated by the blatant horns.

Decidedly a poet must have both courage and
faith to hold himself so steadily aloof from the
competition of the market-place; to work with
such easy cheerfulness in his quiet corner; to remain so manifestly unaffected by the swift cur-
rents of contemporary verse. For fifteen years
he has gone on producing his own favourite kind
of poetry, dealing with children, with flowers, with
autumn and winter, with ghosts of memory, with
figures in literature, and has finally obtained a
respectable audience without once raising his
voice. He has written surprisingly little love
poetry; the notes of passion, as we are accus-
tomed to hear them, seldom sound from his lute;
nor do we hear the agonizing cries of doubt, re-

morse, or despair. There is nothing turbulent and nothing truculent; he has made no contribution to the literature of revolt. Yet many of his poems make an irresistible appeal to our more reflective moods; and once or twice, his fancy, always winsome and wistful, rises to a height of pure imagination, as in *The Listeners*—which I find myself returning to muse over again and again.

His studies of humanity—both from observation and from books—are descriptive rather than dramatic. I do not know a contemporary poet whose published works contain so few quotation marks. The dramatic monologue, which Emerson back in the 'forties prophesied would be the highest class of poetry in the immediate future (which prophecy was fulfilled), does not interest Mr. De La Mare; maybe he feels that it has been done so well that he prefers to let it alone. His remarkable thirteen poems dealing with Shakespearean characters—where he attempts with considerable success to pluck out the heart of the mystery—are all descriptive. Perhaps the most original and beautiful of these is

MERCUTIO

Along an avenue of almond-trees
Came three girls chattering of their sweethearts three.
And lo! Mercutio, with Byronic ease,
Out of his philosophic eye cast all
A mere flow'r'd twig of thought, whereat. . . .
Three hearts fell still as when an air dies out
And Venus falters lonely o'er the sea.

But when within the further mist of bloom
His step and form were hid, the smooth child Ann
Said, "La, and what eyes he had!" and Lucy said,
"How sad a gentleman!" and Katharine,
"I wonder, now, what mischief he was at."
And these three also April hid away,
Leaving the spring faint with Mercutio.

There are immense tracts of Shakespeare which Walter De La Mare never could even have remotely imitated; but I know of no poet today who could approach the wonderful Queen Mab speech more successfully than he.

The same method of interpretative description that he employs in dealing with Shakespearean characters he uses repeatedly in making portraits from life. One of the most vivid and delightful of these is

OLD SUSAN

When Susan's work was done she'd sit,
With one fat guttering candle lit,
And window opened wide to win
The sweet night air to enter in;
There, with a thumb to keep her place
She'd read, with stern and wrinkled face,
Her mild eyes gliding very slow
Across the letters to and fro,
While wagged the guttering candle flame
In the wind that through the window came.
And sometimes in the silence she
Would mumble a sentence audibly,
Or shake her head as if to say,
"You silly souls, to act this way!"
And never a sound from night I'd hear,
Unless some far-off cock crowed clear;
Or her old shuffling thumb should turn

> Another page; and rapt and stern,
> Through her great glasses bent on me
> She'd glance into reality;
> And shake her round old silvery head,
> With—"You!—I thought you was in bed!"—
> Only to tilt her book again,
> And rooted in Romance remain.

I am afraid that Rupert Brooke could not have written a poem like *Old Susan*; he would have made her ridiculous and contemptible; he would have accentuated physical defects so that she would have been a repugnant, even an offensive, figure. But Mr. De La Mare has the power—possessed in the supreme degree by J. M. Barrie —of taking just such a person as Old Susan, living in a world of romance, and making us smile with no trace of contempt and with no descent to pity. One who can do this loves his fellow-men.

Poems like *Old Susan* prepare us for one of the most happy exhibitions of Mr. De La Mare's talent—his verses written for and about children. Every household ought to have that delightful quarto, delightfully and abundantly illustrated, called *Peacock Pie: A Book of Rhymes. With Illustrations by W. Heath Robinson.* There is a picture for each poem, and the combination demands and will obtain an unconditional surrender.

If the poetry of James Flecker and Walter De La Mare live after them, it will not be because of sensational qualities, in matter or in manner. Fancy is bred either in the heart or in the head —and the best poetry should touch either one or the other or both. Mr. De La Mare owes his present eminence simply to merit—his endeavour has been to write just as well as he possibly could. His limit has been downward, not upward. He may occasionally strike over the heads of his audience, for his aim is never low.

The poetry of D. H. Lawrence (born 1885) erupts from the terrible twenties. In spite of his school experience, he has never sent his mind to school; he hates discipline. He has an undeniable literary gift, which has met—as it ought to—with glad recognition. He has strength, he has fervour, he has passion. But while his strength is sometimes the happy and graceful play of rippling muscles, it is often contortion. If Mr. De La Mare may seem too delicate, too restrained, Mr. Lawrence cares comparatively little for delicacy; and the word restraint is not in his bright lexicon. In other words, he is aggressively "modern." He is one of the most skilful manipulators of free verse—he can drive four horses abreast, and somehow or other reach the goal.

He sees his own turbulent heart reflected stormily in every natural spectacle. He observes flowers in an anti-Wordsworthian way. He mentions with appreciation roses, lilies, snapdragons, but to him they are all passion-flowers. And yet—if he only knew it—his finest work is in a subdued mood. He is a master of colouring—and I like his quieter work as a painter better than his feverish, hectic cries of desire. Despite his dialect poems, he is more successful at description than at drama. I imagine Miss Harriet Monroe may think so too; it seems to me she has done well in selecting his verses, to give three out of the five from his colour-pieces, of which perhaps the best is

SERVICE OF ALL THE DEAD

Between the avenue of cypresses,
All in their scarlet capes and surplices
Of linen, go the chaunting choristers,
The priests in gold and black, the villagers.

And all along the path to the cemetery
The round dark heads of men crowd silently;
And black-scarfed faces of women-folk wistfully
Watch at the banner of death, and the mystery.

And at the foot of a grave a father stands
With sunken head and forgotten, folded hands;
And at the foot of a grave a mother kneels
With pale shut face, nor neither hears nor feels.

The coming of the chaunting choristers
Between the avenue of cypresses,
The silence of the many villagers,
The candle-flames beside the surplices.

(Remember the English pronunciation of "cemetery" is not the common American one.) He is surely better as a looker-on at life than when he tries to present the surging passions of an actor-in-chief. Then his art is full of sound and fury, and instead of being thrilled, we are, as Stevenson said of Whitman's poorer poems, somewhat indecorously amused. All poets, I suppose, are thrilled by their own work; they read it to themselves with shudders of rapture; but it is only when this *frisson* is felt by others than blood-relatives that they may feel some reasonable assurance of success. The London *Times* quite properly refuses to surrender to lines like these:

> And if I never see her again?
> I think, if they told me so,
> I could convulse the heavens with my horror.
> I think I could alter the frame of things in my agony.
> I think I could break the System with my heart.
> I think, in my convulsion, the skies would break.

He should change his gear from high to low; he will never climb Parnassus on this speed, not even with his muffler so manifestly open.

The *Times* also quotes without appreciation from the same volume the following passage, where the woman, looking back, stirs a biblical reminiscence.

> I have seen it, felt it in my mouth, my throat, my chest, my belly,
> Burning of powerful salt, burning, eating through my defenceless nakedness,
> I have been thrust into white sharp crystals,
> Writhing, twisting, superpenetrated,
> Ah, Lot's wife, Lot's wife!
> The pillar of salt, the whirling, horrible column of salt, like a waterspout
> That has enveloped me!

Most readers may not need a whole pillar, but they will surely take the above professions *cum grano salis*. It is all in King Cambyses' vein; and I would that we had Pistol to deliver it. I

cite it here, not for the graceless task of showing
Mr. Lawrence at his worst, but because such stuff
is symptomatic of many of the very "new" poets,
who wander, as Turgenev expressed it, "aimless
but declamatory, over the face of our long-suffering mother earth."

John Drinkwater, born on the first of June,
1882, has had varied experiences both in business
and in literature, and is at present connected with
the management of the Birmingham Repertory
Theatre. Actively engaged in commercial life,
he has found time to publish a number of volumes
of poems, plays in verse, critical works in prose,
and a long string of magazine articles. He has
wisely collected in one volume—though I regret
the omission of *Malvern Lyrics*—the best of his
poems that had previously appeared in four separate works, containing the cream of his production
from 1908 to 1914. His preface to this little book,
published in 1917, is excellent in its manly modesty.
"Apart from the Cromwell poem itself, the present selection contains all that I am anxious to preserve from those volumes, and there is nothing before 1908 which I should wish to be reprinted now
or at any time." One of the earlier books had
been dedicated to John Masefield, to whom in the
present preface the author pays an affectionate
compliment—"John Masefield, who has given a
poet's praise to work that I hope he likes half as
well as I like his."

The first poem, *Symbols,* prepares the reader for what is to follow, though it is somewhat lacking in the technique that is characteristic of most of Mr. Drinkwater's verse.

> I saw history in a poet's song,
>   In a river-reach and a gallows-hill,
> In a bridal bed, and a secret wrong,
>   In a crown of thorns: in a daffodil.
>
> I imagined measureless time in a day,
>   And starry space in a wagon-road,
> And the treasure of all good harvests lay
>   In the single seed that the sower sowed.
>
> My garden-wind had driven and havened again
>   All ships that ever had gone to sea,
> And I saw the glory of all dead men
>   In the shadow that went by the side of me.

The West of England looms large in contemporary poetry. A. E. Housman, John Masefield, W. W. Gibson, J. E. Flecker have done their best to celebrate its quiet beauty; and some of the finest work of Mr. Drinkwater is lovingly devoted to these rural scenes. We know how Professor Housman and John Masefield regard Bredon Hill —another tribute to this "calm acclivity, salubrious spot" is paid in Mr. Drinkwater's cheerful song, *At Grafton.* The spirit of his work in general is the spirit of health—take life as it is, and enjoy it. It is the open-air verse of broad, windswept English counties. Its surest claim to distinction lies in its excellent, finished workmanship

—he is a sound craftsman. But he has not yet shown either sufficient originality or sufficient inspiration to rise from the better class of minor poets. His verse-drama, *The Storm,* which was produced in Birmingham in 1915, shows strong resemblances to the one-act plays of Mr. Gibson and is not otherwise impressive.

William Henry Davies, the Welsh poet, exhibits in his half-dozen miniature volumes an extraordinary variety of subjects. Everything is grist. He was born of Welsh parentage in Monmouthshire on the twentieth of April, 1870. He became an American tramp, and practised this interesting profession six years; he made eight or nine trips to England on cattle-ships, working his passage; he walked about England selling pins and needles. He remarks that "he sometimes varied this life by singing hymns in the street." At the age of thirty-four he became a poet, and he insists—not without reason—that he has been one ever since. Readers may be at times reminded of the manner of John Davidson, but after all, Mr. Davies is as independent in his poetry as he used to be on the road.

Sometimes his verse is banal—as in the advice *To a Working Man.* But oftener his imagination plays on familiar scenes in town and country with a lambent flame, illuminating and glorifying common objects. He has the heart of the child, and tries to see life from a child's clear eyes.

THE TWO FLOCKS

Where are you going to now, white sheep,
  Walking the green hill-side;
To join that whiter flock on top,
  And share their pride?

Stay where you are, you silly sheep:
  When you arrive up there,
You'll find that whiter flock on top
  Clouds in the air!

Yet much of his poetry springs from his wide
knowledge and experience of life. An original
defence of the solitary existence is seen in *Death's
Game,* although possibly the grapes are sour.

Death can but play one game with me—
  If I do live alone;
He cannot strike me a foul blow
  Through a belovèd one.

Today he takes my neighbour's wife,
  And leaves a little child
To lie upon his breast and cry
  Like the Night-wind, so wild.

And every hour its voice is heard—
  Tell me where is she gone!
Death cannot play that game with me—
  If I do live alone.

The feather-weight pocket-volumes of verse that
this poet puts forth, each containing a crop of tiny
poems—have an excellent virtue—they are interesting, good companions for a day in the country.
There is always sufficient momentum in page 28
to carry you on to page 29—something that cannot
be said of all books.

English literature suffered a loss in the death of Edward Thomas, who was killed in France on the ninth of April, 1917. He was born on the third of March, 1878, and had published a long list of literary critiques, biographies, interpretations of nature, and introspective essays. He took many solitary journeys afoot; his books *The South Country, The Heart of England,* and others, show both observation and reflection. Although English by birth and education, he had in his veins Welsh and Spanish blood.

In 1917 a tiny volume of his poems appeared. These are unlike any other verse of the past or present. They cannot be called great poetry, but they are original, imaginative, whimsical, and reveal a rich personality. Indeed we feel in reading these rimes that the author was greater than anything he wrote or could write. The difficulty in articulation comes apparently from a mind so full that it cannot run freely off the end of a pen.

Shyness was undoubtedly characteristic of the man, as it often is of minute observers of nature. I am not at all surprised to learn from one who knew him of his "temperamental melancholy." He was austere and aloof; but exactly the type of mind that would give all he had to those who possessed his confidence. It must have been a privilege to know him intimately. I have said that his poems resemble the work of no other poet; this is true; but there is a certain kinship between him and Robert Frost, indicated not only in the verses, but in the fact that his book is dedicated to the American.

His death accentuates the range of the dragnet of war. This intellectual, quiet, introspective, slightly ironical temperament would seem almost ideally unfitted for the trenches. Yet, although no soldier by instinct, and having a family dependent upon his writings for support, he gave himself freely to the Great Cause. He never speaks in his verses of his own sacrifice, and indeed says little about the war; but the first poem in the volume expresses the universal call.

> Rise up, rise up,
> And, as the trumpet blowing
> Chases the dreams of men,
> As the dawn glowing
> The stars that left unlit
> The land and water,
> Rise up and scatter
> The dew that covers
> The print of last night's lovers—
> Scatter it, scatter it!
>
> While you are listening
> To the clear horn,
> Forget, men, everything
> On this earth newborn,
> Except that it is lovelier
> Than any mysteries.
> Open your eyes to the air
> That has washed the eyes of the stars
> Through all the dewy night:
> Up with the light,
> To the old wars;
> Arise, arise!

In reading Edward Thomas, Rupert Brooke, Alan Seeger, we recognize how much greater were the things they sacrificed than the creature comforts ordinarily emphasized in the departure from home to the trenches; these men gave up their imagination.

A thoroughly representative poem by Edward Thomas is *Cock-Crow;* beauty of conception mingled with the inevitable touch of homeliness at the end.

> Out of the wood of thoughts that grows by night
> To be cut down by the sharp axe of light,—
> Out of the night, two cocks together crow,
> Cleaving the darkness with a silver blow:
> And bright before my eyes twin trumpeters stand,
> Heralds of splendour, one at either hand,
> Each facing each as in a coat of arms;
> The milkers lace their boots up at the farms.

This is his favourite combination, seen on every page of his work,—fancy and fact.

Another poet in khaki who writes powerful and original verse is Robert Nichols (born 1893), an Oxford man who has already produced two volumes—*Invocation,* and, in 1918, *Ardours and Endurances.* Accompanying the second is a portrait made in 1915, exhibiting the face of a dreamy-looking boy. No one who reads the pages of this book can doubt the author's gift. In his trench-poetry he somehow manages to combine the realism of Barbusse with an almost holy touch of imagination; and some of the most beautiful pieces are manly laments for friends killed in battle. He was himself severely wounded. His poems of strenuous action are mostly too long to quote; occasionally he writes in a more quiet mood of contemplation.

THE FULL HEART

Alone on the shore in the pause of the nighttime
I stand and I hear the long wind blow light;
I view the constellations quietly, quietly burning;
I hear the wave fall in the hush of the night.

Long after I am dead, ended this bitter journey,
Many another whose heart holds no light
Shall your solemn sweetness hush, awe, and comfort,
O my companions, Wind, Waters, Stars, and Night.

Other Oxford poets from the front are Siegfried Sassoon, Robert Graves and Willoughby Weaving, whose two volumes *The Star Fields* and *The Bubble* are as original in their way as the work of Mr. Nichols, though inferior in beauty of expression. Mr. Weaving was invalided home in 1915, and his first book has an introduction by Robert Bridges. In *The Bubble* (1917) there are many poems so deeply meditative that their full force does not reach one until after repeated readings. He has also a particular talent for the last line.

TO ——

(Winter 1916)

Thou lover of fire, how cold is it in the grave?
Would I could bring thee fuel and light thee a fire as of old!
Alas! how I think of thee there, shivering out in the cold,
Till my own bright fire lacketh the heat which it gave!

Oh, would I could see thee again, as in days gone by,
Sitting hands over the fire, or poking it to a bright blaze
And clearing the cloggy ash from the bars in thy careful ways!
Oh, art thou the more cold or here by the fire am I?

B. H. Blackwell, the Oxford publisher, seems to have made a good many "finds"; besides producing some of the work of Mr. Nichols and Mr. Weaving—both poets now have American publishers as well—the four volumes *Oxford Verse*, running from 1910 to 1917, contain many excellent things. And in addition to these, there are original adventures in the art of poetry, sometimes merely bizarre, but interesting as experiments, exhibited in the two volumes *Wheels 1916,* and *Wheels 1917,* and also in the books called *Initiates: a Series of Poetry by Proved Hands.*

CHAPTER VI

THE IRISH POETS

Irish poetry a part of English Literature—common-sense the basis of romanticism—misapprehension of the poetic temperament—William Butler Yeats—his education—his devotion to art—his theories—his love poetry—resemblance to Maeterlinck—the lyrical element paramount—the psaltery—pure rather than applied poetry—John M. Synge—his mentality—his versatility—a terrible personality—his capacity for hatred—his subjectivity—his interesting Preface—brooding on death—A. E.—The Master of the island—his sincerity and influence—disembodied spirits—his mysticism—homesickness—true optimism—James Stephens—poet and novelist—realism and fantasy—Padraic Colum—Francis Ledwidge—Susan Mitchell—Thomas MacDonagh—Joseph Campbell—Seumas O'Sullivan—Herbert Trench—Maurice Francis Egan—Norreys Jephson O'Conor—F. Carlin—The advance in Ireland.

In what I have to say of the work of the Irish poets, I am thinking of it solely as a part of English literature. I have in mind no political bias whatever, though I confess I have small admiration for extremists. During the last forty years Irishmen have written mainly in the English language, which assures to what is good in their compositions an influence bounded only by the dimensions of the earth. Great creative writers are such an immense and continuous blessing to the world that the locality of their birth pales in comparison with the glory of it, a glory in which we

157

all profit. We need original writers in America; but I had rather have a star of the first magnitude appear in London than a star of lesser power appear in Los Angeles. Every one who writes good English contributes something to English literature and is a benefactor to English-speaking people. An Irish or American literary aspirant will be rated not according to his local flavour or fervour, but according to his ability to write the English language. The language belongs to Ireland and to America as much as it belongs to England; excellence in its command is the only test by which Irish, American, Canadian, South African, Hawaiian and Australian poets and novelists will be judged. The more difficult the test, the stronger the appeal to national pride.

In a recent work, called *The Celtic Dawn,* I found this passage: "The thesis of their contention is that modern English, the English of contemporary literature, is essentially an impoverished language incapable of directly expressing thought." I am greatly unimpressed by such a statement. The chief reason why there is really a Celtic Dawn, or a Celtic Renaissance, is because Irishmen like Synge, Yeats, Russell and others have succeeded in writing English so well that they have attracted the attention of the world.

Ireland has never contributed to English literature a poet of the first class. By a poet of the first class I mean one of the same grade with the leading half-dozen British poets of the nineteenth century. This dearth of great Irish poets is the more noticeable when we think of Ireland's contributions to English prose and to English drama. Possibly, if one had prophecy rather than history to settle the question, one might predict that Irishmen would naturally write more and better poetry than Englishmen; for the common supposition is that the poetic temperament is romantic, sentimental, volatile, reckless. If this were true, then the lovable, careless, impulsive Irish would completely outclass in original poetry the sensible, steady-headed, cautious Englishman. What are the facts about the so-called poetic temperament?

Chaucer, Shakespeare, Milton, Gray, Wordsworth, Keats, Tennyson, Browning, Arnold, were in character, disposition, and temperament precisely the opposite of what is superficially supposed to be "poetic." Some of them were deeply erudite; all of them were deeply thoughtful. They were clear-headed, sensible men—in fact, common sense was the basis of their mental life. And no one can read the letters of Byron without seeing how well supplied he was with the shrewd common sense of the Englishman. He was more selfish than any one of the men enumerated above—but he was no fool. There is nothing inconsistent in his being at once the greatest romantic poet and the greatest satirist of his age. His masterpiece, *Don Juan,* is the expression of a nature at the farthest possible remove from sentimentality. And the author of *Faust* was remarkable among

all the children of men for his poise, balance, calm
—in other words, for common sense.

It is by no accident that the British—whom for-
eigners delight to call stodgy and slow-witted,—
have produced more high-class poetry than any
other nation in the history of the world. English
literature is instinctively romantic, as French
literature is instinctively classic. The glory of
French literature is prose; the glory of English
literature is poetry.

As the tallest tree must have the deepest roots,
so it would seem that the loftiest edifices of verse
must have the deepest foundations. Certainly
one of the many reasons why American poetry is
so inferior to British is because our roots do not
go down sufficiently deep. Great poetry does not
spring from natures too volatile, too susceptible,
too easily swept by gusts of emotion. Landor was
one of the most violent men we have on record;
he was a prey to uncontrollable outbursts of rage,
caused by trivial vexations; but his poetry aimed
at cold, classical correctness. In comparison with
Landor, Tennyson's reserve was almost glacial—
yet out of it bloomed many a gorgeous garden
of romance. Splendid imaginative masterpieces
seem to require more often than not a creative
mind marked by sober reason, logical processes,
orderly thinking.

John Morley, who found the management of
Ireland more than a handful, though he loved Ireland and the Irish with an affection greater than

that felt by any other Englishman of his time, has, in his *Recollections,* placed on opposite pages—all the more striking to me because unintentional— illuminating testimony to the difference between the Irish and the British temperament. And this testimony supports the point I am trying to make —that the "typical" logicless, inconsequential Irish mind, so winsome and so exasperating, is not the kind of brain to produce permanent poetry.

A peasant was in the dock for a violent assault. The clerk read the indictment with all its legal jargon. The prisoner to the warder: "What's all that he says?" *Warder:* "He says ye hit Pat Curry with yer spade on the side of his head." *Prisoner:* "Bedad an' I did." *Warder:* "Then plade not guilty." This dialogue, loud and in the full hearing of the court.

Read Wordsworth's two poems on Burns; kind, merciful, steady, glowing, manly they are, with some strong phrases, good lines, and human feeling all through, winding up in two stanzas at the close. These are among the pieces that make Wordsworth a poet to live with; he repairs the daily wear and tear, puts back what the fret of the day has rubbed thin or rubbed off, sends us forth in the morning *whole.*

Robert Browning, whose normality in appearance and conversation pleased sensible folk and shocked idolaters, summed up in two stanzas the difference between the popular conception of a poet and the real truth. One might almost take the first stanza as representing the Irish and the second the English temperament.

"Touch him ne'er so lightly, into song he broke:
Soil so quick-receptive,—not one feather-seed,
Not one flower-dust fell but straight its fall awoke

> Vitalising virtue: song would song succeed
> Sudden as spontaneous—prove a poet-soul!"
>
> >Indeed?
>
> Rock's the song-soil rather, surface hard and bare:
> Sun and dew their mildness, storm and frost their rage
> Vainly both expend,—few flowers awaken there:
> Quiet in its cleft broods—what the after age
> Knows and names a pine, a nation's heritage.

People who never grow up may have a certain kind of fascination, but they will not write great poetry. It is exactly the other way with creative artists; they grow up faster than the average. The maturity of Keats is astonishing. . . . Mr. Yeats's wonderful lamentation, *September 1913*, that sounds like the wailing of the wind, actually gives us a reason why Irishmen are getting the attention of the world in poetry, as well as in fiction and drama.

> What need you, being come to sense,
> But fumble in a greasy till
> And add the halfpence to the pence
> And prayer to shivering prayer, until
> You have dried the marrow from the bone;
> For men were born to pray and save,
> Romantic Ireland's dead and gone,
> It's with O'Leary in the grave.
>
> Yet they were of a different kind.
> The names that stilled your childish play
> They have gone about the world like wind,
> But little time had they to pray
> For whom the hangman's rope was spun,
> And what, God help us, could they save;
> Romantic Ireland's dead and gone,
> It's with O'Leary in the grave.

Was it for this the wild geese spread
The grey wing upon every tide;
For this that all that blood was shed,
For this Edward Fitzgerald died,
And Robert Emmet and Wolfe Tone,
All that delirium of the brave;
Romantic Ireland's dead and gone,
It's with O'Leary in the grave.

Yet could we turn the years again,
And call those exiles as they were,
In all their loneliness and pain
You'd cry "some woman's yellow hair
Has maddened every mother's son:"
They weighed so lightly what they gave,
But let them be, they're dead and gone,
They're with O'Leary in the grave.

William Butler Yeats has done more for English poetry than any other Irishman, for he is the greatest poet in the English language that Ireland has ever produced. He is a notable figure in contemporary literature, having made additions to verse, prose and stage-plays. He has by no means obliterated Clarence Mangan, but he has surpassed him.

Mr. Yeats was born at Dublin, on the thirteenth of June, 1865. His father was an honour man at Trinity College, taking the highest distinction in Political Economy. After practising law, he became a painter, which profession he still adorns. The future poet studied art for three years, but when twenty-one years old definitely devoted himself to literature. In addition to his original work, one of his foremost services to humanity was

his advice to that strange genius, John Synge—
for it was partly owing to the influence of his
friend that Synge became a creative writer, and
he had, alas! little time to lose.

Mr. Yeats published his first poem in 1886.
Since that date, despite his preoccupation with the
management of the Abbey Theatre, he has produced a long list of works in verse and prose, decidedly unequal in merit, but shining with the light
of a luminous mind.

From the first, Mr. Yeats has seemed to realize
that he could serve Ireland best by making beautiful and enduring works of art, rather than by any
form of political agitation. This is well; for despite the fact that a total ineptitude for statesman-
ship seldom prevents the enthusiast from issuing
and spreading dogmatic propaganda, a merely
elementary conception of the principle of division
of labour should make us all rejoice when the artist
confines himself to art. True artists are scarce
and precious; and although practical men of business often regard them as superfluous luxuries,
the truth is that we cannot live without them. As
poet and dramatist, Mr. Yeats has done more for
his country than he could have accomplished in
any other way.

Never was there more exclusively an artist. He
writes pure, not applied poetry. I care little for
his theories of symbolism, magic and what not.
Poets are judged not by their theories, not by the
"schools" to which they give passionate adher-

ence, but simply and solely by the quality of their work. No amount of theory, no correctness of method, no setting up of new or defence of old standards, no elevated ideals can make a poet if he have not the divine gift. Theories have hardly more effect on the actual value of his poetry than the colour of the ink in which he writes. The reason why it is interesting to read what Mr. Yeats says about his love of magic and of symbols is not because there is any truth or falsehood in these will-o'-the-wisps, but because he is such an artist that even when he writes in prose, his style is so beautiful, so harmonious that one is forced to listen. Literary art has enormous power in propelling a projectile of thought. I do not doubt that the chief reason for the immense effect of such a philosophy as that of Schopenhauer or that of Nietzsche is because each man was a literary artist—indeed I think both were greater writers than thinkers. A good thing this is for their fame, for art lasts longer than thought. The fashion of a man's thought may pass away; his knowledge and his ideas may lose their stamp, either because they prove to be false or because they become universally current. Everybody believes Copernicus, but nobody reads him. Yet when a book, no matter how obsolete in thought, is marked by great beauty of style, it lives forever. Consider the case of Sir Thomas Browne. Art is the great preservative.

Mr. Yeats has a genius for names and titles.

His names, like those of Rossetti's, are sweet symphonies. *The Wind Among the Reeds, The Shadowy Waters, The Secret Rose, The Land of Heart's Desire, The Island of Statues* are poems in themselves, and give separate pleasure like an overture without the opera. Perhaps it is not too fanciful to observe that *The Wind Among the Reeds* suggests better than any other arrangement of words the lovely minor melodies of our poet, while *The Shadowy Waters* gives exactly the picture that comes into one's mind in thinking of his poems. There is an extraordinary fluidity in his verse, like running water under the shade of overhanging branches. One feels that Mr. Yeats loves these titles, and chooses them with affectionate solicitude, like a father naming beautiful children.

The love poetry of Mr. Yeats, like the love poetry of Poe, is swept with passion, but the passion is mingled with unutterable reverence. It is unlike much modern love poetry in its spiritual exaltation. Just as manners have become more free, and intimacies that once took months to develop, now need only minutes, so much contemporary verse-tribute to women is so detailed, so bold, so cock-sure, that the elaborate compliments only half-conceal a sneer. In all such work love is born of desire—its sole foundation—and hence is equally short-lived and fleeting. In the poems of Mr. Yeats, desire seems to follow rather than to precede love. Love thus takes on, as it ought to, something of the beauty of holiness.

Fasten your hair with a golden pin,
And bind up every wandering tress;
I bade my heart build these poor rhymes:
It worked at them, day out, day in,
Building a sorrowful loveliness
Out of the battles of old times.

You need but lift a pearl-pale hand,
And bind up your long hair and sigh;
And all men's hearts must burn and beat;
And candle-like foam on the dim sand,
And stars climbing the dew-dropping sky,
Live but to light your passing feet.

A still more characteristic love-poem is the one which gleams with the symbols of the cloths of heaven.

Had I the heavens' embroidered cloths,
Enwrought with golden and silver light,
The blue and the dim and the dark cloths
Of night and light and the halflight,
I would spread the cloths under your feet;
But I, being poor, have only my dreams;
I have spread my dreams under your feet;
Tread softly because you tread on my dreams.

In mysticism, in symbolism, and in the quality of his imagination, Mr. Yeats of course reminds us of Maeterlinck. He has the same twilit atmosphere, peopled with elusive dream-footed figures, that make no more noise than the wings of an owl. He is of imagination all compact. He is neither a teacher nor a prophet; he seems to turn away from the real sorrows of life, yes, even from its real joys, to dwell in a world of his own creation. He invites us thither, if we care to go; and if we go not, we cannot understand either his art or his ideas. But if we wander with him in the shadowy darkness, like the lonely man in Titanic alleys accompanied only by Psyche, we shall see strange visions. We may be led to the door of a legended tomb; we may be led along the border of dim waters; but we shall live for a time in the realm of Beauty, and be the better for the experience, even though it resemble nothing in the town and country that we know.

Mr. Yeats, like Browning, writes both lyrical poems and dramas; but he is at the opposite remove from Browning in everything except the gift of song. Browning was so devoted to the dramatic aspect of art, that he carried the drama even into its seemingly contradictory form, the lyric. Every lyric is a little one-act play, and he called them dramatic lyrics. Mr. Yeats, on the other hand, is so essentially a lyric poet, that instead of writing dramatic lyrics, he writes lyric dramas. Even his stage-plays are primarily lyrical.

Those who are interested in Mr. Yeats's theory of speaking, reciting, or chanting poetry to the psaltery should read his book, *Ideas of Good and Evil*, which contains some of his most significant articles of faith, written in shining prose. Mr. Yeats cannot write on any subject without illu-

minating it by the light of his own imagination;
and I find his essays in criticism full of original
thought—the result of years of brooding reflection.
In these short pieces his genius is as clear as it is
in his poems.

He is, in fact, a master of English. His latest
work, with its musical title, *Per Amica Silentia
Lunae* (1918), has both in spirit and form something of the ecstasy and quaint beauty of Sir
Thomas Browne. I had supposed that such a
style as that displayed in *Urn-Burial* was a lost
art; but Mr. Yeats comes near to possessing its
secret. This book is like a deep pool in its lim-
pidity and mystery; no man without genius could
have written it. I mean to read it many times, for
there are pages that I am not sure that I understand. One looks into its depths of suggestion as
one looks into a clear but very deep lake; one can
see far down, but not to the bottom of it, which
remains mysterious. He invites his own soul, but
there is no loafing. Indeed his mind seems preter-
naturally active, as in a combination of dream and
cerebration.

We make out of the quarrel with others, rhetoric, but of
the quarrel with ourselves, poetry. Unlike the rhetoricians,
who get a confident voice from remembering the crowd they
have won or may win, we sing amid our uncertainty; and,
smitten even in the presence of the most high beauty by the
knowledge of our solitude, our rhythm shudders. I think,
too, that no fine poet, no matter how disordered his life, has
ever, even in his mere life, had pleasure for his end. . . . The
other self, the anti-self or antithetical self, as one may choose

to name it, comes but to those who are no longer deceived, whose passion is reality. The sentimentalists are practical men who believe in money, in position, in a marriage bell, and whose understanding of happiness is to be so busy whether at work or at play, that all is forgotten but the momentary aim. They will find their pleasure in a cup that is filled from Lethe's wharf, and for the awakening, for the vision, for the revelation of reality, tradition offers us a different word— ecstasy. . . . We must not make a false faith by hiding from our thoughts the causes of doubt, for faith is the highest achievement of the human intellect, the only gift man can make to God, and therefore it must be offered in sincerity. Neither must we create, by hiding ugliness, a false beauty as our offer- ing to the world. He only can create the greatest imaginable beauty who has endured all imaginable pangs, for only when we have seen and foreseen what we dread shall we be rewarded by that dazzling unforeseen wing-footed wanderer.

I admire his devotion to the art of poetry. He will not turn Pegasus into a dray-horse, and make him haul cart-loads of political or moral propa- ganda. In his fine apologia, *The Cutting of an Agate,* he states and restates his creed: "Litera- ture decays when it no longer makes more beauti- ful, or more vivid, the language which unites it to all life, and when one finds the criticism of the student, and the purpose of the reformer, and the logic of the man of science, where there should have been the reveries of the common heart, en- nobled into some raving Lear or unabashed Don Quixote. . . . I have been reading through a bundle of German plays, and have found every- where a desire not to express hopes and alarms common to every man that ever came into the

world, but politics or social passion, a veiled or
open propaganda. . . . If Homer were alive today,
he would only resist, after a deliberate struggle,
the temptation to find his subject not in Helen's
beauty, that every man has desired, nor in the
wisdom and endurance of Odysseus that has been
the desire of every woman that has come into the
world, but in what somebody would describe, perhaps, as 'the inevitable contest,' arising out of
economic causes, between the country-places and
small towns on the one hand, and, upon the other,
the great city of Troy, representing one knows
not what 'tendency to centralization.' "

In other words, if I understand him correctly,
Mr. Yeats believes that in writing pure rather
than applied poetry, he is not turning his back on
great issues to do filigree work, but is merely turning aside from questions of temporary import to
that which is fixed and eternal, life itself.

John Millington Synge was born near Dublin on
the sixteenth of April, 1871, and died in Dublin on
the twenty-fourth of March, 1909. It is a curious
thing that the three great Irishmen of the Celtic
renaissance—the only men who were truly inspired by genius—originally studied another form
of art than literature. Mr. Yeats studied painting
for years; A. E. is a painter of distinction; Synge
was an accomplished musician before he became a
man of letters. There is not the slightest doubt
that the effect of these sister arts upon the literary

work of the Great Three is pervasive and powerful. The books of Mr. Yeats and Mr. Russell are full of word-pictures; and the rhythm of Synge's strange prose, which Mr. Ernest Boyd ingeniously compares with Dr. Hyde's translations, is full of harmonies.

Dr. Hyde has not only witnessed a new and wonderful literary revival in his country, but he has the satisfaction of knowing that he is vitally connected with its birth and bloom.

Synge had the greatest mental endowment of all the Irish writers of his time. He had an amazingly powerful mind. At Trinity College he took prizes in Hebrew and in Irish, and at the same time gained a scholarship in harmony and counterpoint at the Royal Irish Academy of Music. As a boy, "he knew the note and plumage of every bird, and when and where they were to be found." As a man, he could easily have mastered the note of every human being, as in addition to his knowledge of ancient languages, he seems to have become proficient in German, French, and Italian with singular speed and ease. He was an excellent performer on the piano, flute, and violin, did conjuring tricks, and delighted the natives of the Aran Islands with his penny whistle. He must have had a positive genius for concentration, obtaining a command over anything to which he cared to devote his attention. Mr. Yeats found him in that ramshackle old Hôtel Corneille in the Latin Quar-

ter, busily writing literary criticism in French and
English, and told him as an inspired messenger to
go to the primitive folk in Ireland and become a
creative artist. He went; and in a few years
reached the summit of dramatic achievement.

Synge was a terrible person, as terrible in his
way as Swift. When Carlyle saw Daniel Webster,
he said, "I should hate to be that man's nigger."
I do not envy any of the men or women who, for
whatever reason, incurred the wrath of Synge.
He was never noisy or explosive, like a dog whose
barks are discounted, to whom one soon ceases to
pay any attention; we all know the futile and petty
irascibility of the shallow-minded. Synge was
like a mastiff who bites without warning. Irony
was the common chord in his composition. He
studied life and hated death; hated the gossip of
the world, which seemed to him the gabble of
fools. Physically he was a sick man, and felt his
tether. He thought it frightful that he should
have to die, while so many idiots lived long. He
never forgave men and women for their folly, and
the only reason why he did not forgive God was
because he was not sure of His existence. The
lady addressed in the following "poem" must
have read it with queasy emotion, and have unwillingly learned it by heart. A photograph of her
face immediately after its perusal would look like
futurist art; but who knows the expression on
the face of the poet while preparing this
poison?

THE CURSE

*To a sister of an enemy of the author's who disapproved of
"The Playboy."*

> Lord, confound this surly sister,
> Blight her brow with blotch and blister,
> Cramp her larynx, lung, and liver,
> In her guts a galling give her.
>
> Let her live to earn her dinners
> In Mountjoy with seedy sinners:
> Lord, this judgment quickly bring,
> And I'm your servant, John M. Synge.

(Mountjoy is a prison.)

Irish exaggeration is as often seen in plenary curses as in plenary blessings; both have the quality of humour. The curses are partly compounded of robust delight, like the joy of London cabmen in repartee; and the blessings are doubtless commingled with irony. But Synge had a savage heart. He was essentially a wild man, and a friend of mine had a vision of him that seems not without significance. He was walking in a desolate part of Ireland in a bleak storm of rain; when suddenly over the hills came the solitary figure of Synge, dressed in black, with a broad hat pulled over his brows.

As a stranger and sojourner he walked this earth. In the midst of Dublin he never mentioned politics, read no newspapers, and little contemporary literature, not even the books of his few intimate friends. Every one who knew him had such immense respect for the quality of his intellect that it is almost laughable to think how eagerly they must have awaited criticism of the books they gave him—criticism that never came. Yet he never seems to have given the impression of surliness; he was not surly, he was silent. He must have been the despair of diagnosticians; even in his last illness, it was impossible for the doctors and nurses to discover how he felt, for he would not tell. I think his burning mind consumed his bodily frame.

Synge wrote few poems, and they came at intervals during a period of sixteen or seventeen years. Objectively, they are unimportant; his contributions to English literature are his dramas and his prose sketches. But as revelations of his personality they have a deep and melancholy interest; and every word of his short Preface, written in December, 1908, a few months before his death, is valuable. He knew he was a dying man, and not only wished to collect these fugitive bits of verse, but wished to leave behind him his theory of poetry. With characteristic bluntness, he says that the poems which follow the Preface were mostly written "before the views just stated, with which they have little to do, had come into my head."

No discussion of modern verse should omit consideration of this remarkable Preface—for while it has had no effect on either Mr. Yeats or Mr. Russell—it has influenced other Irish poets, and many that are not Irish. Indeed much aggressively "modern" work is trying, more or less successfully, to fit this theory.   In the advance, Synge was more prophet than poet.

Many of the older poets, such as Villon and Herrick and Burns, used the whole of their personal life as their material, and the verse written in this way was read by strong men, and thieves, and deacons, not by little cliques only.   Then, in the town writing of the eighteenth century, ordinary life was put into verse that was not poetry, and when poetry came back with Coleridge and Shelley, it went into verse that was not always human.   [This last clause shows the difference between Synge and his friends, Yeats and Russell.]

In these days poetry is usually a flower of evil or good; but it is the timbre of poetry that wears most surely, and there is no timbre that has not strong roots among the clay and worms.

Even if we grant that exalted poetry can be kept successful by itself, the strong things in life are needed in poetry also, to show that what is exalted or tender is not made by feeble blood. It may almost be said that before verse can be human again it must learn to be brutal.

Like Herrick, he wrote verse about himself, for he knew that much biography and criticism would follow his funeral.

ON AN ANNIVERSARY

After reading the dates in a book of Lyrics.

With Fifteen-ninety or Sixteen-sixteen
We end Cervantes, Marot, Nashe or Green:
Then Sixteen-thirteen till two score and nine,
Is Crashaw's niche, that honey-lipped divine.
And so when all my little work is done
They'll say I came in Eighteen-seventy-one,
And died in Dublin. . . . What year will they write
For my poor passage to the stall of night?

A QUESTION

I asked if I got sick and died, would you
With my black funeral go walking too,
If you'd stand close to hear them talk or pray
While I'm let down in that steep bank of clay.

And, No, you said, for if you saw a crew
Of living idiots pressing round that new
Oak coffin—they alive, I dead beneath
That board—you'd rave and rend them with your teeth.

The love of brutal strength in Synge's work may have been partly the projection of his sickness, just as the invalid Stevenson delighted in the creation of powerful ruffians; but the brooding on his own death is quite modern, and is, I think, part of the egoism that is so distinguishing a feature in contemporary poetry. So many have abandoned all hope of a life beyond the grave, that they cling to bodily existence with almost gluttonous passion, and are filled with self-pity at the thought of their own death and burial. To my mind, there is something unworthy, something childish, in all this. When a child has been rebuked or punished by its father or mother, it plays a trump card—"You'll be sorry when I am dead!" It is better for men and women to attack the daily task with what cheerful energy they can command, and let the interruption of death come when it must. If life is short, it seems unwise to spend so much of our time in rehearsals of a tragedy that can have only one performance.

In the modern Tempest of Ireland, Yeats is

Ariel and A. E. is Prospero. He is the Master of the island. As a literary artist, he is not the equal of either of the two men whose work we have considered; but he is by all odds the greatest Personality. He holds over his contemporaries a spiritual sway that many a monarch might envy. Perhaps the final tribute to him is seen in the fact that even George Moore treats him with respect.

One reason for this predominance is the man's sincerity. All those who know him regard him with reverence; and to us who know him only through his books and his friends, his sincerity is equally clear and compelling. He has done more than any other man to make Dublin a centre of intellectual life. At one time his house was kept open every Sunday evening, and any friend, stranger, or foreigner had the right to walk in without knocking, and take a part in the conversation. A. E. used to subscribe to every literary journal, no matter how obscure, that was printed in Ireland; every week he would scan the pages, hoping to discover a man of promise. It was in this way he "found" James Stephens, and not only found him, but founded him. Many a struggling painter or poet has reason to bless the gracious assistance of George W. Russell.

It is a singular thing that the three great men of modern Ireland seem more like disembodied spirits than carnal persons. Synge always seems to those who read his books like some ghost, waking the echoes with ironical laughter; I cannot imagine A. E. putting on coat and trousers; and although I once had the honour—which I gratefully remember—of a long talk with W. B. Yeats, I never felt that I was listening to a man of flesh and blood. It is fitting that these men had their earthly dwelling in a sea-girt isle, where every foot of ground has its own superstition, and where the constant mists are peopled with unearthly figures.

I do not really know what mysticism is; but I know that Mr. Yeats and Mr. Russell are both mystics and of a quite different stamp. Mr. Yeats is not insincere, but his mysticism is a part of his art rather than a part of his mind. He is artistically, rather than intellectually, sincere. The mysticism of Mr. Russell is fully as intellectual as it is emotional; it is more than his creed; it is his life. His poetry and his prose are not shadowed by his mysticism, they emanate from it. He does not have to live in another world when he writes verse, and then come back to earth when the dinner or the door bell rings; he lives in the other world all the time. Or rather, the earth and common objects are themselves part of the Universal Spirit, reflecting its constant activities.

DUST

I heard them in their sadness say
  "The earth rebukes the thought of God;
We are but embers wrapped in clay,
  A little nobler than the sod."

> But I have touched the lips of clay,
>   Mother, thy rudest sod to me
> Is thrilled with fire of hidden day,
>   And haunted by all mystery.

The above poem, taken from the author's first volume, *Homeward: Songs by the Way*, does not reflect that homesickness of which A. E. speaks in his Preface. Homesickness is longing, yearning; and there is little of any such quality in the work of A. E. Or, if he is really homesick, he is homesick not like one who has just left home, but more like one who is certain of his speedy return thither. This homesickness has more anticipation than regret; it is like healthy hunger when one is assured of the next meal. For assurance is the prime thing in A. E.'s temperament and in his work; it partly accounts for his strong influence. Many writers today are like sheep having no shepherd; A. E. is a shepherd. To turn from the wailing so characteristic of the poets, to the books of this high-hearted, resolute, candid, cheerful man, is like coming into harbour after a mad voyage. He moves among his contemporaries like a calm, able surgeon in a hospital. I suspect he has been the recipient of many strange confessions. His poetry has healing in its wings.

Has any human voice ever expressed more wisely or more tenderly the reason why Our Lord was a man of sorrows? Why He spake to humanity in the language of pain, rather than in the language of delight? Was it not simply because, in talking to us, He who could speak all languages, used our own, rather than that of His home coun-

A LEADER

Though your eyes with tears were blind,
  Pain upon the path you trod:
Well we knew, the hosts behind,
  Voice and shining of a god.

For your darkness was our day,
  Signal fires, your pains untold,
Lit us on our wandering way
  To the mystic heart of gold.

Naught we knew of the high land,
  Beauty burning in its spheres;
Sorrow we could understand
  And the mystery told in tears.

Something of the secret of his quiet strength is seen in the following two stanzas, which close his poem *Apocalyptic* (1916):

It shall be better to be bold
  Than clothed in purple in that hour;
The will of steel be more than gold;
  For only what we are is power.
Who through the starry gate would win
Must be like those who walk therein.

You, who have made of earth your star,
  Cry out, indeed, for hopes made vain:
For only those can laugh who are
  The strong Initiates of Pain,
Who know that mighty god to be
Sculptor of immortality.

It is a wonderful thing—a man living in a house in Dublin, living a life of intense, ceaseless, and extraordinarily diversified activity, travelling on life's common way in cheerful godliness, and shedding abroad to the remotest corners of the earth a masculine serenity of soul.

James Stephens was not widely known until the year 1912, when he published a novel called *The Crock of Gold;* this excited many readers in Great Britain and in America, an excitement considerably heightened by the appearance of another work of prose fiction, *The Demi-Gods,* in 1914; and general curiosity about the author became rampant. It was speedily discovered that he was a poet as well as a novelist; that three years before his reputation he had issued a slim book of verse, boldly named *Insurrections,* the title being the boldest thing in it. By 1915 this neglected work had passed through four editions, and during the last six years he has presented to an admiring public five more volumes of poems, *The Hill of Vision,* 1912; *Songs from the Clay,* 1915; *The Adventures of Seumas Beg,* 1915; *Green Branches,* 1916, and *Reincarnations,* 1918.

A. E. believed in him from the start; and it was owing to the influence of A. E. that *Insurrections* took the form of a book, gratefully dedicated to its only begetter. Both patron and protégé must have been surprised by its lack of impact, and still more surprised by the immense success of *The Crock of Gold.* The poems are mainly realistic, pictures of slimy city streets with slimy creatures crawling on the pavements. It is an interesting fact that they appeared the same year of Synge's *Poems* with Synge's famous Preface counselling brutality, counselling anything to bring poetry away from the iridescent dreams of W. B. Yeats down to the stark realities of life and nature. They bear testimony to the catholic breadth of A. E.'s sympathetic appreciation, for they are as different as may be imagined from the spirit of mysticism. It must also be confessed that their absolute merit as poetry is not particularly remarkable; all the more credit to the discernment of A. E., who described behind them an original and powerful personality.

The influence of Synge is strong in the second book of verses, called *The Hill of Vision,* particularly noticeable in such a poem as *The Brute.* Curiously enough, *Songs from the Clay* is more exalted in tone than *The Hill of Vision.* The air is clearer and purer. But the author of *The Crock of Gold* and *The Demi-Gods* appears again in *The Adventures of Seumas Beg.* In these charming poems we have that triple combination of realism, humour, and fantasy that gave so original a flavour to the novels. They make a valuable addition to child-poetry; for men, women, angels, fairies, God and the Devil are treated with easy familiarity, in practical, definite, conversational language. These are the best fruits of his imagination in rime.

THE DEVIL'S BAG

I saw the Devil walking down the lane
Behind our house.— There was a heavy bag
Strapped tightly on his shoulders, and the rain
Sizzled when it hit him. He picked a rag
Up from the ground and put it in his sack,
And grinned and rubbed his hands. There was a thing
Moving inside the bag upon his back—
It must have been a soul! I saw it fling
And twist about inside, and not a hole
Or cranny for escape. Oh, it was sad.
I cried, and shouted out, *"Let out that soul!"*
But he turned round, and, sure, his face went mad,
And twisted up and down, and he said *"Hell!"*
And ran away. . . . Oh, mammy! I'm not well.

In 1916 Mr. Stephens published a threnody, *Green Branches*, which illustrates still another side of his literary powers. There is organ-like music in these noble lines. The sting of bitterness is drawn from death, and sorrow changes into a solemn rapture.

In commenting on Synge's poem, *The Curse*, I spoke of the delight the Irish have in hyperbolic curses; an excellent illustration of this may be found in Mr. Stephens' latest volume, *Reincarnations*. There is no doubt that the poet as well as his imaginary imprecator found real pleasure in the production of the following ejaculations:

RIGHTEOUS ANGER

The lanky hank of a she in the inn over there
Nearly killed me for asking the loan of a glass of beer;
May the devil grip the whey-faced slut by the hair,
And beat bad manners out of her skin for a year.

That parboiled imp, with the hardest jaw you will see
On virtue's path, and a voice that would rasp the dead,
Came roaring and raging the minute she looked at me,
And threw me out of the house on the back of my head!

If I asked her master he'd give me a cask a day;
But she, with the beer at hand, not a gill would arrange!
May she marry a ghost and bear him a kitten, and may
The High King of Glory permit her to get the mange.

Padraic Colum has followed the suggestion of Synge, and made deep excavations for the foundations of his poetry. It grows up out of the soil like a hardy plant; and while it cannot be called major work, it has a wholesome, healthy earthiness. It is realistic in a different way from the town eclogues of James Stephens; it is not merely in the country, it is agricultural. His most important book is *Wild Earth,* published in Dublin in 1901, republished with additions in New York in 1916. The smell of the earth is pungent in such poems as *The Plougher* and *The Drover;* while his masterpiece, *An Old Woman of the Roads,* voices the primeval and universal longing for the safe shelter of a home. I wonder what those who believe in the abolition of private property are going to do with this natural, human passion? Private property is not the result of an artificial social code—it is the result of an instinct. The first three stanzas of this poem indicate its quality, expressing the all but inexpressible love of women for each stick of furniture and every household article.

O, to have a little house!
  To own the hearth and stool and all!
The heaped up sods upon the fire,
  The pile of turf against the wall!

To have a clock with weights and chains
  And pendulum swinging up and down!
A dresser filled with shining delft,
  Speckled and white and blue and brown!

I could be busy all the day
  Clearing and sweeping hearth and floor,
And fixing on their shelf again
  My white and blue and speckled store!

Lord Dunsany brought to public attention a new poet, Francis Ledwidge, whose one volume, *Songs of the Fields,* is full of promise. In October, 1914, he enlisted in Kitchener's first army, and was killed on the thirty-first of August, 1917. Ledwidge's poetry is more conventional than that of most of his Irish contemporaries, and he is at his best in describing natural objects. Such poems as *A Rainy Day in April,* and *A Twilight in Middle March* are most characteristic. But occasionally he arrests the ear with a deeper note. The first four lines of the following passage, taken from *An Old Pain,* might fittingly apply to a personality like that of Synge:

I hold the mind is the imprisoned soul,
And all our aspirations are its own
Struggles and strivings for a golden goal,
That wear us out like snow men at the thaw.
And we shall make our Heaven where we have sown
Our purple longings. Oh! can the loved dead draw

Anear us when we moan, or watching wait
Our coming in the woods where first we met,
The dead leaves falling in their wild hair wet,
Their hands upon the fastenings of the gate?

A direct result of the spiritual influence of A. E.
is seen in the poetry of Susan Mitchell. She is
not an imitator of his manner, but she reflects the
mystical faith. Her little volume, *The Living
Chalice,* is full of the beauty that rises from suffering. It is not the spirit of acquiescence or of
resignation, but rather dauntless triumphant af-
firmation. Her poems of the Christ-child have
something of the exaltation of Christina Rossetti;
for to her mind the road to victory lies through the
gate of Humility. Here is a typical illustration:

THE HEART'S LOW DOOR

O Earth, I will have none of thee.
  Alien to me the lonely plain,
And the rough passion of the sea
  Storms my unheeding heart in vain.

The petulance of rain and wind,
  The haughty mountains' superb scorn,
Are but slight things I've flung behind,
  Old garments that I have out-worn.

Bare of the grudging grass, and bare
  Of the tall forest's careless shade,
Deserter from thee, Earth, I dare
  See all thy phantom brightness fade.

And, darkening to the sun, I go
  To enter by the heart's low door,
And find where Love's red embers glow
  A home, who ne'er had home before.

Thomas MacDonagh (1878–1916) was, like so many of the young Irish writers of the twentieth century, both scholar and poet. In 1916 he published a prose critical work, *Literature in Ireland,* in which his two passions, love of art and love of country, are clearly displayed. His books of original verse include *The Golden Joy,* 1906; *Songs of Myself,* 1910, and others. He was a worshipper of Beauty, his devotion being even more religious than æsthetic. The poems addressed to Beauty —of which there are comparatively many—exhibit the familiar yet melancholy disparity between the vision in the poet's soul and the printed image of it. This disparity is not owing to faulty technique, for his management of metrical effects shows ease and grace; it is simply the lack of sufficient poetic vitality. Although his ambition as an artist appears to have been to write great odes and hymns to Beauty, his simple poems of Irish life are full of charm. The *Wishes to My Son* has a poignant tenderness. One can hardly read it without tears. And the love of a wife for "her man" is truly revealed in the last two stanzas of *John-John.*

> The neighbours' shame of me began
>   When first I brought you in;
> To wed and keep a tinker man
>   They thought a kind of sin;
> But now this three years since you're gone
>   'Tis pity me they do,
> And that I'd rather have, John-John,
>   Than that they'd pity you.

Pity for me and you, John-John,
  I could not bear.

Oh, you're my husband right enough,
  But what's the good of that?
You know you never were the stuff
  To be the cottage cat,
To watch the fire and hear me lock
  The door and put out Shep—
But there now, it is six o'clock
  And time for you to step.
God bless and keep you far, John-John!
  And that's my prayer.

Joseph Campbell, most of whose work has been published under the Irish name Seosamh Maccathmhaoil, writes both regular and free verse. He is close to the soil, and speaks the thoughts of the peasants, articulating their pleasures, their pains, and their superstitions. No deadness of conventionality dulls the edge of his art—he is an original man. His fancy is bold, and he makes no attempt to repress it. Perhaps his most striking poem is *I am the Gilly of Christ*—strange that its reverence has been mistaken for sacrilege! And in the little song, *Go, Ploughman, Plough,* one tastes the joy of muscle, the revelation of the upturned earth, and the promise of beauty in fruition.

Go, ploughman, plough
The mearing lands,
The meadow lands:
The mountain lands:
All life is bare
Beneath your share,
All love is in your lusty hands.

Up, horses, now!
And straight and true
Let every broken furrow run:
The strength you sweat
Shall blossom yet
In golden glory to the sun.

In 1917 Mr. Campbell published a beautiful volume, signed with his English name, embellished with his own drawings—one for each poem—called *Earth of Cualann.* Cualann is the old name for the County of Wicklow, but it includes also a stretch to the northwest, reaching close to Dublin. Mr. Campbell's description of it in his preface makes a musical overture to the verses that follow. "Wild and unspoilt, a country of cairn-crowned hills and dark, watered valleys, it bears even to this day something of the freshness of the heroic dawn."

The work of Seumas O'Sullivan, born in 1878, has often been likened to that of W. B. Yeats, but I can see little similarity either in spirit or in manner. The younger poet has the secret of melody and his verses show a high degree of technical excellence; but in these respects he no more resembles his famous countryman than many another master. His best poems are collected in a volume published in 1912, and the most interesting of these give pictures of various city streets, *Mercer Street* (three), *Nelson Street, Cuffe Street,* and so on. In other words, the most original part of this poet's production is founded on reality. This does not mean that he lacks imagination; for it is only by imagination that a writer can portray and interpret familiar scenes. The more widely and easily their veracity can be verified by readers, the greater is the challenge to the art of the poet.

Although the work of Herbert Trench is not particularly identified with Ireland, he was born in County Cork, in 1865, and his first volume of poems (1901) was called *Deirdre Wedded*. He completed his formal education at Oxford, taking a first class in the Final Honour Schools, and becoming a Fellow of All Souls. His poetical reputation, which began with the appearance of *Apollo and the Seaman*, in 1907, has been perceptibly heightened by the publication in 1918 of his collected works in two volumes, *Poems, with Fables in Prose*, saluted rapturously by a London critic under the heading "Unforgettable Accents." No one can now tell whether they are unforgettable or not; but his poems are certainly memorable for individual lines rather than for complete architectural beauty. In the midst of commonplace composition single phrases stand out in a manner that almost startles the reader.

We may properly add to our list the names of three Irish poets who are Americans. Maurice Francis Egan, full of years and honours, a scholar and statesman, giving notable service to America as our Minister to Denmark, has written poetry marked by tenderness of feeling and delicacy of art. His little book, *Songs and Sonnets*, pub-

lished in 1892, exhibits the range of his work as
well as anything that he has written. It is
founded on a deep and pure religious faith. . . .
Norreys Jephson O'Conor is a young Irish-Ameri-
can, a graduate of Harvard, and has already published three volumes of verse, *Celtic Memories,*
which appeared in England in 1913, *Beside the
Blackwater,* 1915, and *Songs of the Celtic Past,*
1918; in 1916 he published a poetic play, *The Fairy
Bride,* which was produced for the benefit of Irish
troops at the front.   American by birth and residence, of Irish ancestry, he draws his inspiration
almost wholly from Celtic lore and Celtic scenes.
He is a natural singer, whose art is steadily increasing in authority.

In 1918 immediate attention was aroused by a
volume of poems called *My Ireland,* from Francis
Carlin.   This is the work of a young Irishman, a
New York business man, who, outside of the shop,
has dreamed dreams.   Many of these verses are
full of beauty and charm.

It will be seen from our review of the chief figures among contemporary Irish poets that the
jolly, jigging Irishman of stage history is quite
conspicuous by his absence.   He still gives his
song and dance, and those who prefer musical-
comedy to orchestral compositions can find him in
the numerous anthologies of Anglo-Irish verse;
but the tone of modern Irish poetry is spiritual
rather than hearty.

Whatever may be thought of the appropriateness of the term "Advance of English Poetry" for my survey of the modern field as a whole, there is no doubt that it applies fittingly to Ireland. The last twenty-five years have seen an awakening of poetic activity in that island unlike anything known there before; and Dublin has become one of the literary centres of the world. When a new movement produces three men of genius, and a long list of poets of distinction, it should be recognized with respect for its achievement, and with faith in its future.

CHAPTER VII

AMERICAN VETERANS AND FORERUNNERS

American Poetry in the eighteen-nineties—William Vaughn
Moody—his early death a serious loss to literature—George
Santayana—a master of the sonnet—Robert Underwood Johnson—his moral idealism—Richard Burton—his healthy optimism—his growth—Edwin Markham and his famous poem—
Ella Wheeler Wilcox—her additions to our language—Edmund
Vance Cooke—Edith M. Thomas—Henry van Dyke—George E.
Woodberry—his spiritual and ethereal quality—William Dudley Foulke—translator of Petrarch—the late H. K. Vielé—his
whimsicality—Cale Young Rice—his prolific production—his
versatility—Josephine P. Peabody—*Sursum Corda*—her child
poems—Edwin Arlington Robinson—a forerunner of the modern advance—his manliness and common sense—intellectual
qualities.

To compel public recognition by a fresh volume of
poems is becoming increasingly difficult. The
country fields and the city streets are full of singing birds; and after a few more springs have
awakened the earth, it may become as impossible
to distinguish the note of a new imagist as the
note of an individual robin. When the publishers
advertise the initial appearance of a poet, we
simply say *Another!* The versifiers and their
friends who study them through a magnifying
glass may ultimately force us to classify the
songsters into wild poets, gamy poets, barnyard
poets, poets that hunt and are hunted.

But in the last decade of the last century, poets other than migratory, poets who were winter residents, were sufficiently uncommon. Indeed the courage required to call oneself a poet was considerable.

Of the old leaders, Whitman, Whittier, and Holmes lived into the eighteen-nineties; and when, in 1894, the last leaf left the tree, we could not help wondering what the next Maytime would bring forth. Had William Vaughn Moody lived longer, it is probable that America would have had another major poet. He wrote verse to please himself, and plays in order that he might write more verse; but at the dawning of a great career, the veto of death ended both. As it is, much of his work will abide.

Indiana has the honour of his birth. He was born at Spencer, on the eighth of July, 1869. He was graduated at Harvard, and after teaching there, he became a member of the English Department of the University of Chicago. He died at Colorado Springs, on the seventeenth of October, 1910.

The quality of high seriousness, so dear to Matthew Arnold, was characteristic of everything that Mr. Moody gave to the public. At his best, there is a noble dignity, a pure serenity in his work, which make for immortality. This dignity is never assumed; it is not worn like an academic robe; it is an integral part of the poetry. *An Ode in Time of Hesitation* has already become a classic, both for its depth of moral feeling and for its sculptured style. Like so many other poets, Mr, Moody was an artist with pencil and brush as well as with the pen; his study of form shows in his language.

George Santayana was born at Madrid, on the sixteenth of December, 1863. His father was a Spaniard, and his mother an American. He was graduated from Harvard in 1886, and later became Professor of Philosophy, which position he resigned in 1912, because academic life had grown less and less congenial, although his resignation was a matter of sincere regret on the part of both his colleagues and his pupils. Latterly he has lived in France.

He is a professional philosopher but primarily a man of letters. His philosophy is interesting chiefly because the books that contain it are exquisitely written. He is an artist in prose and verse, and it seems unfortunate that his professorial activity—as in the case of A. E. Housman—choked his Muse. For art has this eternal advantage over learning. Nobody knows whether or not philosophical truth is really true; but Beauty is really beautiful.

In 1894 Mr. Santayana produced—in a tiny volume limited to four hundred and fifty copies on small paper—*Sonnets and Other Poems;* and in 1899 a less important book, *Lucifer: a Theological Tragedy.* No living American has written finer sonnets than our philosopher. In sincerity of feeling, in living language, and in melody they reach distinction.

> A wall, a wall around my garden rear,
> And hedge me in from the disconsolate hills;
> Give me but one of all the mountain rills,
> Enough of ocean in its voice I hear.
> Come no profane insatiate mortal near
> With the contagion of his passionate ills;
> The smoke of battle all the valley fills,
> Let the eternal sunlight greet me here.
> This spot is sacred to the deeper soul
> And to the piety that mocks no more.
> In nature's inmost heart is no uproar,
> None in this shrine; in peace the heavens roll,
> In peace the slow tides pulse from shore to shore,
> And ancient quiet broods from pole to pole.

> O world, thou choosest not the better part!
> It is not wisdom to be only wise,
> And on the inward vision close the eyes,
> But it is wisdom to believe the heart.
> Columbus found a world, and had no chart,
> Save one that faith deciphered in the skies;
> To trust the soul's invincible surmise
> Was all his science and his only art.
> Our knowledge is a torch of smoky pine
> That lights the pathway but one step ahead
> Across a void of mystery and dread.
> Bid, then, the tender light of faith to shine
> By which alone the mortal heart is led
> Unto the thinking of the thought divine.

ON A VOLUME OF SCHOLASTIC PHILOSOPHY

What chilly cloister or what lattice dim
Cast painted light upon this careful page?
What thought compulsive held the patient sage
Till sound of matin bell or evening hymn?

> Did visions of the Heavenly Lover swim
> Before his eyes in youth, or did stern rage
> Against rash heresy keep green his age?
> Had he seen God, to write so much of Him?
> Gone is that irrecoverable mind
> With all its phantoms, senseless to mankind
> As a dream's trouble or the speech of birds.
> The breath that stirred his lips he soon resigned
> To windy chaos, and we only find
> The garnered husks of his disusèd words.

Robert Underwood Johnson was born at Washington, on the twelfth of January, 1853, and took his bachelor's degree at Earlham College, in Indiana, at the age of eighteen. When twenty years old, he became a member of the editorial staff of the *Century Magazine,* and remained there exactly forty years. His first volume of poems, *The Winter Hour,* was published in 1891, since which time he has produced many others. Now he is his own publisher, and two attractive books "published by the author" appeared in 1917—*Poems of War and Peace* and *Italian Rhapsody.*

Mr. Johnson is a conservative, by which he would mean that as editor, publicist, and poet, he has tried to maintain the highest standards in art, politics, morality, and religion. Certainly his services to his country have been important; and many good causes that he advocated are now realities. There is no love lost between him and the "new" school in poetry, and possibly each fails to appreciate what is good in the other.

Moral idealism is the foundation of much of Mr.

Johnson's verse; he has written many occasional poems, poems supporting good men and good works, and poems attacking the omnipresent and well-organized forces of evil. I am quite aware that in the eyes of many critics such praise as that damns him beyond hope of redemption; but the interesting fact is, that although he has toiled for righteousness all his life, he is a poet.

His poem, *The Voice of Webster,* although written years ago, is not only in harmony with contemporary historical judgment (1918) but has a Doric dignity worthy of the subject. There are not a few memorable lines:

> Forgetful of the father in the son,
> Men praised in Lincoln what they blamed in him.

Always the friend of small and oppressed nations, whose fate arouses in him an unquenchable indignation, he published in 1908 paraphrases from the leading poet of Servia. In view of what has happened during the last four years, the first sentence of the preface to these verses, written by Nikola Tesla, has a reinforced emphasis—"Hardly is there a nation which has met with a sadder fate than the Servian." How curious today seems the individual or national pessimism that was so common *before* 1914! Why did we not realize how (comparatively) happy we were then? Hell then seems like paradise now. It is as though an athletic pessimist should lose both legs. Shall we never learn anything from Edgar's wisdom?

O gods! Who is't can say "I am at the worst"?
I am worse than e'er I was.

Another poet, who has had a long and honourable career, is Richard Burton. He was born at
Hartford, Connecticut, on the fourteenth of March,
1859, and was educated at Trinity and at Johns
Hopkins, where he took the doctor's degree in
Anglo-Saxon. For the last twenty years he has
been Professor of English Literature at the University of Minnesota, and is one of the best teachers and lecturers in the country. He paradoxi-
cally found his voice in a volume of original poems
called *Dumb in June,* which appeared in 1895.
Since then he has published many books of verse
and prose—plays, stories, essays, and lyrics.

He has shown steady development as a poet—
Poems of Earth's Meaning (he has the habit of
bad titles), which came out in 1917, is his high-
water mark. I am glad that he reprinted in this
volume the elegy on the death of Arthur Upson,
written in 1910; there is not a false note in it.

The personality of Richard Burton shines
clearly through his work; cheerful manliness and
cheerful godliness. He knows more about human
nature than many pretentious diagnosticians; and
his gladness in living communicates itself to the
reader. Occasionally, as in *Spring Fantasies,*
there is a subtlety easy to miss on a first or careless reading. On the edge of sixty, this poet is
doing his best singing and best thinking.

Sometimes an author who has been writing all

his life will, under the flashlight of inspiration, reveal deep places by a few words formed into some phrase that burns its way into literature. This is the case with Edwin Markham (born 1852) who has produced many books, but seems destined to be remembered for *The Man With the Hoe* (1899). His other works are by no means negligible, but that one poem made the whole world kin.

To a certain extent, the same may be said of Ella Wheeler Wilcox (born 1855). In spite of an excess of sentimentality, which is her besetting sin, she has written much excellent verse. Two sayings, however, will be remembered long after many of her contemporaries are forgotten:

> Laugh and the world laughs with you,
> Weep, and you weep alone.

Furthermore, in these days of world-tragedy, we all owe her a debt of gratitude for being the author of the phrase written many years ago:

> No question is ever settled
> Until it is settled right.

The legitimate successor to James Whitcomb Riley is Edmund Vance Cooke (born 1866). He has the same philosophy of cheerful kindliness, founded on a shrewd knowledge of human nature. Verse is his mother tongue; and occasionally he rises above fluency and ingenuity into the pure air of imagination.

Among America's living veterans should be

named with respect Edith M. Thomas, who has been bravely singing for over thirty years. She was born in Ohio on the twelfth of August, 1854, and her first book of poems appeared in 1885. She is an excellent illustration of just how far talent can go unaccompanied by the divine breath of inspiration. She has perhaps almost too much facility; she has dignity, good taste, an excellent command of a wide variety of metrical effects; she has read ancient and modern authors, she is a keen observer, she is as alert and inquisitive now, as in the days of her youth; and loves to use her abilities in cultivating the fruits of the spirit. I suspect that with the modesty that so frequently accompanies good taste, she understands her own limitations better than any critic could do.

Her long faithfulness to the Muse ought to be remembered, now that poetry has come into its kingdom.

Among our veteran poets should be numbered also Henry Van Dyke (born 1852). His versatility is so remarkable that it has somewhat obscured his particular merit. His lyric *Reliance* is spiritually as well as artistically true:

> Not to the swift, the race:
> Not to the strong, the fight:
> Not to the righteous, perfect grace:
> Not to the wise, the light.
>
> But often faltering feet
> Come surest to the goal;
> And they who walk in darkness meet
> The sunrise of the soul.

A thousand times by night
The Syrian hosts have died;
A thousand times the vanquished right
Hath risen, glorified.

The truth by wise men sought
Was spoken by a child;
The alabaster box was brought
In trembling hands defiled.

Not from the torch, the gleam,
But from the stars above:
Not from my heart, life's crystal stream,
But from the depths of love.

George E. Woodberry (born 1855), graduate of
Harvard, a scholar, literary biographer, and critic
of high standing, has been eminent among contemporary American poets since the year 1890,
marked by his book of verse, *The North Shore
Watch*. In 1917 an interesting and valuable *Study*
of his poetry appeared, written by Louis V.
Ledoux, and accompanied by a carefully minute
bibliography. I do not mean to say anything un-
pleasant about Mr. Woodberry or the public, when
I say that his poetry is too fine for popularity. It
is not the raw material of poetry, like that of Carl
Sandburg, yet it is not exactly the finished product
that passes by the common name. It is rather the
essence of poetry, the spirit of poetry, a clear
flame—almost impalpable. "You may not be
worthy to smoke the Arcadia mixture," well—we
may not be worthy to read all that Mr. Woodberry
writes. And I am convinced that it is not his

fault. His poems of nature and his poems of love
speak out of the spirit. He not only never
"writes down" to the public, it seems almost as if
he intended his verse to be read by some race superior to the present stage of human development.

> But in his motion like an angel sings,
> Still quiring to the young-eyed cherubins;
> Such harmony is in immortal souls;
> But whilst this muddy vesture of decay
> Doth grossly close it in, we cannot hear it.

William Dudley Foulke may fairly be classed
with the Indiana group. He was born at New
York in 1848, but has lived in Indiana since 1876.
He has been conspicuous in much political and
social service, but the soul of the man is found in
his books of verse, most of which have been first
printed in England. He is a lifelong student of
Petrarch, and has made many excellent translations. His best independent work may be found
in a group of poems properly called *Ad Patriam*.
I think such a sonnet as *The City's Crown* is fairly
representative:

> What makes a city great? Huge piles of stone
>   Heaped heavenward? Vast multitudes who dwell
> Within wide circling walls? Palace and throne
>   And riches past the count of man to tell,
>
> And wide domain? Nay, these the empty husk!
>   True glory dwells where glorious deeds are done,
> Where great men rise whose names athwart the dusk
>   Of misty centuries gleam like the sun!

In Athens, Sparta, Florence, 'twas the soul
  That was the city's bright, immortal part,
The splendour of the spirit was their goal,
  Their jewel, the unconquerable heart!

So may the city that I love be great
Till every stone shall be articulate.

The early death of Herman Knickerbocker Vielé robbed America not only of one of her most brilliant novelists, but of a poet of fine flavour. In 1903 he published a tall, thin book, *Random Verse*, that has something of the charm and beauty of *The Inn of the Silver Moon*. In everything that he wrote, Mr. Vielé revealed a winsome whimsicality, and a lightness of touch impossible except to true artists. It should also be remembered to his credit that he loved France with an ardour not so frequently expressed then as now. Indeed, he loved her so much that the last four years of agony might have come near to breaking his heart. He was one of the finest spirits of the twentieth century.

Cale Young Rice was born in Kentucky, on the seventh of December, 1872. He is a graduate of Cumberland University and of Harvard, and his wife is the famous creator of Mrs. Wiggs. He has been a prolific poet, having produced many dramas and lyrics, which were collected in two stout volumes in 1915. In 1917 appeared two new works, *Trails Sunward* and *Wraiths and Realities*, with interesting prefaces, in which the anthologies of the "new" poetry, their makers, editors, and defenders, are heartily cudgelled. Mr. Rice is a conservative in art, and writes in the orthodox manner; although he is not afraid to make metrical experiments.

I like his lyrical pieces better than his dramas. His verse-plays are good, but not supremely good; and I find it difficult to read either blank verse or rimed drama, unless it is in the first class, where assuredly Mr. Rice's meritorious efforts do not belong.

His songs are spontaneous, not manufactured. He is a natural singer with such facility that it is rather surprising that the average of his work is so good. A man who writes so much ought, one would think, to be more often than not, commonplace; but the fact is that most of his poems could not be turned into prose without losing their life. He has limitations instead of faults; within his range he may be counted on to give a satisfactory performance. By range I mean of course height rather than breadth. He is at home all over the earth, and his subjects are as varied as his style.

Josephine Preston Peabody (Mrs. Marks) was born at New York, and took her degree at Radcliffe in 1894. For two years she was a member of the English department of Wellesley (two syllables only). Her drama *Marlowe* (1901) gave her something like fame, though I have always thought it was overrated; it is certainly inferior to *The Death of Marlowe* (1837), by Richard Hengist Horne. In 1910 her play *The Piper* won the Stratford-on-Avon prize, and subsequently proved to be one of the most successful plays seen on the American stage in the twentieth century. It was produced by the New Theatre, the finest stock company ever known in America.

Josephine Peabody has written other dramas, and has an enviable reputation as a lyric poet. The burden of her poetry is *Sursum Corda!* As I read modern verse, I am forced to the conclusion that men and women require a vast deal of comforting. The years preceding the war seem in the retrospect happy, almost a golden age; homesickness for the England, France, Italy, America that existed before 1914 is almost a universal sentiment; yet when we read the verse composed during those days of prosperous tranquillity, when youth seemed comic rather than tragic, we find that half the poets spent their time in lamentation, and the other half in first aid. An enormous number of lyrics speak as though despondency were the normal condition of men and women; are we really all sad when alone, engaged in reading or writing? "Every man is grave alone," said Emerson. I wonder.

So many poets seem to tell us that we ought not absolutely to abandon all hope. The case for living is admittedly a bad one; but the poets beseech us to stick it. Does every man really go down to business in the morning with his jaw set? Does every woman begin the day with compressed

lips, determined somehow to pull through till afternoon? Even the nature poets are always telling us to look at the birds and flowers and cheer
up. Is that all botany and zoology are good for?
Have we nothing to learn from nature but—buck
up?

I do not mean that Josephine Peabody's poems
resemble glad Polyanna, but I was driven to these
divagations by the number of cheery lyrics that
she has felt it necessary to write. Now I find it
almost as depressing to be told that there *is* hope
as to be told that there isn't.

> I met Poor Sorrow on the way
>   As I came down the years;
> I gave him everything I had
>   And looked at him through tears.
>
> "But, Sorrow, give me here again
>   Some little sign to show;
> For I have given all I own;
>   Yet have I far to go."
>
> Then Sorrow charmed my eyes for me
>   And hallowed them thus far;
> "Look deep enough in every dark,
>   And you shall see the star."

The first two poems in *The Harvest Moon*
(1916) are very fine; but sometimes I think her
best work is found in a field where it is difficult to
excel—I mean child poetry. Her *Cradle Song* is
as good as anything of hers I know, though I could
wish she had omitted the parenthetical refrain. I
hope readers will forgive me—though I know they

won't—for saying that *Dormi, dormi tu* sounds like a triumphant exclamation at the sixteenth hole.

An American poet who won twenty-two years ago a reputation with a small volume, who ten years later seemed almost forgotten, and who now deservedly stands higher than ever before is Edwin Arlington Robinson. He was born in Maine, on the twenty-second of December, 1869, and studied at Harvard University. In 1896 he published two poems, *The Torrent* and *The Night Before;* these were included the next year in a volume called *The Children of the Night.* His successive books of verse are *Captain Craig,* 1902; *The Town Down the River,* 1910; *The Man Against the Sky,* 1916; *Merlin,* 1917; and he has printed two plays, of which *Van Zorn* (1914) despite its chilling reception, is exceedingly good.

Mr. Robinson is not only one of our best known American contemporary poets, but is a leader and recognized as such. Many write verses today because the climate is so favourable to the Muse's somewhat delicate health. But if Mr. Robinson is not a germinal writer, he is at all events a precursor of the modern advance. The year 1896 was not opportune for a venture in verse, but the Gardiner poet has never cared to be in the rearward of a fashion. The two poems that he produced that year he has since surpassed, but they clearly demonstrated his right to live and to be heard.

The prologue to the 1897 volume contained his platform, which, so far as I know, he has never seen cause to change. Despite the title, he is not an infant crying in the night; he is a full-grown man, whose voice of resonant hope and faith is heard in the darkness. His chief reason for believing in God is that it is more sensible to believe in Him than not to believe. His religion, like his art, is founded on common sense. Everything that he writes, whether in drama, in lyrics, or in prose criticism, is eminently rational.

> There is one creed, and only one,
> That glorifies God's excellence;
> So cherish, that His will be done,
> The common creed of common sense.
>
> It is the crimson, not the grey,
> That charms the twilight of all time;
> It is the promise of the day
> That makes the starry sky sublime.
>
> It is the faith within the fear
> That holds us to the life we curse;—
> So let us in ourselves revere
> The Self which is the Universe!
>
> Let us, the Children of the Night,
> Put off the cloak that hides the scar!
> Let us be Children of the Light,
> And tell the ages what we are!

This creed is repeated in the sonnet *Credo*, later in the same volume, which also contains those rather striking portraits of individuals, of which the most impressive is *Richard Cory*. More than one critic has observed that these dry sketches are in a way forerunners of the *Spoon River Anthology*.

The next book, *Captain Craig,* rather disappointed the eager expectations of the poet's admirers; like Carlyle's Frederick, the man finally turns out to be not anywhere near worth the intellectual energy expended on him. Yet this volume contained what is on the whole, Mr. Robinson's masterpiece—*Isaac and Archibald*. We are given a striking picture of these old men, and I suppose one reason why we recognize the merit of this poem so much more clearly than we did sixteen years ago, is because this particular kind of character-analysis was not in demand at that time.

The figure of the man against the sky, which gives the name to the work published in 1916, does not appear, strictly speaking, till the end of the book. Yet in reality the first poem, *Flammonde,* is the man against the sky-line, who looms up biggest of all in his town as we look back. This fable teaches us to appreciate the unappreciated.

Mr. Robinson's latest volume, *Merlin,* may safely be neglected by students of his work. It adds nothing to his reputation, and seems uncharacteristic. I can find little in it except diluted Tennyson, and it won't do to dilute Tennyson. One might almost as well try to polish him. It is of course possible that Mr. Robinson wished to try something in a romantic vein; but it is not his vein. He excels in the clear presentment of char-

acter; in pith; in sharp outline; in solid, masculine effort; his voice is baritone rather than
tenor.

To me his poetry is valuable for its moral
stimulus; for its unadorned honesty and sincerity; for its clear rather than warm singing. He
is an excellent draughtsman; everything that he
has done has beauty of line; anything pretentious
is to him abhorrent. He is more map-maker than
painter. He is of course more than a maker of
maps. He has drawn many an intricate and accurate chart of the deeps and shallows of the
human soul.

CHAPTER VIII

VACHEL LINDSAY AND ROBERT FROST

Lindsay the Cymbalist—first impression—Harriet Monroe's Magazine—training in art—the long vagabond tramps—correct order of his works—his drawings—the "Poem Game"—*The Congo*—*General William Booth*—wide sweep of his imagination—sudden contrasts in sound—his prose works—his interest in moving pictures—an apostle of democracy—a wandering minstrel—his vitality—a primary man—art plus morality—his geniality—a poet and a missionary—his fearlessness—Robert Frost—the poet of New England—his paradoxical birth—his education—his career in England—his experiences on a farm—his theory of the spoken word—an out-door poet—not a singer—lack of range—interpreter as well as observer—pure realism—rural tragedies—centrifugal force—men and women—suspense—the building of a poem—the pleasure of recognition—his sincerity—his truthfulness.

"But you—you can help so much more. You can help spiritually. You can help to shape things, give form and thought and poignancy to the most matter-of-fact existence; show people how to think and live and appreciate beauty. What does it matter if some of them jeer at you, or trample on your work? What matters is that those for whom your message is intended will know you by your work."
—STACY AUMONIER, *Just Outside.*

Of all living Americans who have contributed to the advance of English poetry in the twentieth century, no one has given more both as prophet and priest than Vachel Lindsay. His poems are notable for originality, pictorial beauty, and thrilling music. He belongs to no modern school, but

is doing his best to found one; and when I think
of his love of a loud noise, I call him a Cymbalist.

Yet when I use the word *noise* to describe
his verse, I use it not only in its present, but in
its earlier meaning, as when Edmund Waller
saluted Chloris with

> While I listen to thy voice,
>   Chloris! I feel my life decay;
> That powerful noise
>   Calls my flitting soul away.

This use of the word, meaning an agreeable,
harmonious sound, was current from Chaucer to
Coleridge.

My first acquaintance with Mr. Lindsay's poetry
began with a masterpiece, *General William Booth
Enters into Heaven.*   Early in the year 1913, before I had become a subscriber to Harriet Monroe's *Poetry,* I found among the clippings in the
back of a copy of the *Independent* this extraordinary burst of music.   I carried it in my pocket for
months.   Nothing since Francis Thompson's *In No
Strange Land* had given me such a spinal chill.
Later I learned that it had appeared for the first
time in the issue of *Poetry* for January, 1913.   All
lovers of verse owe a debt of gratitude to Miss
Monroe for bringing the new poet to the attention
of the public; and all students of contemporary
movements in metre ought to subscribe to her
monthly magazine; the numbers naturally vary in
value, but almost any one may contain a ''find'';

as I discovered to my pleasure in reading *Niagara* in the summer of 1917.

Nicholas Vachel Lindsay—Vachel rimes with Rachel—was born at Springfield, Illinois—which rimes with boy—on the tenth of November, 1879. His pen name omits the Nicholas. For three years he was a student at Hiram College in Ohio, and for five years an art student, first at Chicago, and then at New York. This brings us to the year 1905. From that year until 1910 he drew strange pictures, lectured on various subjects, and wrote defiant and peculiar "bulletins." At the same time he became a tramp, making long pilgrimages afoot in 1906 through Florida, Georgia, the Carolinas, and in 1908 he invaded in a like manner some of the Northern and Eastern States. These wanderings are described with vigour, vivacity, and contagious good humour in his book called *A Handy Guide for Beggars*. His wallet contained nothing but printed leaflets—his poems —which he exchanged for bed and board. He was the Evangelist of Beauty, preaching his gospel everywhere by reciting his verses. In the summer of 1912 he walked from Illinois to New Mexico.

To understand his development, one should read his books not according to the dates of formal publication, but in the following order: *A Handy Guide for Beggars, Adventures While Preaching the Gospel of Beauty, The Art of the Moving Picture*—these three being mainly in prose. Then one is ready for the three volumes of poetry,

General William Booth Enters into Heaven
(1913), *The Congo* (1914), and *The Chinese Night-ingale* (1917). Another prose work is well under way, *The Golden Book of Springfield,* concerning which Mr. Lindsay tells me, "The actual Golden Book is a secular testament about Springfield, to be given to the city in 2018, from a mysterious source. My volume is a hypothetical forecast of the times of 2018, as well as of the Golden Book. Frankly the Lindsay the reviewers know came nearer to existing twelve years ago than today, my manuscripts are so far behind my notes. And a thing that has helped in this is that through changing publishers, etc., my first prose book is called my latest. If you want my ideas in order, assume the writer of the *Handy Guide for Beggars* is just out of college, of *Adventures While Preaching* beginning in the thirties, and the *Art of the Moving Picture* half-way through the thirties. The Moving Picture book in the last half embodies my main social ideas of two years ago. In mood and method, you will find *The Golden Book of Springfield* a direct descendant of the general social and religious philosophy which I crowded into the photoplay book whether it belonged there or not. I hope you will do me the favour and honour to set my work in this order in your mind, for many of my small public still think *A Handy Guide for Beggars* the keynote of my present work. But it was really my first wild dash."

The above letter was written 8 August, 1917.

Like many creative writers, Mr. Lindsay is an artist not only with the pen, but with the pencil. He has made drawings since childhood; drawing and writing still divide his time and energy. The first impression one receives from the pictures is like that produced by the poems—strangeness. The best have that Baconian element of strangeness in the proportion which gives the final touch to beauty; the worst are merely bizarre. He says, "My claim for them is that while laboured and struggling in execution, they represent a study of Egyptian hieroglyphics and Japanese art, two most orthodox origins for art, and have no relation whatever to cubism, post-impressionism, or futurism. . . . I have been very fond of Swinburne all my life, and I should say my drawing is nearer to his ornate mood than any of my writing has been. But that is a matter for your judgment." I find his pictures so interesting that I earnestly hope he will some day publish a large collection of them in a separate volume.

One of his latest developments is the idea of the *Poem Game*, which is elaborated with interesting poetic illustrations in the volume called *The Chinese Nightingale*. In giving his directions and suggestions in the latter part of this book, he remarks, "The present rhymer has no ambitions as a stage manager. The Poem Game idea, in its rhythmic picnic stage, is recommended to amateurs, its further development to be on their own initiative. Informal parties might divide into groups of dancers and groups of chanters. The whole might be worked out in the spirit in which children play King William was King James's Son, London Bridge. . . . The main revolution necessary for dancing improvisers, who would go a longer way with the Poem Game idea, is to shake off the Isadora Duncan and the Russian precedents for a while, and abolish the orchestra and piano, replacing all these with the natural meaning and cadences of English speech. The work would come closer to acting than dancing is now conceived.''

Here is a good opportunity for house parties, in the intervals of Red Cross activities; and at the University of Chicago, 15 February, 1918, *The Chinese Nightingale* was given with a full chorus of twelve girls, selected for their speaking voices. From the testimony of one of the professors at the university, it is clear that the performance was a success, realizing something of Mr. Lindsay's idea of the union of the arts, with Poetry at the centre.

Among the games given in verse by the author in the latter part of *The Chinese Nightingale* volume is one called *The Potatoes' Dance,* which appears to me to approach most closely to the original purpose. It is certainly a jolly poem. But whether these games are played by laughing choruses of youth or only by the firelight in the fancy of a solitary reader, the validity of Vachel

Lindsay's claim to the title of Poet may be settled at once by witnessing the transformation of a filthy rumhole into a sunlit forest. As Edmond Rostand looked at a dunghill, and saw the vision of Chantecler, so Vachel Lindsay looked at some drunken niggers and saw the vision of the Congo.

Fat black bucks in a wine-barrel room,
Barrel-house kings, with feet unstable,
Sagged and reeled and pounded on the table,
Pounded on the table,
Beat an empty barrel with the handle of a broom,
Hard as they were able,
Boom, boom, Boom,
With a silk umbrella and the handle of a broom,
Boomlay, boomlay, boomlay, Boom.
Then I had religion, Then I had a vision,
I could not turn from their revel in derision.
Then I saw the Congo, creeping through the black,
Cutting through the forest with a golden track.
Then along that river bank
A thousand miles
Tattooed cannibals danced in files;
Then I heard the boom of the blood-lust song
And a thigh-bone beating on a tin-pan gong. . . .
A negro fairyland swung into view,
A minstrel river
Where dreams come true.
The ebony palace soared on high
Through the blossoming trees to the evening sky.
The inlaid porches and casements shone
With gold and ivory and elephant-bone. . . .
Just then from the doorway, as fat as shotes,
Came the cake-walk princes in their long red coats,
Canes with a brilliant lacquer shine,
And tall silk hats that were red as wine.
And they pranced with their butterfly partners there,
Coal-black maidens with pearls in their hair,

Knee-skirts trimmed with the jassamine sweet,
And bells on their ankles and little black-feet.

There are those who call this nonsense and its
author a mountebank. I call it poetry and its
author a poet. You never heard anything like it
before; but do not be afraid of your own enjoyment. Read it aloud a dozen times, and you, too,
will hear roaring, epic music, and you will see the
mighty, golden river cutting through the forest.

I do not know how many towns I have visited
where I have heard "What do you think of Vachel
Lindsay? He was here last month and recited
his verses. Most of his audience were puzzled."
Yet they remembered him. What would have
happened if I had asked them to give me a brief
synopsis of the lecture they heard yesterday on
"The Message of John Ruskin"? Fear not, little
flock. Vachel Lindsay is an authentic wandering
minstrel. The fine phrases you heard yesterday
were like snow upon the desert's dusty face, light-
ing a little hour or two, is gone.

General William Booth Enters into Heaven—
with the accompanying instruments, which blare
out from the printed page—is a sublime interpretation of one of the varieties of religious experience. Two works of genius have been written
about the Salvation Army—*Major Barbara* and
General William Booth Enters into Heaven. But
Major Barbara, with its almost appalling cleverness—Granville Barker says the second act is the
finest thing Shaw ever composed—is written,

after all, from the seat of the scornful, like a
metropolitan reporter at a Gospel tent; Mr. Lindsay's poem is written from the inside, from the
very heart of the mystery. It is interpretation,
not description. "Booth was blind," says Mr.
Lindsay; "all reformers are blind." One must
in turn be blind to many obvious things, blind to
ridicule, blind to criticism, blind to the wisdom
of this world, if one would understand a phenom-
enon like General Booth.

> Booth led boldly with his big bass drum—
> (Are you washed in the blood of the Lamb?)
> The Saints smiled gravely and they said: "He's come."
> (Are you washed in the blood of the Lamb?) . . . .
> Walking lepers followed, rank on rank,
> Lurching bravoes from the ditches dank,
> Drabs from the alleyways and drug fiends pale—
> Minds still passion-ridden, soul-powers frail:—
> Vermin-eaten saints with mouldy breath,
> Unwashed legions with the ways of Death—
> (Are you washed in the blood of the Lamb?) . . . .
> And when Booth halted by the curb for prayer
> He saw his Master thro' the flag-filled air.
> Christ came gently with a robe and crown
> For Booth the soldier, while the throng knelt down.
> He saw King Jesus. They were face to face,
> And he knelt a-weeping in that holy place.
> (Are you washed in the blood of the Lamb?)

Dante and Milton were more successful in making pictures of hell than of heaven—no one has
ever made a common conception of heaven more
permanently vivid than in this poem.

See how amid the welter of crowds and the

deafening crash of drums and banjos the individual faces stand out in the golden light.

> Big-voiced lassies made their banjos bang,
> Tranced, fanatical they shrieked and sang. . . .
> Bull-necked convicts with that land make free. . . .
> The lame were straightened, withered limbs uncurled
> And blind eyes opened on a new, sweet world. . . .
> Gone was the weasel-head, the snout, the jowl!
> Sages and sibyls now, and athletes clean,
> Rulers of empires, and of forests green!

It is a pictorial, musical, and spiritual masterpiece. I am not afraid to call it a spiritual masterpiece; for to any one who reads it as we should read all true poetry, with an unconditional surrender to its magic, General William Booth and his horde will not be the only persons present who will enter into heaven.

Vachel Lindsay needs plenty of room for his imagination—the more space he has in which to disport himself, the more impressive he becomes. His strange poem, *How I Walked Alone in the Jungles of Heaven,* has the vasty sweep congenial to his powers. *Simon Legree* is as accurate an interpretation of the negro's conception of the devil and of hell as *General William Booth* is of the Salvation Army's conception of heaven, though it is not so fine a poem. When he rises from hell or descends from heaven, he loves big, boundless things on the face of the earth, like the Western Plains and the glory of Niagara. The contrast between the bustling pettiness of the

artificial city of Buffalo and the eternal fresh
beauty of Niagara is like Bunyan's vision of the
man busy with the muck-rake while over his head
stood an angel with a golden crown.

> Within the town of Buffalo
> Are prosy men with leaden eyes.
> Like ants they worry to and fro,
> (Important men, in Buffalo).
> But only twenty miles away
> A deathless glory is at play:
> Niagara, Niagara. . . .
>
> Above the town a tiny bird,
> A shining speck at sleepy dawn,
> Forgets the ant-hill so absurd,
> This self-important Buffalo.
> Descending twenty miles away
> He bathes his wings at break of day—
> Niagara, Niagara.

True poet that he is, Vachel Lindsay loves to
show the contrast between transient noises that
tear the atmosphere to shreds and the eternal
beauty of unpretentious melody. After the thunder and the lightning comes the still, small voice.
Who ever before thought of comparing the roar
of the swiftly passing motor-cars with the sweet
singing of the stationary bird? Was there ever
in a musical composition a more startling change
from fortissimo to pianissimo?

> Listen to the iron-horns, ripping, racking,
> Listen to the quack-horns, slack and clacking.
> Way down the road, trilling like a toad,
> Here comes the *dice*-horn, here comes the *vice*-horn,
> Here comes the *snarl*-horn, *brawl*-horn, *lewd*-horn,

Followed by the *prude*-horn, bleak and squeaking:—
(Some of them from Kansas, some of them from Kansas.)
Here comes the *hod*-horn, *plod*-horn, *sod*-horn,
Nevermore-to-*roam*-horn, *loam*-horn, *home*-horn,
(Some of them from Kansas, some of them from Kansas.)

> Far away the Rachel-Jane
> Not defeated by the horns,
> Sings amid a hedge of thorns:—
> "Love and life,
> Eternal youth—
> Sweet, sweet, sweet, sweet,
> Dew and glory,
> Love and truth,
> Sweet, sweet, sweet, sweet."

Of Mr. Lindsay's prose works the one first written, *A Handy Guide for Beggars,* is by all odds the best. Even if it did not contain musical cadenzas, any reader would know that the author was a poet. It is full of the spirit of joyous young manhood and reckless adventure, and laughs its way into our hearts. There is no reason why Mr. Lindsay should ever apologize for this book, even if it does not represent his present attitude; it is as individual as a diary, and as universal as youth. His later prose is more careful, possibly more thoughtful, more full of information; but this has a touch of genius. Its successor, *Adventures While Preaching the Gospel of Beauty,* does not quite recapture the first fine careless rapture. Yet both must be read by students of Mr. Lindsay's verse, not only because they display his personality, but because the original data of many poems can be found among these experiences of the road. For example, *The Broncho That Would Not Be Broken,* which first appeared in 1917, is the rimed version of an incident that happened in July, 1912. It made an indelible impression on the amateur farmer, and the poem has a poignant beauty that nothing will ever erase from the reader's mind. I feel certain that I shall have a vivid recollection of this poem to the last day of my life, assuming that on that last day I can remember anything at all.

A more ambitious prose work than either of the tramp books is *The Art of the Moving Picture.* It is rather singular that Mr. Lindsay, whose poetry primarily appeals to the ear, should be so profoundly interested in an art whose only appeal is to the eye. The reason, perhaps, is twofold. He is professionally a maker of pictures as well as of chants, and he is an apostle of democracy. The moving picture is the most democratic form of art that the world has ever seen. Maude Adams reaches thousands; Mary Pickford reaches millions. It is clear that Mr. Lindsay wishes that the limitless influence of the moving picture may be used to elevate and ennoble America; for here is the greatest force ever known through which his gospel may be preached—the gospel of beauty.

Like so many other original artists, Mr. Lindsay's poetry really goes back to the origins of the art. As John Masefield is the twentieth century Chaucer, so Vachel Lindsay is the twentieth century minstrel. On the one occasion when he

met W. B. Yeats, the Irishman asked him point-
blank, "What are we going to do to restore the
primitive singing of poetry?" and would not stay
for an answer. Fortunately the question was put
to a man who answered it by accomplishment; the
best answer to any question is not an elaborate
theory, but a demonstration. As it is sometimes
supposed that Mr. Lindsay's poetry owes its inspiration to Mr. Yeats, it may be well to state
here positively that our American owes nothing to
the Irishman; his poetry developed quite inde-
pendently of the other's influence, and would have
been much the same had Mr. Yeats never risen
above the horizon. When I say that he owes
nothing, I mean he owes nothing in the manner
and fashion of his art; he has a consuming admiration for Mr. Yeats's genius; for Mr. Lindsay con-
siders him of all living men the author of the
most beautiful poetry.

Chants are only about one-tenth of Vachel Lindsay's work. However radical in subject, they
are conservative in form, following the precedents
of the ode from its origin. It is necessary to insist that while the material is new, the method is
consciously old. He is no innovator in rime or
rhythm. But the chants, while few in number, are
the most individual part of his production; and
up to the year 1918—the most impressive.

For in *The Congo* we have real minstrelsy.
The shoulder-notes, giving detailed directions for
singing, reciting, intoning, are as charming in

their way as the stage-directions of J. M. Barrie. They not only show the aim of the poet; they admit the reader immediately into an inner communion with the spirit of the poem.

Every one who reads *The Congo* or who hears it read cannot help enjoying it; which is one reason why so many are afraid to call it a great poem. For a similar reason, some critics are afraid to call Percy Grainger a great composer, because of his numerous and delightful audacities. Yet *The Congo* is a great poem, possessing as it does many of the high qualities of true poetry. It shows a splendid power of imagination, as fresh as the forests it describes; it blazes with glorious colours; its music transports the listener with climax after climax; it interprets truthfully the spirit of the negro race.

I should not think of attempting to determine the relative position of Percy Grainger in music and of Vachel Lindsay in poetry; but it is clear that both men possess an amazing vitality. Is it not the lack of vital force which prevents so many accomplished artists from ever rising above the crowd? I suppose we have all read reams on reams of magazine verse exhibiting technical correctness, exactitude in language, and pretty fancy; and after a momentary unspoken tribute to the writer's skill, we straightway forget. But when a poem like *Danny Deever* appears, it is vain to call it a music-hall ballad, or to pretend that it is not high art; the fact is that the worst memory in the world will retain it. Such a poem comes like a breeze into a close chamber; it is charged with vitality. We are in contact with a new force—a force emanating from that mysterious and inexhaustible stream whence comes every manifestation of genius. To have this supervitality is to have genius; and although one may have with it many distressing faults of expression and an unlimited supply of bad taste, all other qualities combined cannot atone for the absence of this one primal element. Indeed the excess of wealth in energy is bound to produce shocking excrescences; our Springfield poet is sometimes absurd when he means to be sublime, bizarre when he means to be picturesque. The same is true of Walt Whitman—it is true of all creative writers whom John Burroughs calls *primary* men, in distinction from excellent artists who remain in the secondary class. Mark Twain, Rudyard Kipling, Walt Whitman, John Masefield, Vachel Lindsay are primary men.

I have often wondered who would write a poem worthy of the Grand Canyon of the Colorado. Vachel Lindsay is the only living American who could do it, and I hope he will accept this challenge. Its awful majesty can be revealed only in verse; for it is one of the very few wonders of the world which no photograph and no painting can ever reproduce. Who ever saw a picture that gave him any conception of this incomparable spectacle?

In order to understand the primary impulse
that drove Mr. Lindsay into writing verse and
making pictures, one ought to read first of all his
poem *The Tree of Laughing Bells, or The Wings
of the Morning*. The first half of the title exhibits his love of resounding harmonies; the second gives an idea of the range of his imagination.
His finest work always combines these two elements, melody and elevation, "and singing still
dost soar, and soaring ever singest." I hope that
the picture he drew for *The Tree of Laughing
Bells* may some time be made available for all
students of his work, as it was his first serious
design.

Vachel Lindsay is essentially honest, for he
tries to become himself exactly what he hopes
the future American will be. He is a Puritan with
a passion for Beauty; he is a zealous reformer
filled with Falstaffian mirth; he goes along the
highway, singing and dancing, distributing tracts.
"Apollo's first, at last the true God's priest."

We know that two mighty streams, the Renaissance and the Reformation, which flowed side by
side without mingling, suddenly and completely
merged in Spenser's *Faery Queene*. That immortal song is a combination of ravishing sweetness and moral austerity. Later the Puritan became the Man on Horseback, and rode roughshod
over every bloom of beauty that lifted its delicate
head. Despite the genius of Milton, supreme
artist plus supreme moralist, the Puritans man-

aged somehow to force into the common mind an antagonism between Beauty and Morality which persists even unto this day. There is no reason why those two contemporaries, Oscar Wilde and the Rev. Charles H. Spurgeon, should stand before the London public as the champions of contending armies; for Beauty is an end in itself, not a means, and so is Conduct.

In the best work of Vachel Lindsay, we find these two qualities happily married, the zest for beauty and the hunger and thirst after righteousness. He made a soap-box tour for the Anti-Saloon League, preaching at the same time the Gospel of Beauty. As a rule, reformers are lacking in the two things most sedulously cultivated by commercial travellers and life-insurance agents, tact and humour. If these interesting orders of the Knights of the Road were as lacking in geniality as the typical reformer, they would lose their jobs. And yet fishers of men, for that is what all reformers are, try to fish without bait, at the same time making much loud and offensive speech. Then they are amazed at the callous indifference of humanity to "great moral issues."

Vachel Lindsay is irresistibly genial. Nor is any of this geniality made up of the professionally ingratiating smile; it is the foundation of his temperament. What has this got to do with his poetry? It has everything to do with it. It gives him the key to the hearts of children; to the basic savagery of a primitive black or a poor white; to peripatetic harvesters; to futurists, imagists, blue-stockings, pedants of all kinds; to evangelists, college professors, drunken sailors, tramps whose robes are lined with vermin. He is the great American democrat, not because that is his political theory, but simply because he cannot help it.

His attitude toward other schools of art, even when he has nothing in common with them, is positively affectionate. Could there be two poets more unlike in temperament and in style than Mr. Lindsay and Mr. Masters? Yet in the volume, *The Chinese Nightingale*, we have a poem dedicated "to Edgar Lee Masters, with great respect." He speaks of "the able and distinguished Amy Lowell," and of his own poems "parodied by my good friend, Louis Untermeyer." He says, "I admire the work of the Imagist Poets. We exchange fraternal greetings. . . . But neither my few heterodox pieces nor my many struggling orthodox pieces conform to their patterns. . . . The Imagists emphasize pictorial effects, while the Higher Vaudeville exaggerates musical effects. Imagists are apt to omit rhyme, while in my Higher Vaudeville I often put five rhymes on a line."

Impossible to quarrel with Vachel Lindsay. His stock of genial tolerance is inexhaustible, and makes him regard not only hostile humans, but even destructive insects, with inquisitive affection.

> I want live things in their pride to remain.
> I will not kill one grasshopper vain
> Though he eats a hole in my shirt like a door.
> I let him out, give him one chance more.
> Perhaps, while he gnaws my hat in his whim,
> Grasshopper lyrics occur to him.

During his tramps, the parents who unwillingly received him discovered, when he began to recite stories to their children, that they had entertained an angel unawares; and I have not the slightest doubt that on the frequent occasions when his application for food and lodging was received with a volley of curses, he honestly admired the noble fluency of his enemy. When he was harvesting, the singing stacker became increasingly and distressingly pornographic; instead of rebuking him for foulness, which would only have bewildered the stacker, Mr. Lindsay taught him the first stanza of Swinburne's chorus. "The next morning when my friend climbed into our barge to ride to the field he began:

> When the hounds of spring are on winter's traces,
> The mother of months, in meadow or plain,
> Fills the shadows—

'Dammit, what's the rest of it? I've been trying to recite that piece all night.' Now he has the first four stanzas. And last evening he left for Dodge City to stay overnight and Sunday. He was resolved to purchase *Atalanta in Calydon* and find in the Public Library *The Lady of Shalott* and *The Blessed Damozel,* besides paying the usual visit to his wife and children.''

If a man cannot understand music, painting, and poetry without loving these arts, neither can a man understand men and women and children without loving them. This is one reason why even the cleverest cynicism is never more than half the truth, and usually less.

Mr. Lindsay is a poet, and a missionary. As a missionary, he wishes all Americans to be as good judges of poetry as they are, let us say, of baseball. One of the numerous joys of being a professional ball-player must be the knowledge that you are exhibiting your art to a prodigious assembly of qualified critics. John Sargent knows that the majority of persons who gaze at his picture of President Wilson are incompetent to express any opinion; his subtlety is lost or quite misunderstood; but Tyrus Raymond Cobb knows that the thousands who daily watch him during the summer months appreciate his consummate mastery of the game. Vachel Lindsay, I suppose, wants millions not merely to love, but to detect the finer shades of the poetic art.

If he set out to accomplish this dream by lowering the standards of poetry, then he would debase the public and be a traitor to his guild. But his method is uncompromising—he taught the harvester not Mrs. Hemans, but Swinburne. He calls his own verse the higher vaudeville. But *The*

Congo is the higher vaudeville as *Macbeth* is the higher melodrama. And there is neither melodrama nor vaudeville in *Abraham Lincoln Walks at Midnight*—a poem of stern and solemn majesty.

Mr. Lindsay is true to the oldest traditions of poetry in his successful attempts to make his verses ring and sing. He is both antique and antic. But he is absolutely contemporary, "modern," "new," in his fearlessness. He has this in common with the practicers of free verse, with the imagists, with the futurists; he is not in the least afraid of seeming ridiculous. There can be no progress in art until artists overcome wholly this blighting fear. It is the lone individual, with his name stamped all over him, charging into the safely anonymous mass; but that way lies the Advance.

When Thomas Carlyle took up the study of Oliver Cromwell, he found that all previous historians had tried to answer this question: What is the mask that Oliver wore? And suddenly the true answer came to him in the form of another question: What if it should prove to be no mask at all, but just the man's own face? So there are an increasingly large number of readers who are discerning in the dauntless gambols of Vachel Lindsay, not the mask of buffoonery, worn to attract attention, but a real poet, dancing gaily with bronchos, children, field-mice and potatoes.

Such unquenchable vitality, such bubbling exuberance, cannot always be graceful, cannot al-

ways be impressive. But the blunders of an original man are sometimes more fruitful than the
correctness of a copyist. Furthermore, blunders
sometimes make for wisdom and truth. Let us
not forget Vachel Lindsay's poem on Columbus:

> Would that we had the fortunes of Columbus,
> Sailing his caravels a trackless way,
> He found a Universe—he sought Cathay.
> God give such dawns as when, his venture o'er,
> The Sailor looked upon San Salvador.
> God lead us past the setting of the sun
> To wizard islands, of august surprise;
> God make our blunders wise.

COLD PASTORAL!

The difference between Vachel Lindsay and
Robert Frost is the difference between a drum-
major and a botanist. The former marches gaily
at the head of his big band, looking up and around
at the crowd; the latter finds it sweet

> with unuplifted eyes
> To pace the ground, if path be there or none.

Robert Frost, the poet of New England, was
born at San Francisco, and published his first volume in London. Midway between these two cities
lies the enchanted ground of his verse; for he belongs to New England as wholly as Whittier, as
truly as Mr. Lindsay belongs to Illinois. He
showed his originality so early as the twenty-sixth
of March, 1875, by being born at San Francisco;
for although I have known hundreds of happy

Californians, men and women whose love for their great State is a religion, Robert Frost is the only person I ever met who was born there. That beautiful country is frequently used as a springboard to heaven; and that I can understand, for the transition is less violent than from some other points of departure. But why so few natives?

Shamelessly I lift the following biographical facts from Miss Amy Lowell's admirable essay on our poet. At the age of ten, the boy was moved to Lawrence, Massachusetts. He went to school, and disliked the experience. He tried Dartmouth and later Harvard, staying a few months at the first and two years at the second. Between these academic experiences he was married. In 1900 he began farming in New Hampshire. In 1911 he taught school, and in 1912 went to England. His first book of poems, *A Boy's Will,* was published at London in 1913. The review in *The Academy* was ecstatic. In 1914 he went to live at Ledbury, where John Masefield was born, and where in the neighbourhood dwelt W. W. Gibson. His second volume, *North of Boston,* was published at London in 1914. Miss Lowell quotes a sentence, full of insight, from the review in the *Times.* "Poetry burns up out of it, as when a faint wind breathes upon smouldering embers." In March, 1915, Mr. Frost returned to America, bringing his reputation with him. He bought a farm in New Hampshire among the mountains, and in 1916 appeared his third volume, *Mountain Interval*.

Was there ever a better illustration of the uncritical association of names than the popular coupling of Robert Frost with Edgar Lee Masters? They are similar in one respect; they are both poets. But in the glorious army of poets, it would be difficult to find two contemporaries more wholly unlike both in the spirit and in the form of their work than Mr. Frost and Mr. Masters. Mr. Frost is as far from free verse as he can stretch, as far as Longfellow; and while he sometimes writes in an ironical mood, he never indulges himself in cynicism. As a matter of fact, Mr. Frost is nearer in his art to Mr. Lindsay than to Mr. Masters; for his theory of poetry, which I confess I cannot understand, requires the poet to choose words entirely with reference to their spoken value.

His poetry is more interesting and clearer than his theories about it. I once heard him give a combination reading-lecture, and after he had read some of his poems, all of which are free from obscurity, he began to explain his ideas on how poetry should be written. He did this with charming modesty, but his "explanations" were opaque. After he had continued in this vein for some time, he asked the audience which they would prefer to have him do next—read some more of his poems, or go on talking about poetry? He obtained from his hearers an immediate response, picked up his book, and read in admirable fashion his excellent verse. We judge poets by their poems, not by their theories.

Robert Frost is an out-door poet. Even when he gives a picture of an interior, the people are always looking out of the windows at something or other. In his poems we follow the procession of the seasons, with the emphasis on autumn and winter. One might be surprised at the infrequency of his poems on spring, were it not for the fact that his knowledge of the country is so precise and definite. Spring is more beautiful in the city than in the country; it comes with less alloy. No one has ever drawn a better picture of a country road in the pouring rain, where "the hoof-prints vanish away."

In spite of his preoccupation with the exact value of oral words, he is not a singing lyrist. There is not much *bel canto* in his volumes. Nor do any of his poems seem spontaneous. He is a thoughtful man, given to meditation; the meanest flower or a storm-bedraggled bird will lend him material for poetry. But the expression of his poems does not seem naturally fluid. I suspect he has blotted many a line. He is as deliberate as Thomas Hardy, and cultivates the lapidary style. Even in the conversations frequently introduced into his pieces, he is as economical with words as his characters are with cash. This gives to his work a hardness of outline in keeping with the New England tempera-

ment and the New Hampshire climate. There is
no doubt that much of his peculiarly effective
dramatic power is gained by his extremely careful expenditure of language.

It is, of course, impossible to prescribe bound-
ary lines for a poet, although there are critics who
seem to enjoy staking out a poet's claim. While
I have no intention of building futile walls around
Mr. Frost's garden, nor erecting a sign with the
presumptuous prohibition of trespassing beyond
them, it is clear that he has himself chosen to
excel in quality of produce rather than in variety
and range. In the first poem of the first volume,
he concludes as follows:

> They would not find me changed from him they knew—
> Only more sure of all I thought was true.

This is certainly a precise statement of the impression made on the reader who studies his three
books in chronological order. *A Boy's Will,* as
befits a youth who has lived more in himself than
in the world, is more introspective than either
North of Boston or *Mountain Interval;* but this
habit of introspection gave him both the method
and the insight necessary for the accurate study
of nature and neighbours. He discovered what
other people were like, simply by looking into his
own heart. And in *A Boy's Will* we find that
same penetrating examination of rural scenes and
common objects that gives to the two succeeding
works the final stamp of veracity. I do not re-

member ever having seen a phrase like the following, though the phrase instantly makes the familiar picture leap into that empty space ever before the reader's eye—that space, which like bare wall-paper, seems to demand a picture on its surface.

Or highway where the slow wheel pours the sand.

It is fortunate that the law of diminishing returns—which every farmer is forced to heed—does not apply to pastoral poets. Out of the same soil Robert Frost has successfully raised three crops of the same produce. He might reply that in the intervals he has let the ground lie fallow—but my impression is that he is really working it all the time.

The sharp eye of the farmer sees nothing missed by our poet, but the poet has interpretation as well as vision. He not only sees things but sees things in their relations; and he knows that not only is everything related to every other thing, but that all things are related to the eternal mystery, their source and their goal. This is why the yellow primrose is so infinitely more than a yellow primrose. This also explains why the poems of Mr. Frost, after stirring us to glad recognition of their fidelity, leave us in a revery.

His studies of human nature are the purest realism. They are conversations rather than arias, for he uses the speaking, not the singing voice. Poets are always amazing us, and some day Robert Frost may astonish me by writing a romantic ballad. It would surely be a surprise, for with his lack of operatic accomplishment, and his fondness for heroes in homespun, he would seem almost ideally unfitted for the task. This feeling I find strengthened by his poem called *An Equal Sacrifice*, the only one of his pieces where anything like a ballad is attempted, and the only one in all three books which seems to be an undeviating failure. It is as flat as a pancake, and ends with flat moralizing. Mr. Frost is particularly unsuccessful at preaching.

No, apart from his nature poems, his studies of men and women are most impressive when they follow the lines of Doric simplicity in the manner of the powerful stage-plays written by Susan Glaspell. The rigidity of the mould seems all the better fitted for the suppressed passion it contains, just as liquid fire is poured into a vessel with unyielding sides. His two most successful poems of this kind are *Home Burial*, in *North of Boston*, and *Snow*, in *Mountain Interval*. The former is not so much a tragedy as the concentrated essence of tragedy. There is enough pain in it to furnish forth a dozen funerals. It has that centrifugal force which Mr. Calderon so brilliantly suggests as the main characteristic of the dramas of Chekhov. English plays are centripetal; they draw the attention of the audience to the group of characters on the stage; but Chekhov's, says Mr. Calderon, are centrifugal; they throw our regard off from the actors to the whole class of humanity they represent. Just such a remark applies to *Home Burial;* it makes the reader think of the thousands of farmhouses darkened by similar tragedies. Nor is it possible to quote a single separate passage from this poem, for each line is so necessary to the total effect that one must read every word of it to feel its significance. It is a masterpiece of tragedy. And it is curious, as one continues to think about it, as one so often does on finishing a poem by Robert Frost, that we are led first to contemplate the number of such tragedies, and finally to contemplate a stretch of life of far wider range— the broad, profound difference between a man and a woman. Are there any two creatures on God's earth more unlike? In this poem the man is true to himself, and for that very reason cannot in his honest, simple heart comprehend why he should appear to his own wife as if he were some frightful monster. He is perplexed, amazed, and finally enraged at the look of loathing in the wide eyes of his own mate. It was a little thing—his innocent remark about a birch fence—that revealed to her that she was living with a stranger. Grief never possesses a man as it does a woman, except when the grief is exclusively concerned with his own bodily business, as when he discovers that he has cancer or toothache. To the last day of human life on earth, it will seem incomprehensible to a woman that a man, on the occasion of a death in the family, can sit down and eat with gusto a hearty meal. For bodily appetite, which is the first thing to leave a woman, is the last to leave a man; and when it has left every other part of his frame, it sometimes has a repulsive survival in his eyes. The only bridge that can really cross this fathomless chasm between man and woman is the bridge of love.

The dramatic quality of *Snow* is suspense. The object through which the suspense is conveyed to the reader is the telephone, employed with such tragic effect at the Grand Guignol. Mr. Frost's art in colloquial speech has never appeared to better advantage than here, and what a wave of relief when the voice of Meserve is heard! It is like a resurrection.

In order fully to appreciate a poem like *Mending Wall,* one should hear Mr. Frost read it. He reads it with such interpretative skill, with subtle hesitations and pauses for apparent reflection, that the poem grows before the audience even as the wall itself. He hesitates as though he had a word in his hands, and was thinking what would be exactly the best place to deposit it—even as the farmer holds a stone before adding it to the structure. For this poem is not written, it is built. It is built of separate words, and like the wall it describes, it takes two to build it, the author and the reader. When the last line is reached, the poem is finished.

Nearly every page in the poetry of Robert Frost gives us the pleasure of recognition. He is not only sincere, he is truthful—by which I mean that he not only wishes to tell the truth, but succeeds in doing so. This is the fundamental element in his work, and will, I believe, give it permanence.

GOOD HOURS

I had for my winter evening walk—
No one at all with whom to talk,
But I had the cottages in a row
Up to their shining eyes in snow.

And I thought I had the folk within:
I had the sound of a violin;
I had a glimpse through curtain laces
Of youthful forms and youthful faces.

I had such company outward bound.
I went till there were no cottages found.
I turned and repented, but coming back
I saw no window but that was black.

Over the snow my creaking feet
Disturbed the slumbering village street
Like profanation, by your leave,
At ten o'clock of a winter eve.

A poem like that gives not only the pleasure of recognition; it has an indescribable charm. It is the charm when joy fades, not into sorrow, but into a deep, abiding peace.

CHAPTER IX

AMY LOWELL, ANNA BRANCH, EDGAR LEE MASTERS, LOUIS UNTERMEYER

Amy Lowell—a patrician—a radical—her education—her years of preparation—vigour and versatility—definitions of free verse and of poetry—Whitman's influence—the imagists —*Patterns*—her first book—her rapid improvement—sword blades—her gift in narrative—polyphonic prose—Anna Hempstead Branch—her dramatic power—domestic poems— tranquil meditation—an orthodox poet—Edgar Lee Masters— his education—Greek inspiration—a lawyer—*Reedy's Mirror* —the *Anthology*—power of the past—mental vigour—similarity and variety—irony and sarcasm—passion for truth— accentuation of ugliness—analysis—a masterpiece of cynicism —an ideal side—the dramatic monologue—defects and limitations—Louis Untermeyer—his youth—the question of beauty —three characteristics—a gust of life—*Still Life*—old maids —burlesques and parodies—the newspaper humourists—F. P. A.—his two books—his influence on English composition.

Among the many American women who are writing verse in the twentieth century, two stand out —Amy Lowell and Anna Branch. And indeed I can think of no woman in the history of our poetry who has surpassed them. Both are bone-bred New Englanders. No other resemblance occurs to me.

It is interesting that a cosmopolitan radical like Amy Lowell should belong ancestrally so exclusively to Massachusetts, and to so distinguished a family. She is a born patrician, and a reborn Liberal. James Russell Lowell was a cousin of Miss Lowell's grandfather, and her maternal grandfather, Abbott Lawrence, was also Minister to England. Her eldest brother, nineteen years older than she, was the late Percival Lowell, a scientific astronomer with a poetic imagination; he was one of the most interesting and charming personalities I ever knew. His constant encouragement and example were powerful formative influences in his sister's development. Another brother is the President of Harvard, Abbott Lawrence Lowell, through whose dignified, penetrating, sensible, authoritative speeches and writings breathes the old Massachusetts love of liberty.

Courage is a salient characteristic in Amy Lowell. She is afraid of nothing, not even of her birthday. She was born at Brookline, on the ninth of February, 1874. "Like all young poets, I was influenced by everybody in turn, but I think the person who affected me most profoundly was Keats, although my later work resembles his so little. I am a collector of Keats manuscripts, and have spent much time in studying his erasures and corrections, and they taught me most of what I know about poetry; they, and a very interesting book which is seldom read today—Leigh Hunt's *Imagination and Fancy*. I discovered the existence of Keats through that volume, as my family read very little of what was considered in those days 'modern poetry'; and, although my father had Keats in his library, Shelley was barred, on account of his being an atheist. I ran across this volume of Leigh Hunt's when I was about fifteen and it turned me definitely to poetry." (*Letter of March, 1918.*)

When she was a child, her family took her on a long European tour; in later years she passed one winter on the Nile, another on a fruit ranch in California, another in visiting Greece and Turkey. In 1902 she decided to devote her life to writing poetry, and spent eight years in faithful study, effort, and practice without publishing a word. In the *Atlantic Monthly* for August, 1910, appeared her first printed verse; and in 1912 came her first volume of poems, *A Dome of Many-Coloured Glass,* the title being a quotation from the forbidden Shelley. Since that year she has been a notable figure in contemporary literature. Her reputation was immensely heightened and widened by the publication of her second book, *Sword Blades and Poppy Seed,* in 1914. In 1916 came the third volume, *Men, Women, and Ghosts.*

She has been a valiant fighter for poetic theory, writing many articles on Free Verse, Imagism, and kindred themes; and she is the author of two works in prose criticism, *Six French Poets,* in 1915, and *Tendencies in Modern American Poetry,* in 1917, of which the former is the more valuable and important. In five years, then, from 1912 to 1917, she produced three books of original verse, two tall volumes of literary criticism, and a large number of magazine poems and essays—a remarkable record both in quantity and quality.

Vigour and versatility are the words that rise in one's mind when thinking of the poetry of Amy Lowell. It is absurd to class her as a disciple of free verse, or of imagism, or of polyphonic prose; she delights in trying her hand at all three of these styles of composition, for she is an experimentalist; but much of her work is in the strictest orthodox forms, and when she has what the Methodists used to call *liberty,* no form or its absence can prevent her from writing poetry.

I can see no reason for either attacking or defending free verse, and if I had any influence with Miss Lowell, I should advise her to waste no more time in the defence of any school or theory, because the ablest defence she or any one else can make is actually to write poetry in the manner in which some crystallized critics say it cannot be done. True poetry is recognizable in any garment; and ridicule of the clothes can no more affect the identity of the article than the attitude of Penelope's suitors toward the rags of Ulysses affected his kingship. Let the journalistic wits have their fling; it is even permissible to enjoy their wit, when it is as cleverly expressed as in the following epigram, which I believe appeared in the Chicago *Tribune:* "Free verse is a form of theme unworthy of pure prose embodiment developed by a person incapable of pure poetic expression." Not at all bad; but as some one said

of G. K. Chesterton, it would be unfair to apply
to wit the test of truth. It is better to remember
Coleridge's remark on poetry: ''The opposite
of poetry is not prose but science; the opposite of
prose is not poetry but verse.'' Perhaps we could
say of the polyphonic people that they are well
versed in prose.

The amazing growth of free verse during the
last ten years has surprised no one more than me,
and it has convinced me of my lack of prophetic
clairvoyance. Never an idolater of Walt Whitman, I have also never been blind to his genius;
as he recedes in time his figure grows bigger and
bigger, like a man in the moving pictures leaving the screen. But I used to insist rather em-
phatically that although he was said to be both
the poet of democracy and the poet of the future,
he was in fact admired mostly by literary aristo-
crats; and that the poets who came after him were
careful to write in strict composition. In the
'nineties I looked around me and behold, Kipling,
Phillips, Watson and Riley were in their work
at the opposite extreme from Walt Whitman; he
had not a single disciple of unquestioned poetic
standing. Now, in the year of grace 1918, though
he is not yet read by the common people—a thousand of whom read Longfellow to one who reads
Whitman—he has a tribe of followers and imita-
tors, many of whom do their utmost to reach his
results by his methods, and some of whom enjoy
eminence.

Those who are interested in the growth of imagist poetry in English should read the three slender anthologies published respectively in 1915, 1916, and 1917, called *Some Imagist Poets,* each containing poems nowhere previously printed. The short prefaces to the first two volumes are models of modesty and good sense, whether one likes imagist poetry or hates it. According to this group of poets, which is not a coterie or a mutual admiration society, but a few individuals engaged in amicable rivalry at the same game, the principles of imagism are mainly six, of which only the second is a departure from the principles that have governed the production of poetry in the past. First, to use the exact word: second, to create new rhythms: third, to allow absolute freedom in the choice of subject; fourth, to present an image: fifth, to produce poetry that is hard and clear: sixth, to study concentration.

There are six poets adequately represented in each volume; but the best poem of all is *Patterns,* by Amy Lowell. In spite of having to carry six rules in her head while writing it—for if one is determined to be "free" one must sufficiently indicate the fact—she has written a real poem. It strictly conforms to all six requirements, and is at the same time simple, sensuous, passionate. I like it for many reasons—because it is real, intimate, confidential; because it narrates a tragic experience that is all too common in actual life; because its tragedy is enhanced by dramatic contrasts, the splendour of the bright, breezy, sunlit garden contrasting with the road of ashen spiritual desolation the soul must take; the splendour of the gorgeous stiff brocade and the futility of the blank, soft, imprisoned flesh; the obstreperous heart, beating in joyous harmony with the rhythm of the swaying flowers, changed by one written word into a desert of silence. It is the sudden annihilation of purpose and significance in a body and mind vital with it; so that as we close the poem we seem to see for ever moving up and down the garden path a stiff, brocaded gown, moving with no volition. The days will pass: the daffodils will change to roses, to asters, to snow; but the unbroken pattern of desolation will change not.

Publication is as essential to a poet as an audience to a playwright; Keats realized this truth when he printed *Endymion*. He knew it was full of faults and that he could not revise it. But he also knew that its publication would set him free, and make it possible for him immediately to write something better. This seems to have been the case with Amy Lowell. Her first book, *A Dome of Many-Coloured Glass,* does not compare for a moment with *Sword Blades and Poppy Seed*. It seems a harsh judgment, but I find under the dome hardly one poem of unusual merit, and some of them are positively bad. Could anything be flatter than the first line of the sonnet *To John Keats?*

Great master! Boyish, sympathetic man!

The second volume, *Sword Blades and Poppy Seed,* which came two years later, showed a remarkable advance, and gave its author an enviable position in American literature. An admirable preface reveals three characteristics—reverence for the art of poetry, determination not to be confined to any school, and a refreshingly honest confession of hard labour in learning how to make poems. As old Quarles put it in the plain-spoken seventeenth century,

I see no virtues where I smell no sweat.

The first poem, which gives its name to the volume, is written in the lively octosyllabics made famous by *Christmas Eve.* The sharpness of her drawings, one of her greatest gifts, is evident in the opening lines:

A drifting, April, twilight sky,
A wind which blew the puddles dry,
And slapped the river into waves
That ran and hid among the staves
Of an old wharf. A watery light
Touched bleak the granite bridge, and white
Without the slightest tinge of gold,
The city shivered in the cold.

Soon the traveller meets a man who takes him to an old room, full of the symbols of poetry—edged weapons, curiously and elegantly wrought, together with seeds of poppy. Poems may be divided into two classes, stimulants and sedatives.

> All books are either dreams, or swords,
>   You can cut, or you can drug, with words.

Tennyson's poetry is mainly soothing, which is what lazy and tired people look for in any form of art, and are disappointed when they do not find it; the poetry of Donne, Browning, Emerson is the sword of the spirit; it is the opposite of an anæsthetic. Hence when readers first meet it, the effect is one of disturbance rather than repose, and they think it cannot be poetry. Yet in this piece of symbolism, which itself is full of beauty, Amy Lowell seems to say that both reveillé and taps are wrought by music—one is as much the legitimate office of poetry as the other. But although she classifies her poems in this volume according to the opening pair of symbols, and although she gives twice as much space to poppies as to swords, her poetry is always more stimulating than soothing. Her poppy seeds won't work; there is not a soporific page in the whole book.

One of the reasons why her books are so interesting is because she knows how to tell a story in verse. In her romances style waits on matter, like an attentive and thoroughly trained handmaid. Both poetry and incident are sustained from beginning to end; and the reader would stop more often to admire the flowers along the path if he were not so eager to know the event. In this particular kind of verse-composition, she has shown a steady development. The first real illustration of her powers is seen in *The Great Adventure of Max Brueck,* in *Poppy Seed,* though why so stirring a poem is thus classified is to me quite mysterious; yet when we compare this "effort" with later poems like *Pickthorn Manor* and *The Cremona Violin* we see an advance both in vigour and in technique which is so remarkable* that she makes her earlier narrative seem almost immature. A poet is indeed fortunate who can defeat that most formidable of all rivals—her younger self. In *The Cremona Violin* we have an extraordinary combination of the varied abilities possessed by the author. It is an absorbing tale full of drama, incident, realism, romanticism, imagism, symbolism and pure lyrical singing. There is everything in fact except polyphonic prose, and although I am afraid she loves her experiments in that form, they are the portion of her complete works that I could most willingly let die.

Her sensitiveness to colours and to sounds is clearly betrayed all through the romantic narrative of the *Cremona Violin,* where the instrument is a symbol of the human heart. Those who, in the old days before the Germans began their career of wholesale robbery and murder, used to hear Mozart's operas in the little rococo *Residenz-Theater* in Munich, will enjoy reminiscently these stanzas.

> The *Residenz-Theater* sparkled and hummed
> With lights and people. Gebnitz was to sing,
> That rare soprano. All the fiddles strummed

With tuning up; the wood-winds made a ring
Of reedy bubbling noises, and the sting
Of sharp, red brass pierced every eardrum; patting
From muffled tympani made a dark slatting

Across the silver shimmering of flutes;
A bassoon grunted, and an oboe wailed;
The 'celli pizzicato-ed like great lutes,
And mutterings of double basses trailed
Away to silence, while loud harp-strings hailed
Their thin, bright colours down in such a scatter
They lost themselves amid the general clatter.

Frau Altgelt, in the gallery, alone,
Felt lifted up into another world.
Before her eyes a thousand candles shone
In the great chandeliers. A maze of curled
And powdered periwigs past her eyes swirled.
She smelt the smoke of candles guttering,
And caught the scent of jewelled fans fluttering.

Her most ambitious attempt in polyphonic prose
is *Guns as Keys: and the Great Gate Swings,*
whereof the title is like a trumpet fanfare. The
thing itself is a combination of a moving picture
and a calliope. Written with immense gusto, full
of comedy and tragedy, it certainly is not lacking
in vitality; but judged as poetry, I regard it as
inferior to her verse romances and lyrics.

Rhythmical prose is as old as the Old Testament; the best modern rhythmical prose that I
have seen is found in the earlier plays of Maurice
Maeterlinck, written a quarter of a century ago.
It is unnecessary to enquire whether those dramas
are poetry or not; for although nearly all his work
is in the printed form of prose, the author is

almost invariably spoken of as "the poet Maeterlinck."

The versatility of Amy Lowell is so notable
that it would be vain to predict the nature of her
future production, or to attempt to set a limit to
her range. In her latest and best book, *Men,
Women, and Ghosts,* besides the two admirable
long narratives, we have poems of patriotism, out-
door lyrics, town eclogues, pictures of still life,
tragic pastorals in the manner of Susan Glaspell,
and one delightful *revenant, Nightmare,* which
takes us back to Dickens, for it is a verse comment on a picture by George Cruikshank. Her
robust vitality is veined with humour; she watches
a roof-shingler with active delight, discovering
poetry in cheerful manual toil. One day life
seems to her depressing; another day, beautiful;
another, inspiring; another, downright funny.

In spite of her assured position in contemporary
literature, one feels that her career has not
reached its zenith.

Some twelve years ago, I was engaged in earn-
est conversation with James Whitcomb Riley concerning the outlook for American poetry. The
chronic optimist for once was filled with woe.
"There is not a single person among the younger
writers," said he, "who shows any promise of
greatness, except"—and then his face recovered
its habitual cheerfulness—"Anna Hempstead
Branch. She is a poet."

In justification of his gloom, it should be remembered that the present advance in American
poetry began some time after he uttered these
words; and although he was a true poet and wrote
poems that will live for many years to come, he
was, in everything that had to do with the art of
poetry, the most conservative man I ever knew.

Anna Branch was born at Hempstead House,
New London, Connecticut, and was graduated
from Smith College in 1897. In 1898 she won a
first prize for the best poem awarded by the *Century Magazine* in a competition open to college
graduates. Since then she has published three
volumes of verse, *The Heart of the Road*, 1901,
The Shoes That Danced, 1905, *Rose of the Wind*,
1910. I fear that her ambition to be a dramatist
may have prevented her from writing lyrical
poetry (her real gift) during these last eight
years. If it is true, 'tis pity; for a good poem
is a better thing than a successful play and will
live longer.

Like many poets who cannot write plays, she is
surcharged with dramatic energy. But, to use a
familiar phrase, it is action in character rather
than character in action which marks her work
most impressively, and the latter is the essential
element for the footlights. Shakespeare, Rostand, and Barrie have both, and are naturally
therefore great dramatists. Two of the most
dramatic of Miss Branch's poems are *Lazarus*
and *Ora Pro Nobis*. These are fruitful subjects

for poetry, the man who came back from the grave
and the passionate woman buried alive. In the
short piece *Lazarus,* cast into the form of dialogue,
Lazarus answers the question put to him by Tennyson in *In Memoriam.*

> Where wert thou, brother, those four days?

Various members of the group, astounded at his
resurrection, try in vain to have their curiosity
satisfied. What do the dead do? Are they
happy? *Has my baby grown?* What overpowering motive brought you back from peace to live
once more in sorrow?

This last question Lazarus answers in a positive but unexpected way.

> A great desire led me out alone
> From those assured abodes of perfect bliss. . . .
> And by the way I went came seeking earth,
> Seeing before my eyes one only thing—
> > *The Crowd*
> What was it, Lazarus? Let us share that thing!
> What was it, brother, thou didst see?
> > *Lazarus*
>
> > > A cross.

Another dynamic poem, glowing with passion, is
Ora Pro Nobis. It is difficult to select passages
from it, for it is sustained in power and beauty
from the first line to the last; yet some idea of its
form and colour may be obtained by citation. A
little girl was put into a convent with only two
ways of passing the time; stitching and praying.
She has never seen her face—she never will see it,

for no mirror is permitted; but she sees one day
the reflection of its beauty in the hungry eyes of a
priest.

> Long years I dwelt in that dark hall,
> There was no mirror on the wall,
> I never saw my face at all,
>   (Hail Mary.)
> In a great peace they kept me there,
> A straight white robe they had me wear,
> And the white bands about my hair.
> I did not know that I was fair.
>   (Hail Mary.) . . .
> The sweet chill fragrance of the snow,
> More fine than lilies all aglow
> Breathed around—he saw me so,
> In garments spun of fire and snow.
>   (Holy Mother, pray for us.)
> His hands were on my face and hair,
> His high, stern eyes that would forswear
> All earthly beauty, saw me there.
> Oh, then I knew that I was fair!
>   (Mary, intercede for us.) . . .
> Then I raised up to God my prayer,
> I swept its strong and circling air,
> Betwixt me and the great despair.
>   (Sweet Mary, pray for us.)
> But when before the sacred shrine
> I knelt to kiss the cross benign,
> Mary, I thought his lips touched mine.
>   (Ave Maria, Ora Pro Nobis.)

Although some of her poems have an intensity almost terrible, Anna Branch has written household lyrics as beautiful in their uncrowded simplicity as an eighteenth century room. The
Songs for My Mother, celebrating her clothes, her
hands, her words, her stories breathe the un-

rivalled perfume of tender memories. And if
Lazarus is a sword, two of her most original pieces
are poppy-seeds, *To Nature* and

THE SILENCE OF THE POETS

I better like that shadowed side of things
In which the Poets wrote not; when they went
Unto the fullness of their great content
Like moths into the grass with folded wings.
The silence of the Poets with it brings
The other side of moons, and it is spent
In love, in sorrow, or in wonderment.
After the silence, maybe a bird sings.
I have heard call, as Summer calls the swallow,
A leisure, bidding unto ways serene
To be a child of winds and the blue hazes.
"Dream"—quoth the Dreamer—and 'tis sweet to follow!
So Keats watched stars rise from his meadows green,
And Chaucer spent his hours among the daisies.

This productive leisure has borne much fruit in
the poetry of Anna Branch; her work often has
the quiet beauty rising from tranquil meditation.
She is an orthodox poet. She uses the old material—God, Nature, Man—and writes songs with
the familiar notation. She has attracted attention not by the strangeness of her ideas, or by the
audacity of her method, but simply by the sincerity of her thought and the superior quality of
her singing voice. There is no difficulty in distinguishing her among the members of the choir,
and she does not have to make a discord to be
noticed.

There are almost as many kinds of poets as there are varieties of human beings; it is a far cry from Anna Branch to Edgar Lee Masters. I do not know whether either reads the other; it may be a mutual admiration exists; it may be that each would be ashamed to have written the other's books; even if that were true, there is no reason why an American critic—with proper reservations —should not be proud of both. For if there is one thing certain about the advance of poetry in America, it is that the advance is a general one along the whole line of composition from free verse and polyphonic prose on the extreme left to sonnets and quatrains on the extreme right.

Edgar Lee Masters was born in Kansas, on the twenty-third of August, 1869. The family moved to Illinois the next year. His father was a lawyer, and the child had access to plenty of good books, which he read eagerly. In spite of his preoccupation with the seamy side of human nature, he is in reality a bookish poet, and most of his work—though not the best part of it—smells of the lamp. Fortunately for him he was brought up on the Bible, for even those who attack the Old Book are glad to be able to tip their weapons with biblical language. Ibsen used to say that his chief reading, even in mature years, was always the Bible; "it is so strong and mighty."

Everything connected with books and literary work fascinated the youth; like so many boys of

his time—before wireless came in—he had his own
printing-press. I wonder if it was a "self-
inker"? In my day, the boy who owned a "self-
inker" and "club-skates" was regarded with envy.
The three generations in this family illustrate the
play *Milestones;* the grandfather vainly tried to
make his son a farmer, but the boy elected to be
a lawyer and carried his point; he in turn was
determined to twist his son into a lawyer, whereas
Edgar wanted to be a writer. As this latter profession is usually without emolument, he was
forced into the law, where the virile energy of his
mind rewarded his zestless efforts with success.
However, at the age of twenty-one, he persuaded
his father to allow him to study at Knox College
for a year, a highly important period in his development; for he resumed the interrupted study
of Latin, and began Greek. Greek is the chief
inspiration of his life, and of his art. He has
read Homer every year since his college days.

Later he went to Chicago, and stayed there,
busying himself not only at his profession, but
taking part in political activities, as any one might
guess from reading his poems. The primal impulse to write was not frustrated; he has written
verse all his life; and in fact has published a considerable number of volumes during the last
twenty years, no one of which attracted any attention until 1915, when *Spoon River Anthology*
made everybody sit up.

Mr. Masters was nearly fifty when this book appeared; it is a long time to wait for a reputation, especially if one is constantly trying to obtain a hearing. It speaks powerfully for his courage, tenacity, and faith that he should never have quit—and his triumph will encourage some good and many bad writers to persevere. Emboldened by the immense success of *Spoon River,* he produced three more volumes in rapid succession; *Songs and Satires* in 1916, *The Great Valley* in the same year, and *Toward the Gulf* in 1918. It is fortunate for him that these works followed rather than preceded the *Anthology;* for although they are not destitute of merit, they seem to require a famous name to ensure a sale. It is the brand, and not the goods, that gives a circulation to these books.

The pieces in *Spoon River Anthology* originally appeared in William Marion Reedy's periodical, called *Reedy's Mirror,* the first one being printed in the issue for 29 May, 1914, and the others following week after week. A grateful acknowledgment is made in a brief preface to the volume, and the full debt is handsomely paid in a dedicatory preface of *Toward the Gulf,* which every one interested in Mr. Masters—and who is not?—should read with attention. The poet manfully lets us know that it was Mr. Reedy who, in 1909, made him read the Greek Anthology, without which *Spoon River* would never have been written. Criticism is forestalled in this preface, because Mr. Masters takes a prose translation of Meleager,

"with its sad revealment and touch of irony"—
exactly the characteristics of *Spoon River*—and
turns it into free verse:

The holy night and thou,
O Lamp,
We took as witness of our vows;
And before thee we swore,
He that [he] would love me always
And I that I would never leave him.
We swore,
And thou wert witness of our double promise.
But now he says that our vows were written on the running
   waters.
And thou, O Lamp,
Thou seest him in the arms of another.

What Mr. Masters did was to transfer the method
and the tone of the Greek Anthology to a twentieth
century village in the Middle West, or as he expresses it, to make "an epic rendition of modern
life."

Even if it were desirable, how impossible it is
to escape from the past! we are ruled by the dead
as truly in the fields of art as in the domain of
morality and religion. The most radical innovator can no more break loose from tradition than a
tree can run away from its roots. John Masefield takes us back to Chaucer; Vachel Lindsay is
a reincarnation of the ancient minstrels; Edgar
Lee Masters owes both the idea and the form of
his masterpiece to Greek literature. Art is as
continuous as life.

This does not mean that he lacks originality. It

was a daring stroke—body-snatching in 1914. To produce a work like *Spoon River Anthology* required years of accumulated experience; a mordant power of analysis; a gift of shrewd speech, a command of hard words that will cut like a diamond; a mental vigour analogous to, though naturally not so powerful, as that displayed by Browning in *The Ring and the Book*. It is still a debatable proposition whether or not this is high-class poetry; but it is mixed with brains. Imagine the range of knowledge and power necessary to create two hundred and forty-six distinct characters, with a revealing epitaph for each one! The miracle of personal identity has always seemed to me perhaps the greatest miracle among all those that make up the universe; but to take up a pen and clearly display the marks that separate one individual from the mass, and repeat the feat nearly two hundred and fifty times, this needs creative genius.

The task that confronted Mr. Masters was this: to exhibit a long list of individuals with sufficient basal similarity for each one to be unmistakably human, and then to show the particular traits that distinguish each man and woman from the others, giving each a right to a name instead of a number. For instinctively we are all alike; it is the way in which we manage our instincts that shows divergence; just as men and women are alike in possessing fingers, whereas no two finger-prints are ever the same.

Mr. Masters has the double power of irony and sarcasm. The irony of life gives the tone to the whole book; particular phases of life like religious hypocrisy and political trimming are treated with vitriolic scorn. The following selection exhibits as well as any the author's poetic power of making pictures, together with the grinning irony of fate.

BERT KESSLER

I winged my bird,
Though he flew toward the setting sun;
But just as the shot rang out, he soared
Up and up through the splinters of golden light,
Till he turned right over, feathers ruffled,
With some of the down of him floating near,
And fell like a plummet into the grass.
I tramped about, parting the tangles,
Till I saw a splash of blood on a stump,
And the quail lying close to the rotten roots.
I reached my hand, but saw no brier,
But something pricked and stunned and numbed it.
And then, in a second, I spied the rattler—
The shutters wide in his yellow eyes,
The head of him arched, sunk back in the rings of him,
A circle of filth, the color of ashes,
Or oak leaves bleached under layers of leaves,
I stood like a stone as he shrank and uncoiled
And started to crawl beneath the stump,
When I fell limp in the grass.

This poem, with its unforgettable pictures and its terrible climax, can stand easily enough by itself; it needs no interpretation; and yet, if we like, the rattler may be taken as a symbol—a symbol of the generation of vipers of which the population of Spoon River is mainly composed.

In the *Anthology,* the driving motive is an almost perverted passion for truth. Conventional
epitaphs are marked by two characteristics; artistically, when in verse, they are the worst specimens of poetry known to man; even good poets
seldom write good epitaphs, and among all the
sins against art perpetrated by the uninspired, the
most flagrant are found here; to a bad poet, for
some reason or other, the temptation to write
them is irresistible. In many small communities,
one has to get up very early in the morning to
die before the village laureate has his poem prepared. This depth of artistic infamy is equalled
only by the low percentage of truth; so if one
wishes to discover literary illustrations where
falsehood is united with crudity, epitaphs would
be the field of literature toward which one would
instinctively turn.

Like Jonathan Swift, Mr. Masters is consumed
with hatred for insincerity in art and insincerity
in life; in the laudable desire to force the truth
upon his readers, he emphasizes the ugly, the
brutal, the treacherous elements which exist, not
only in Spoon River, but in every man born of
woman. The result, viewed calmly, is that we
have an impressive collection of vices—which, although inspired by a sincerity fundamentally
noble—is as far from being a truthful picture of
the village as a conventional panegyric. The ordinary photographer, who irons out the warts and
the wrinkles, gives his subject a smooth lying

mask instead of a face; but a photograph that should make the defects more prominent than the eyes, nose, and mouth would not be a portrait.

A large part of a lawyer's business is analysis; and the analytical power displayed by Mr. Masters is nothing less than remarkable. Each character in Spoon River is subjected to a remorseless autopsy, in which the various vicious elements existing in all men and women are laid bare. But the business of the artist, after preparatory and necessary analysing, is really synthesis. It is to make a complete artistic whole; to produce some form of art.

This is why the *Elegy Written in a Country Churchyard,* by Thomas Gray, is so superior as a poem to *Spoon River Anthology.* The rich were buried in the church; the poor in the yard; we are therefore given the short and simple annals of the poor. The curious thing is that these humble, rustic, unlettered folk were presented to the world sympathetically by a man who was almost an intellectual snob. One of the most exact scholars of his day, one of the most fastidious of mortals, one of the shyest men that ever lived, a born mental aristocrat, his literary genius enabled him to write an immortal masterpiece, not about the Cambridge hierarchy, but about illiterate tillers of the soil. The *Elegy* is the genius of synthesis; without submitting each man in the ground to a ruthless cross-examination, Gray managed to express in impeccable beauty of language the common thoughts and feelings that have ever animated the human soul. His poem will live as long as any book, because it is fundamentally true.

I therefore regard *Spoon River Anthology* not as a brilliant revelation of human nature, but as a masterpiece of cynicism. It took a genius to write the fourth book of *Gulliver's Travels;* but after all, Yahoos are not men and women, and horses are not superior to humanity. The reason why, in reading the *Anthology,* we experience the constant pricking of recognition is because we recognize the baser elements in these characters, not only in other persons, but in ourselves. The reason why the Yahoos fill us with such terror is because they are true incarnations of our worst instincts. There, but for the grace of God, go you and I.

The chief element in the creative work of Mr. Masters being the power of analysis, he is at his best in this collection of short poems. When he attempts a longer flight, his limitations appear. It is distinctly unfortunate that *The Spooniad* and *The Epilogue* were added at the end of this wonderful Rogues' Gallery. They are witless.

Even the greatest cynic has his ideal side. It is the figure of Abraham Lincoln that arouses all the romanticism of our poet, as was the case with Walt Whitman, who, to be sure, was no cynic at all. The short poem *Anne Rutledge* is one of the few that strictly conform to the etymological meaning of the title of the book; for "Anthology" is a union of two Greek words, signifying a collection of flowers.

Like Browning, Mr. Masters forsook the drama for the dramatic monologue. His best work is in this form, where he takes one person and permits him to reveal himself either in a soliloquy or in a conversation. And it must be confessed that the monologues spoken by contemporaries or by those Americans who talk from the graveyard of Spoon River, are superior to the attempts at interpreting great historical figures. The Shakespeare poem *Tomorrow Is My Birthday* is not only one of the worst effusions of Mr. Masters' pen, it is almost sacrilege. Good friend, for Jesus' sake, forbear!

Outside of the monologues and the epitaphs, the work of Mr. Masters is mainly unimpressive. Yet I admire his ambition to write on various subjects and in various metres. Occasionally he produces a short story in verse, characterized by dramatic power and by austere beauty of style. The poem *Boyhood Friends,* recently published in the *Yale Review,* and quite properly included by Mr. Braithwaite in his interesting and valuable Anthology for 1917, shows such a command of blank verse that I look for still finer things in the future. With all his twisted cynicism and perversities of expression, Mr. Masters is a true poet. He has achieved one sinister masterpiece, which has cleansed his bosom of much perilous stuff. Tomorrow to fresh woods and pastures new.

Louis Untermeyer was born at New York, on the first of October, 1885. He produced a volume of original poems at the age of twenty-five. This was followed by three other books, and in addition, he has written many verse-translations, a long list of prose articles in literary criticism, whilst not neglecting his professional work as a designer of jewelry. There is no doubt that this form of art has been a fascinating occupation and an inspiration to poetry. He not only makes sermons in stones, but can manufacture jewels five words long. Should any one be dissatisfied with his designs for the jewel-factory, he can "point with pride" to his books, saying, *Haec sunt mea ornamenta.*

Somewhere or other I read a review of the latest volume of verse from Mr. Untermeyer, and the critic began as follows: "One is grateful to Mr. Untermeyer for doing what almost none of his contemporaries on this side of the water thinks of doing." This sentence stimulated my curiosity, for I wondered what particularly distinguishing feature of his work I had failed to see. "For about the last thing that poets and theorizers about poetry in these days think of is beauty. In discussion and practice beauty is almost entirely left out of consideration. Frequently they do not concern themselves with it at all."

Such criticism as that starts with a preconceived definition of beauty, misses every form of beauty outsid'e of the definition, and gives to Mr. Untermeyer credit for originality in precisely that feature of his work where he most resembles contemporary and past poets. I believe that beauty is now as it always has been the main aim of the majority of American poets; but instead of legendary beauty, instead of traditional beauty, they wish us to see beauty in modern life. For example, it is interesting to observe how completely public opinion has changed concerning the New York sky-scrapers. I can remember when they were regarded as monstrosities of commercialism, an offence to the eye and a torment to the æsthetic sense. But I recall through my reading of history that mountains were also once regarded as hideous deformities—they were hook-shouldered giants, impressive in size—anything you like except beautiful. All the mountain had to do was to go on staying there, confident in its supreme excellence, knowing that some day it would be appreciated:

> Somebody remarks:
> Morello's outline there is wrongly traced,
> His hue mistaken; what of that? or else,
> Rightly traced and well ordered; what of that?
> Speak as they please, what does the mountain care?

We know better today; we know that the New York sky-scrapers are beautiful; just as we know that New York harbour in the night has something of the glory of fairyland.

No, it will not do to say that Mr. Untermeyer is original in his preoccupation with beauty; it would be almost as true to say that the chief feature in his work is the English language.

What is notable in him is the combination of three things; an immense love of life, a romantic interpretation of material things, and a remarkable talent for parody and burlesque.

Sex and Death—the obsessions of so many young poets—are not particularly conspicuous in the poetry of this healthy, happy young man. He writes about swimming, climbing the palisades, willow-trees, children playing in the street. Familiar objects become mysterious and thought-provoking in the light of his fancy. His imagination provides him with no end of fun; he needs no melancholy solitary pilgrimage in the gloaming to give him a pair of rimes; a country farm or a city slum is quite enough. I like his affectionate salutation to the willow; I like his interpretation of a side street. His greatest *tour de force* is his poem, *Still Life*. Of all painted pictures, with the one exception of dead fish, the conventional overturned basket of fruit is to me the most barren of meaning, the least inspiring, in suggestion a blank. Yet somehow Mr. Untermeyer, looking at a bowl of fruit, sees something I certainly never saw and do not ever expect to see except on this printed page, something that a bowl of fruit has for me in the same proportion as the stump of a cigar—*something dynamic*.

I do not understand why so many Americans plaster the walls of their dining-rooms with pictures of overset fruit-baskets and of dead fish, with their ugly mouths open; but in "still life" this paradoxical poet sees something full of demoniacal energy. O Death, where is thy sting?

> Never have I beheld such fierce contempt,
> Nor heard a voice so full of vehement life
> As this that shouted from a bowl of fruit,
> High-pitched, malignant, lusty and perverse—
> Brutal with a triumphant restlessness.

But the fruit in the basket is dead. The energy, the fierce vehemence and the lusty shout are not in the bowl, but in the soul. Subjectivity can no further go.

It is rather curious, that when our poet can behold such passion in a willow-tree or in a mess of plucked fruit, he should be so blind to it in the heart of an old maid; though to be honest, the heroine of his poem is meant for an individual rather than a type. If there is one object on earth that a healthy young man cannot understand, it is an old maid. Who can forget that terrible outburst of the aunt in *Une Vie?* "Nobody ever cared to ask if my feet were wet!" Mr. Untermeyer will live and learn. He is not contemptuous; he is full of pity, but it is the pity of ignorance.

Great joys or sorrows never came
    To set her placid soul astir;
  Youth's leaping torch, Love's sudden flame
    Were never even lit for her.

Don't you believe it, Mr. Untermeyer!

Even in his "serious" volumes of verse, there
is much satire and saline humour; so that his delightful book of parodies, called —— *and Other
Poets* is as spontaneous a product of his Muse as
his utterances *ex cathedra*. The twenty-seven
poems, called *The Banquet of the Bards,* with
which the book begins, are excellent fooling and
genuine criticism. He wrote these things for his
own amusement, one reason why they amuse us.
A roll-call of twenty-seven contemporary poets,
where each one comes forward and "speaks his
piece," is decidedly worth having. John Masefield "tells the true story of Tom, Tom, the Piper's
Son"; William Butler Yeats "gives a Keltic version of Three Wise Men in Gotham"; Robert
Frost "relates the Death of the Tired Man," and
so on. I had rather possess this volume than
any other by the author; it is almost worthy to
rank with the immortal *Fly Leaves*. Furthermore, in his serious work Mr. Untermeyer has
only begun to fight.

And while we are considering poems "in
lighter vein," let us not forget the three famous
initials signed to a column in the Chicago *Tribune,*
Don Marquis of the *Evening Sun,* who can be
either grave or gay but cannot be ungraceful, and

the universally beloved Captain Franklin P. Adams, whose *Conning Tower* increased the circulation of the New York *Tribune* and the blood of its readers. Brightest and best of the sons of the Colyumnists, his classic Muse made the *Evening Mail* an evening blessing, sending the suburbanites home to their wives "always in good humour"; then, like Jupiter and Venus, he changed from evening star to morning star, and gave many thousands a new zest for the day's work. Skilful indeed was his appropriation of the methods of Tom Sawyer; as Tom got his fence whitewashed by arousing an eager competition among the boys to do his work for him, each toiler firmly persuaded that he was the recipient rather than the bestower of a favour, so F. P. A. incited hundreds of well-paid literary artists to compete with one another for the privilege of writing his column without money and without price.

His two books of verse, *By and Large* and *Weights and Measures*, have fairly earned a place in contemporary American literature; and the influence of his column toward precision and dignity in the use of the English language has made him one of the best teachers of English composition in the country.

CHAPTER X

Sara Teasdale—her poems of love—her youth—her finished art—Fannie Stearns Davis—her thoughtful verse—Theodosia Garrison—her war poem—war poetry of Mary Carolyn Davies—Harriet Monroe—her services—her original work—Alice Corbin—her philosophy—Sarah Cleghorn—poet of the country village—Jessie B. Rittenhouse—critic and poet—Margaret Widdemer—poet of the factories—Carl Sandburg—poet of Chicago—his career—his defects—J. C. Underwood—poet of city noises—T. S. Eliot—J. G. Neihardt—love poems—C. W. Stork—*Contemporary Verse*—M. L. Fisher—*The Sonnet*—S. Middleton—J. P. Bishop—W. A. Bradley—nature poems—W. Griffith—*City Pastorals*—John Erskine—W. E. Leonard—W. T. Whitsett—Helen Hay Whitney—Corinne Roosevelt Robinson—M. Nicholson—his left hand—Witter Bynner—a country poet—H. Hagedorn—Percy Mackaye—his theories—his possibilities—J. G. Fletcher—monotony of free verse—Conrad Aiken—his gift of melody—W. A. Percy—the best American poem of 1917—Alan Seeger—an Elizabethan—an inspired poet.

Sara Teasdale (Mrs. Filsinger) was born at St. Louis (pronounced Lewis), on the eighth of August, 1884. Her first book appeared when she was twenty-three, and made an impression. In 1911 she published *Helen of Troy, and Other Poems;* in 1915 a volume of original lyrics called *Rivers to the Sea;* some of these were reprinted, together with new material, in *Love*

277

Poems (1917), which also contained *Songs out of Sorrow*—verses that won the prize offered by the Poetry Society of America for the best unpublished work read at the meetings in 1916; and in 1918 she received the Columbia University Poetry Prize of five hundred dollars, for the best book produced by an American in 1917.

In spite of her youth and the slender amount of her production, Sara Teasdale has won her way to the front rank of living American poets. She is among the happy few who not only know what they wish to accomplish, but who succeed in the attempt. How many manuscripts she burns, I know not; but the comparatively small number of pages that reach the world are nearly fleckless. Her career is beginning, but her work shows a combination of strength and grace that many a master might envy. It would be an insult to call her poems "promising," for most of them exhibit a consummate control of the art of lyrical expression. Give her more years, more experience, wider range, richer content, her architecture may become as massive as it is fine. She thoroughly understands the manipulation of the material of poetry. It would be difficult to suggest any improvement upon

TWILIGHT

The stately tragedy of dusk
　Drew to its perfect close,
The virginal white evening star
　Sank, and the red moon rose.

Although she gives us many beautiful pictures of nature, she is primarily a poet of love. White-hot passion without a trace of anything common or unclean; absolute surrender; whole-hearted devotion expressed in pure singing. Nothing is finer than this—to realize that the primal impulse is as strong as in the breast of a cave-woman, yet illumined by clear, high intelligence, and pouring out its feeling in a voice of gracious charm.

PITY

They never saw my lover's face,
　They only know our love was brief,
Wearing awhile a windy grace
　And passing like an autumn leaf.

They wonder why I do not weep,
　They think it strange that I can sing,
They say, "Her love was scarcely deep
　Since it has left so slight a sting."

They never saw my love nor knew
　That in my heart's most secret place
I pity them as angels do
　Men who have never seen God's face.

A PRAYER

Until I lose my soul and lie
　Blind to the beauty of the earth,
Deaf tho' a lyric wind goes by,
　Dumb in a storm of mirth;

Until my heart is quenched at length
　And I have left the land of men,
Oh, let me love with all my strength
　Careless if I am loved again.

If the two pieces just cited are not poetry, then I have no idea what poetry may be.

Another young woman poet is Fannie Stearns Davis (Mrs. Gifford). The quality of her mind as displayed in her two books indicates possibilities of high development. She was born at Cleveland, on the sixth of March, 1884, is a graduate of Smith College, was a teacher in Wisconsin, and has made many contributions to various magazines. Her first book of poems, *Myself and I*, appeared in 1913; two years later came the volume called *Crack o' Dawn*. She is not much given to metrical adventure, although one of her most original poems, *As I Drank Tea Today*, has an irregular rime-scheme. For the most part, she follows both in subject and style the poetic tradition. She has the gift of song—not indeed in the superlative degree—but nevertheless unmistakable; and she has a full mind. She is neither optimist nor pessimist; I should call her a sympathetic observer. The following poem sums up fairly well her accumulated wisdom:

> I have looked into all men's hearts.
> Like houses at night unshuttered they stand,
> And I walk in the street, in the dark, and on either hand
>   There are hollow houses, men's hearts.
>
> They think that the curtains are drawn,
> Yet I see their shadows suddenly kneel
> To pray, or laughing and reckless as drunkards reel
>   Into dead sleep till dawn.

And I see an immortal child
With its quaint high dreams and wondering eyes
Sleeping beneath the hard worn body that lies
    Like a mummy-case defiled.

And I hear an immortal cry
Of splendour strain through the sodden words,
Like a flight of brave-winged heaven-desirous birds
    From a swamp where poisons lie.

—I have looked into all men's hearts.
Oh, secret terrible houses of beauty and pain!
And I cannot be gay, but I cannot be bitter again,
    Since I looked into all men's hearts.

There is one commandment that all poets under the first class, and perhaps some of those favoured ones, frequently break: the tenth. One cannot blame them, for they know what poetry is, and they love it. They not only know what it is, but their own limited experience has taught them what rapture it must be to write lines of flawless beauty. This unconquerable covetousness is admirably and artistically expressed in Fannie Davis's poem, *After Copying Goodly Poetry*. It is an honest confession; but its author is fortunate in being able to express vain desire so beautifully that many lesser poets will covet her covetousness.

Theodosia Garrison was born at Newark, New Jersey, on the twenty-sixth of November, 1874. She has published three volumes of verse, of which perhaps the best known is *The Joy of Life* (1909). At present she is engaged in war work, where her high faith, serene womanliness, and overflowing humour ought to make her, in the finest sense of the word, efficient. Her short poem on the war is a good answer to detractors of America.

APRIL 2nd

We have been patient—and they named us weak;
We have been silent—and they judged us meek,
Now, in the much-abused, high name of God
    We speak.

Oh, not with faltering or uncertain tone—
With chosen words we make our meaning known,
That like a great wind from the West shall shake
    The double throne.

Our colours flame upon the topmost mast,—
We lift the glove so arrogantly cast,
And in the much-abused, high name of God
    We speak at last.

Another war alchemist is Mary Carolyn Davies, poet of Oregon and Brooklyn. She knows both coasts of America, she understands the American spirit of idealism and self-sacrifice, and her verses have a direct hitting power that will break open the hardest heart. In her book, *The Drums in Our Street* (1918), the glory and the tragedy of the world-struggle are expressed in terms of individual feeling. There is decided inequality in this volume, but the best pieces are so carefully distributed among the commonplace that one must read the whole work.

Harriet Monroe was born in Chicago and went to school in Georgetown, D. C. In connection with the World's Exposition in Chicago she received the honour of being formally invited to write a poem for the dedication. Accordingly at the ceremony commemorating the four hundredth anniversary of the discovery of America, 21 October, 1892, her *Columbian Ode* was given with music.

Harriet Monroe's chief services to the art of poetry are seen not so much in her creative work as in her founding and editing of the magazine called *Poetry*, of which I made mention in my remarks on Vachel Lindsay. In addition to this monthly stimulation—which has proved of distinct value both in awakening general interest and in giving new poets an opportunity to be heard, Miss Monroe, with the assistance of Alice Corbin Henderson, published in 1917 an anthology of the new varieties of verse. Certain poets are somewhat arbitrarily excluded, although their names are mentioned in the Preface; the title of the book is *The New Poetry;* the authors are fairly represented, and with some sins of commission the selections from each are made with critical judgment. Every student of contemporary verse should own a copy of this work.

In 1914 Miss Monroe produced a volume of her original poems, called *You and I.* There are over two hundred pages, and those who look in them for something strange and startling will be disappointed. Knowing the author's sympathy with radicalism in art, and with all modern extremists, the form of these verses is surprisingly conservative. To be sure, the first one, *The Hotel,* is in a kind of polyphonic prose, but it is not at all a fair sample of the contents. Now whether the reading of many manuscripts has dulled Miss Monroe's creative power or not, who can say? The fact is that most of these poems are in no way remarkable either for feeling or expression, and many of them fail to rise above the level of the commonplace. There is happily no straining for effect; but unhappily in most instances there is no effect.

Alice Corbin (Mrs. Henderson) is a native of Virginia and a resident of Chicago. She is co-editor with Miss Monroe of *The New Poetry* anthology, wherein her own poems are represented. These indicate skill in the manipulation of different metrical forms; and they reveal as well a shrewd, healthy acceptance of life as it is. This feeling communicates itself in a charming way to the reader; it is too vigorous for acquiescence, too wise for blind optimism, but nearer optimism than pessimism. It seems perhaps in certain aspects to resemble the philosophy of Ralph Hodgson, although his command of the art of poetry is beyond her range.

Sarah Norcliffe Cleghorn was born at Norfolk, Virginia, on the fourth of February, 1876, but since childhood has lived in Vermont. She studied at Radcliffe College, and has written much verse and prose. In 1915 a number of her lyrics were printed between the short stories in a volume by her friend, Dorothy Canfield, called *Hillsboro People.* In 1917 she published a book of verses, *Portraits and Protests,* where the portraits are better than the protests. No one has more truly or more sympathetically expressed the spirit of George Herbert's poetry than Miss Cleghorn has given it with a handful of words, in the lyric *In Bemerton Church.* But she is above all a country mouse and a country muse; she knows her Vermont neighbours to the skin and bone, and brings out artistically the austere sweetness of their daily lives. I think I like best of all her work the poem

A SAINT'S HOURS

In the still cold before the sun,
Her matins   Her brothers and her sisters small
She woke, and washed and dressed each one.

And through the morning hours all
Prime   Singing above her broom she stood
And swept the house from hall to hall.

Then out she ran with tidings good,
Tierce   Across the field and down the lane,
To share them with the neighbourhood.

Four miles she walked, and home again,
Sexts   To sit through half the afternoon
And hear a feeble crone complain.

But when she saw the frosty moon
Nones   And lakes of shadow on the hill,
Her maiden dreams grew bright as noon.

Vespers

She threw her pitying apron frill
Over a little trembling mouse
When the sleek cat yawned on the sill

Evensong

In the late hours and drowsy house.
At last, too tired, beside her bed
She fell asleep—her prayers half said.

Is not this one of the high functions of poetry, to interpret the life the poet knows best, and to interpret it always in terms of the eleventh and twelfth commandments? Observe she loves the sister-mother, and she loves the mouse as well as the cat. There is no reason why those who love birds should not love cats as well; is a cat the only animal who eats birds? It is a diverting spectacle, a man with his mouth full of squab, insisting that cats should be exterminated.

A woman who has done much for the advance of English poetry in America by her influence on public critical opinion, is Jessie B. Rittenhouse. She is a graduate of Genesee Wesleyan Seminary in Lima, New York, taught Latin and English in Illinois and in Michigan, and for five years was busily engaged in journalism. In 1904 she published a volume of criticism on contemporary verse, and for the last fourteen years has printed many essays of interpretation, dealing with the new poets. I dare say no one in America is more familiar with the English poetry of the twentieth century than she. She has been so occupied with this important and fruitful work that she has had little time to compose original verse; but any one who will read through her volume, *The Door of Dreams,* will find it impossible not to admire her lyrical gift. She has not yet shown enough sustained power to give her a place with Anna Hempstead Branch or with Sara Teasdale; but she has the capacity of putting much feeling into very few words.

Margaret Widdemer, the daughter of a clergyman, was born at Doylestown, Pennsylvania, and was graduated from Drexel Institute Library School in 1909. She has written verse and prose from early childhood, but was not widely known until the appearance of her poem *Factories.* In 1915 this was published in a book with other pieces, and a revised, enlarged edition was printed in 1917, called by the name of the now-famous song, and containing in addition nearly a hundred lyrics. Although her soul is aflame at the omnipresence of injustice in the world, her work covers a wide range of thought and feeling. Her heart is swollen with pity for the sufferings of women; but she is no sentimentalist. There is an intellectual independence, a clear-headed womanly self-reliance about her way of thinking and writing that is both refreshing and stimulating. In hope and in despair she speaks for the many thousands of women, who first found their voice in Ibsen's *Doll's House;* her poem, *The Modern Woman to Her Lover* has a cleanly honesty without any strained pose. And although *Factories* is doubt-less her masterpiece in its eloquent *Inasmuch as ye did it not*, she can portray a more quiet and more lonely tragedy as well. Her poem called *The Two Dyings* might have been named *The Heart Knoweth its own Bitterness*.

> I can remember once, ere I was dead,
>   The sorrow and the prayer and bitter cry
> When they who loved me stood around the bed,
>   Watching till I should die:
>
> They need not so have grieved their souls for me,
>   Grouped statue-like to count my failing breath—
> Only one thought strove faintly, bitterly
>   With the kind drug of Death:
>
> How once upon a time, unwept, unknown,
>   Unhelped by pitying sigh or murmured prayer,
> My youth died in slow agony alone
>   With none to watch or care.

Never in any period of the world's history was the table of life so richly spread as in the years 1900–1914; women were just beginning to realize that places ought to be reserved for them as well as for men, when the war came, and there was no place for any one except a place to fight the Black Plague of Kaiserism; now when the war is over, suppose the women insist? What then? Before the French Revolution, only a few were invited to sit down and eat, while the majority were permitted to kneel and watch from a distance. A Frenchman once remarked, "The great appear to us great because we are kneeling—let us rise." They rose, and out of the turmoil came an enormous enlargement of the dining-hall.

Carl Sandburg sings of Chicago with husky-haughty lips. I like Chicago and I like poetry; but I do not much care for the combination as illustrated in Mr. Sandburg's volume, *Chicago Poems.* I think it has been overrated. It is pretentious rather than important. It is the raw material of poetry, rather than the finished product. Mere passion and imagination are not enough to make a poet, even when accompanied by indignation. If feeling and appreciation could produce poetry, then we should all be poets. But it is also necessary to know how to write.

Carl Sandburg was born at Galesburg, Illinois, on the sixth of January, 1878. He has "worked his own way" through life with courage and ambition, performing any kind of respectable indoor and outdoor toil that would keep him alive. In the Spanish war, he immediately enlisted, and belonged to the first military company that went to Porto Rico. In 1898 he entered Lombard College; after his Freshman year, he tried to enter West Point, succeeding in every test—physical and mental—except that of arithmetic; there he has my hearty sympathy, for in arithmetic I was always slow but not sure. He returned to Lombard, and took the regular course for the next three years, paying his way by hard work. His literary ambition had already been awakened, and he attained distinction among his mates. Since graduation, he has had constant and varied experience in journalism. For a group of poems, of which the first was *Chicago,* he was awarded the Levinson prize as the best poem by an American that had appeared in *Poetry* during the year October 1913–October 1914. In 1916 appeared a substantial volume from his pen, called *Chicago Poems.*

His work gives one the impression of being chaotic in form and content. Miss Lowell quotes him as saying, "I don't know where I'm going, but I'm on my way." According to G. K. Chesterton, this attitude was characteristic of modern life in general before the war. We don't know where we're going,—but let's put on more speed. Perhaps the other extreme, so characteristic of our southern African friends, is no better, yet it has a charm absent in the strenuosity of mere eagerness. A Southern negro, being asked whither he was going, replied "I aint goin' nowhar: Ise been done gone whar I was goin'!" It would appear that there is sufficient room between these extremes for individual and social progress.

In manner Mr. Sandburg is closer to Walt Whitman than almost any other of our contemporary poets. I do not call him an imitator, and certainly he is no plagiarist; but I like that part of his work which is farthest removed from the manner of the man of Camden. Walt Whitman was a genius; and whilst it is quite possible and at times desirable to imitate his freedom in composition, it is not possible to catch the secret of his power. It would be an ungracious task to quote Mr. Sandburg at his worst; we are all pretty bad at our worst, whether we are poets or not; I prefer to cite one of his poems which proves to me that he is not only an original writer, but that he possesses a perceptive power of beauty that transforms the commonplace into something of poignant charm, like the song of the nightingale:

> Desolate and lone
> All night long on the lake
> Where fog trails and mist creeps,
> The whistle of a boat
> Calls and cries unendingly,
> Like some lost child
> In tears and trouble
> Hunting the harbour's breast
> And the harbour's eyes.

He has a notable gift for effective poetic figures of speech; in his *Nocturne in a Deserted Brickyard,* an old pond in the moonlight is a "wide dreaming pansy." This and other pieces show true power of poetic interpretation; which makes me believe that the author ought to and will greatly surpass the average excellence exhibited in *Chicago Poems*.

John Curtis Underwood is not only a dynamic, but an insurgent poet and critic. He has published four volumes of poems, *The Iron Muse* (1910), *Americans* (1912), *Processionals* (1915), and *War Flames* (1917). The roar of city streets and the deafening pounding of machinery resound through his pages; yet he somehow or other makes a singing voice heard amid the din. In fact, he uses the din as an accompaniment; he is a kind of vocal Tubal Cain. He writes about strap-hangers, chorus girls, moving pictures, convicts, hospitals, bridge-builders and construction gangs—a symphony of noise, where everybody plays some instrument. He is no pessimist and he is not sour; there are a good many "damns" and "hells" in his verse, because, whatever he lacks, he does not lack emphasis. His philosophy seems to be similar to that of the last two stanzas of *In Memoriam*, though Mr. Underwood expresses it somewhat more concretely.

> Leading the long procession through the midnight,
> Man that was ether, fire, sea, germ and ape,
> Out of the aeons blind of slime emerging,
> Out of the aeons black where ill went groping,
> Finding the fire, was fused to human shape.
>
> Heading the dreary marches through dark ages;
> Where the rest perished that the rest might be,
> Out of the aeons raw and red of bloodshed,
> Man that was caveman, found the stars. Forever
> Man to the stars goes marching from the sea.

His poem *Central*, in which the telephone girl's work is interpreted, is as typical as any of Mr. Underwood's style; and no one, I think, can fail to see the merit in his method.

> Though men may build their bridges high and plant their piers
> below the sea,

And drive their trains across the sky; a higher task is left to
me.
I bridge the void 'twixt soul and soul; I bring the longing
lovers near.
I draw you to your spirit's goal. I serve the ends of fraud
and fear.

The older fates sat in the sun. The cords they spun were
short and slight.
I set my stitches one by one, where life electric fetters night,
Till it outstrips the planet's speed, and out of darkness leaps
to day;
And men in Maine shall hear and heed a voice from San
Francisco Bay.

There is such a display of cynical cleverness in
the verse of T. S. Eliot that I think he might be
able to write almost anything except poetry. He
has an aggressive champion in the distinguished
novelist, May Sinclair, who says his best work is
equal to the best of Robert Browning.

John G. Neihardt was born in Illinois on the
eighth of January, 1881. From 1901 to 1907 he
lived among the Nebraska Indians, studying their
folklore and characteristics. He has published a
number of books, of which the best is perhaps *A
Bundle of Myrrh*, 1907. In 1915 he produced an
epic of the American Fur Trade, preparing himself for the task as follows: "I descended the
Missouri in an open boat, and also ascended the
Yellowstone for a considerable distance. On the
upper river the country was practically un-
changed; and for one familiar with what had
taken place there, it was no difficult feat of the
imagination to revive the details of that time—

the men, the trails, the boats, the trading posts where veritable satraps once ruled under the sway of the American Fur Company.''

I heartily envy him these experiences; to me every river is an adventure, even the quiet, serious old Connecticut.

Yet the poem that resulted from these visions is not remarkable. Nothing, I suppose, is more difficult than to write a good long poem. Poe disapproved of the undertaking in itself; and only men of undoubted genius have succeeded, whereas writers of hardly more than ordinary talent have occasionally turned off something combining brevity and excellence. I feel sure that Mr. Neihardt talks about this journey more impressively than he writes about it. His love lyrics, in *A Bundle of Myrrh,* are much better. The tendency to eroticism is redeemed by sincerity of feeling.

Charles Wharton Stork was born at Philadelphia, on the twelfth of February, 1881, and studied at Haverford, Harvard, and the University of Pennsylvania. He is a scholar, a member of the English Faculty of the University of Pennsylvania, and has made many translations of Scandinavian poems. Always interested in modern developments of poetry, both in America and Europe, he is at present the editor of *Contemporary Verse,* a monthly magazine exclusively made up of original poems. This periodical has been of considerable assistance to students of con-

temporary poetry, for it has given an opportunity to hitherto unknown writers, and often it
contains some notable contribution from men of
established reputation. Thus the number for
April, 1918, may some day have bibliographical
value, since it leads off with a remarkable poem
by Vachel Lindsay, *The Eyes of Queen Esther*.
I advise collectors to secure this, and to subscribe
to the magazine. Mr. Stork has written much
verse himself, of which *Flying Fish: an Ode,* may
be taken as illustrative of his originality and imagination.

Another excellent magazine of contemporary
poetry is *The Sonnet,* edited and published by
Mahlon Leonard Fisher, at Williamsport, Pennsylvania, of which the first number bears the date
February, 1917. This appears bimonthly; and
while the attempt to publish any magazine whatever displays courage, Mr. Fisher is apparently
on the side of the conservatives in art. "We
have attempted no propagandism, and acknowl-
edged no revolution," is the sentence that forms
the signature to his periodical. Furthermore, we
are informed that "the sole aim of *The Sonnet* is
to publish poetry so well thought of by its makers
that they were willing to place it within strict confines. The magazine will have nothing to say in
defence of its name. It will neither attack nor
respond to attacks." It has certainly printed
some good sonnets, among which are many by the
editor. In 1917 appeared a beautiful little vol-

ume, limited to two hundred copies, and published by the author—*Sonnets: a First Series*. Fifty specimens are included, all written by Mr. Fisher. More than a few have grace and truth.

A new aspirant appeared in 1917 with his first volume, *Streets and Faces*. This is Scudder Middleton, brother of George Middleton, the dramatist. He was born at New York, on the ninth of September, 1888, and studied at Columbia. His little book of poetry contains nothing profound, yet there is evidence of undoubted talent which gives me hope. The best poem of his that I have seen was published in *Contemporary Verse* in 1917, and makes a fine recessional to Mr. Braithwaite's Anthology.

THE POETS

We need you now, strong guardians of our hearts,
  Now, when a darkness lies on sea and land,
When we of weakening faith forget our parts
  And bow before the falling of the sand.
Be with us now or we betray our trust
  And say, "There is no wisdom but in death"—
Remembering lovely eyes now closed with dust—
  "There is no beauty that outlasts the breath."
For we are growing blind and cannot see,
  Beyond the clouds that stand like prison bars,
The changeless regions of our empery,
  Where once we moved in friendship with the stars.
O children of the light, now in our grief
Give us again the solace of belief.

A young Princeton student, John Peale Bishop, First Lieutenant of Infantry in the Officers Re-

serve Corps, who studied the art of verse under
the instruction of Alfred Noyes, published in 1917
a little book of original poems, with the modest
title, *Green Fruit*. These were mostly written
during his last undergraduate year at college, and
would not perhaps have been printed now had he
not entered the service. The subjects range from
the Princeton Inn to Italy. Mr. Bishop is a clear-
voiced singer, and there are original songs here,
which owe nothing to other poets. Such a poem
as *Mushrooms* is convincing proof of ability; and
there is an excellent spirit in him.

William Aspenwall Bradley was born at Hartford, Connecticut, on the eighth of February, 1878.
He was a special student at Harvard, and took his
bachelor's and master's degrees at Columbia. He
is now in the Government War Service. He wrote
an admirable *Life of Bryant* in the English Men of
Letters series, and has made many scholarly contributions to the literature of criticism. He has
issued two volumes of original verse, of which perhaps the better known is *Old Christmas*, 1917.
This is composed of tales of the Cumberland
region in Kentucky. These poem-stories are not
only full of dramatic power, comic and tragic, but
they contain striking portraits. I think, however,
that I like best Mr. Bradley's nature-pictures.
The pleasure of recognition will be felt by every-
one who reads the first few lines of

AUTUMN

Now shorter grow November days,
And leaden ponds begin to glaze
With their first ice, while every night
The hoarfrost leaves the meadows white
Like wimples spread upon the lawn
By maidens who are up at dawn,
And sparkling diamonds may be seen
Strewing the close-clipped golfing green.
But the slow sun dispels at noon
The season's work begun too soon,
Bidding faint filmy mists arise
And fold in softest draperies
The distant woodlands bleak and bare,
Until they seem to melt in air.

William Griffith was born at Memphis, Missouri, on the fifteenth of February 1876, and received his education at the public schools. He has been a "newspaper man" and magazine editor, and has produced a number of books in verse and prose, of which the best example is *City Pastorals,* originally published in 1915, revised and reissued in 1918. The title of this book appears to be a paradox; but its significance is clear enough after one has read a few pages. It is an original and interesting way of bringing the breath of the country into the town. The scene is a New York Club on a side street; the year is 1914; the three speakers are Brown, Gray, Green; the four divisions are Spring, Summer, Autumn, Winter. The style is for the most part rimed stanzas in short metre, which go trippingly on the tongue. Grace and delicacy characterize the pic-

tures of the country that the men bring back to the
smoky city from their travels.

Occultly through a riven cloud
  The ancient river shines again,
Still wandering like a silver road
  Among the cities in the plain.

On far horizons softly lean
  The hills against the coming night;
And mantled with a russet'green,
  The orchards gather into sight.

Through apples hanging high and low,
  In ruddy colours, deeply spread
From core to rind, the sun melts slow,
  With gold upcaught against the red.

And here and there, with sighs and calls,
  Among the hills an echo rings
Remotely as the water falls
  And down the meadow softly sings.

A wind goes by; the air is stirred
  With secret whispers far and near;
Another token—just a word
  Had made the rose's meaning clear.

I see the fields; I catch the scent
  Of pine cones and the fresh split wood,
Where bearded moss and stains are blent
  With autumn rains—and all is good.

An air, arising, turns and lifts
  The fallen leaves where they had lain
Beneath the trees, then weakly shifts
  And slowly settles back again.

While with far shouts, now homeward bound,
  Across the fields the reapers go;
And, with the darkness closing round,
  The lilies of the twilight blow.

Many of the other poems in this volume, that follow the *City Pastorals,* are interpretations of various individuals and of various nationalities. Mr. Griffith has a gift for the making of epigrams; and indeed he has studied concision in all his work. It may be that this is a result of his long years of training in journalism; he must have silently implored the writers of manuscripts he was forced to read to leave their damnable faces and begin. Certain it is, that although he can write smoothly flowing music, there is hardly a page in his whole book that does not contain some idea worth thinking about. His wine of Cyprus has both body and bouquet.

Three professional teachers of youth who write poetry as an avocation are John Erskine, professor at Columbia, whose poems bear the impress of an original and powerful personality, William Ellery Leonard, professor in the University of Wisconsin, the author of a number of volumes of poems, some of which show originality in conception and style, and William Thornton Whitsett, of Whitsett Institute, Whitsett, North Carolina, whose book *Saber and Song* (1917), exhibits such variations in merit that if one read only a few pages one might be completely deceived as to the author's actual ability. His besetting sin as an artist is moralizing. Fully half the contents of the volume are uninspired, commonplace, flat. But when he forgets to preach, he can write true poetry. He has the lyrical gift to a high degree, and has a rather remarkable command of the technique of the art. *An Ode to Expression, The Soul of the Sea,* and some of the *Sonnets,* fully justify their publication. The author is much too fond of the old "poetic diction"; he might do well to study simplicity.

A poet who differs from the two last mentioned in her ability to maintain a certain level of excellence is Helen Hay Whitney. She perhaps inherited her almost infallible good taste and literary tact from her distinguished father, that wholly admirable person, John Hay. His greatness as an international statesman was matched by the extraordinary charm of his character, which expressed itself in everything he wrote, and in numberless acts of kindness. He was the ideal American gentleman. One feels in reading the poems of Mrs. Whitney that each one is written both creatively and critically. I mean that she has the primal impulse to write, but that in writing, and more especially in revising, every line is submitted to her own severe scrutiny. I am not sure that she has not destroyed some of her best work, though this is of course only conjecture. At all events, while she makes no mistakes, I sometimes feel that there is too much repression. She is one of our best American sonnet-writers. Such a poem as *After Rain* is a work of art.

Corinne Roosevelt Robinson (Mrs. Douglas Robinson, sister of Theodore Roosevelt) has published two volumes of poems, *The Call of Broth-*

erhood, 1912, and *One Woman to Another,* 1914.
I hope that she will speedily collect in a third book
the fugitive pieces printed in various magazines
since 1914.   Mrs. Robinson's poetry comes from a
full mind and a full heart.   There is the knowledge born of experience combined with spiritual
revelation.   She is an excellent illustration of
the possibility of living to the uttermost in the
crowded avenues of the world without any loss of
religious or moral values.   It must take a strong
nature to absorb so much of the strenuous activities of metropolitan society while keeping the
heart's sources as clear as a mountain spring.   It
is the exact opposite of asceticism, yet seems not
to lose anything important gained by the ascetic
vocation.   She does not serve God and Mammon:
she serves God, and makes Mammon serve her.
This complete roundness and richness of development could not have been accomplished except
through pain.   She expresses grief's contribution
in the following sonnet:

> Beloved, from the hour that you were born
> I loved you with the love whose birth is pain;
> And now, that I have lost you, I must mourn
> With mortal anguish, born of love again;
> And so I know that Love and Pain are one,
> Yet not one single joy would I forego.—
> The very radiance of the tropic sun
> Makes the dark night but darker here below.
> Mine is no coward soul to count the cost;
> The coin of love with lavish hand I spend,
> And though the sunlight of my life is lost
> And I must walk in shadow to the end,—

I gladly press the cross against my heart—
And welcome Pain, that is Love's counterpart!

Meredith Nicholson, the American novelist, like
Mr. Galsworthy, Mr. Phillpotts and many other
novelists in England, has published a volume of
original verse, *Poems,* 1906. It is possibly a sign
of the growing interest in poetry that so many
who have won distinction in prose should in
these latter days strive for the laurel crown. Mr.
Nicholson's poems are a kind of riming journal
of his heart. It is clear that he is not a born
poet, for the flame of inspiration is not in these
pages, nor do we find the perfect phrase or ravishing music; what we do have is well worth preser-
vation in print—the manly, dignified, imaginative
speculations of a clear and honest mind. Furthermore, although he writes verse with his left
hand, there is displayed in many of these pieces
a mastery of the exact meaning of words, attained possibly by his long years of training in
the other harmony of prose.

Witter Bynner—the spelling of whose name I
defy any one to remember, and envelopes addressed to him must be a collection of curiosities
—was born at Brooklyn on the tenth of August,
1881. He was graduated from Harvard in 1902,
and addressed his *Alma Mater* in an *Ode To Harvard,* published in book form in 1907. In 1917 he
collected in one attractive volume, *Grenstone
Poems,* the best of his production—exclusive of
his plays and prose—up to that date. One who

knew Mr. Bynner only by the terrific white slave drama *Tiger*, would be quite unprepared for the sylvan sweetness of the Grenstone poems. Their environment, mainly rural, does not localize the sentiment overmuch; for the poet's mind is a kingdom, even though he is bounded in a nutshell. The environment, however, may be partly responsible for the spirit of healthy cheerfulness that animates these verses; whatever they lack, they certainly do not lack purity and charm. Far from the madding crowd the singer finds contentment, which is the keynote of these songs; happiness built on firm indestructible foundations. Some of the divisional titles indicate the range of subjects: *Neighbors and the Country-side, Children and Death, Wisdom and Unwisdom, Celia, Away from Grenstone*, where homesickness is expressed while travelling in the Far East. And the tone is clearly sounded in

A GRACE BEFORE THE POEMS

"Is there such a place as Grenstone?"
  Celia, hear them ask!
Tell me, shall we share it with them?—
  Shall we let them breathe and bask

On the windy, sunny pasture,
  Where the hill-top turns its face
Toward the valley of the mountain,
  Our beloved place?

Shall we show them through our churchyard,
  With its crumbling wall
Set between the dead and living?
  Shall our willowed waterfall,

Huckleberries, pines and bluebirds
Be a secret we shall share?—
If they make but little of it,
Celia, shall we care?

It will be seen that the independence of Mr. Bynner is quite different from the independence of Mr. Underwood; but they both have the secret of self-sufficiency.

Another loyal Harvard poet is Herman Hagedorn, who was born at New York in 1882, and took his degree at college in 1907. For some time he was on the English Faculty at Harvard, and has a scholar's knowledge of English literature. He has published plays and books of verse, of which the best known are *A Troop of the Guard* (1909) and *Poems and Ballads,* which appeared the same year. He has a good command of lyrical expression, which ought to enable him in the years to come to produce work of richer content than his verses have thus far shown.

The best known of the Harvard poets of the twentieth century is Percy Mackaye, who is still better known as a playwright and maker of pageants. He was born at New York, on the sixteenth of March, 1875, and was graduated from Harvard in 1897. He has travelled much in Europe, and has given many lectures on dramatic art in America. His poetry may be collectively studied in one volume of appalling avoirdupois, published in 1916. It takes a strong wrist to hold it, but it is worth the effort.

The chief difficulty with Mr. Mackaye is his inability to escape from his opinions. He is far too self-conscious, much too much preoccupied with theory, both in drama and in poetry. He can write nothing without explaining his motive, without trying to show himself and others the aim of poetry and drama. However morally noble all this may be—and it surely is that—it hampers the author. I wish he could for once completely forget all artistic propaganda, completely forget himself, and give his Muse a chance. "She needs no introduction to this audience."

There is no doubt that he has something of the divine gift. His *Centenary Ode on Lincoln,* published separately in 1909, was the best out of all the immense number of effusions I read that year. He rose to a great occasion.

One of his most original pieces is the dog-vivisection poem, called *The Heart in the Jar.* There is a tumultuous passion in it almost overpowering; and no one but a true poet could ever have thought of or have employed such symbolism. Mr. Mackaye's mind is so alive, so inquisitive, so volcanic, that he seems to me always just about to produce something that shall surpass his previous efforts. I have certainly not lost faith in his future.

John Gould Fletcher was born at Little Rock, Arkansas, in 1886. He studied at Andover and at Harvard, and has lived much in London. He has become identified with the Imagists. Personally

I wish that Mr. Fletcher would use his remarkable power to create gorgeous imagery in the production of orthodox forms of verse. Free verse ought to be less monotonous than constantly repeated sonnets, quatrains, and stanza-forms; but the fact is just the other way. A volume made up entirely of free verse, unless written by a man of genius, has a capacity to bore the reader that at times seems almost criminal.

Conrad Aiken was born at Savannah, Georgia, on the fifth of August, 1889, is a graduate of Harvard and lives in Boston. He has published several volumes of poems, among which *Earth Triumphant* (1914) is representative of his ability and philosophy. It certainly represents his ability more fairly than *The Jig of Forslin* (1916), which is both pretentious and dull. I suspect few persons have read every page of it. I have.

Not yet thirty, Mr. Aiken is widely known; but the duration of his fame will depend upon his future work. He has thus far shown the power to write melodious music, to paint nature pictures in warm colours; he is ever on the quest of Beauty. His sensible preface to *Earth Triumphant* calls attention to certain similarities between his style in verse-narrative and that of John Masefield. But he is not a copier, and his work is his own. Some poets are on the earth; some are in the air; some, like Shelley, are in the aether. Conrad Aiken is firmly, gladly on the earth. He believes that our only paradise is here and now.

He surely has the gift of singing speech, but his poetry lacks intellectual content. In the volume, *Nocturne of Remembered Spring* (1917), there is a dreamy charm, like the hesitating notes of Chopin.

Although his contribution to the advance of poetry is not important, he has the equipment of a poet. When he has more to say, he will have no difficulty in making us listen; for he understands the magic of words. Thus far his poems are something like librettos; they don't mean much without the music. Let him remember the bitter cry of old Henry Vaughan: every artist, racked by labour-pains, will understand what Vaughan meant by calling this piece *Anguish:*

> O! 'tis an easy thing
>   To write and sing;
> But to write true, unfeignèd verse
> Is very hard!　O God, disperse
> These weights, and give my spirit leave
> To act as well as to conceive!

Among our young American poets there are few who have inherited in richer or purer measure than William Alexander Percy. He was born at Greenville, Mississippi, on the fourth of May, 1885, and studied at the University of the South and at the Harvard Law School. He is now in military service. In 1915, his volume of poems, *Sappho in Leukas,* attracted immediately the attention of discriminating critics. The prologue shows that noble devotion to art, that high faith in it, entirely beyond the understanding of the

Philistine, but which awakens an instant and accurate vibration in the heart of every lover of poetry.

O singing heart, think not of aught save song;
  Beauty can do no wrong.
 Let but th' inviolable music shake
  Golden on golden flake,
  Down to the human throng,
And one, one surely, will look up, and hear and wake.

Weigh not the rapture; measure not nor sift
  God's dark, delirious gift;
 But deaf to immortality or gain,
  Give as the shining rain,
  Thy music pure and swift,
And here or there, sometime, somewhere, 'twill reach the grain.

There is a wide range of subjects in this volume, Greek, mediaeval, and modern—inspiration from books and inspiration from outdoors. But there is not a single poem that could be called crude or flat. Mr. Percy is a poet and an artist; he can be ornate and he can be severe; but in both phases there is a dignity not always characteristic of contemporary verse. I do not prophesy—but I feel certain of this man.

One day in 1917, I clipped a nameless poem from a daily newspaper, and carried it in my pocketbook for months. Later I discovered that it was written by Mr. Percy, and had first appeared in *The Bellman*. I know of no poem by any American published in the year 1917 that for combined beauty of thought and beauty of expression is superior to this little masterpiece.

OVERTONES

I heard a bird at break of day
    Sing from the autumn trees
A song so mystical and calm,
    So full of certainties,
No man, I think, could listen long
    Except upon his knees.
Yet this was but a simple bird,
    Alone, among dead trees.

Alan Seeger—whose heroic death glorified his youth—was born at New York on the twenty-second of June, 1888. He studied at Harvard; then lived in Paris, and no one has ever loved Paris more than he. He enlisted in the Foreign Legion of France at the outbreak of the war in 1914, and fell on the fourth of July, 1916. His letters show his mind and heart clearly.

He knew his poetry was good, and that it would not die with his body. In the last letter he wrote, we find these words: "I will write you soon if I get through all right. If not, my only earthly care is for my poems. Add the ode I sent you and the three sonnets to my last volume and you will have *opera omnia quae existant.*"

He wrote his autobiography in one of his last sonnets, paying poetic tribute to Philip Sidney—lover of woman, lover of battle, lover of art.

Sidney, in whom the heydey of romance
Came to its precious and most perfect flower,
Whether you tourneyed with victorious lance
Or brought sweet roundelays to Stella's bower,

I give myself some credit for the way
I have kept clean of what enslaves and lowers,
Shunned the ideals of our present day
And studied those that were esteemed in yours;
For, turning from the mob that buys Success
By sacrificing all life's better part,
Down the free roads of human happiness
I frolicked, poor of purse but light of heart,
And lived in strict devotion all along
To my three idols—Love and Arms and Song.

His most famous poem, *I Have a Rendezvous with Death,* is almost intolerably painful in its tragic beauty, in its contrast between the darkness of the unchanging shadow and the apple-blossoms of the sunny air—above all, because we read it after both Youth and Death have kept their word, and met at the place appointed.

He was an inspired poet. Poetry came from him as naturally as rain from clouds. His magnificent *Ode in Memory of the American Volunteers Fallen in France* has a nobility of phrase that matches the elevation of thought. Work like this cannot be forgotten.

Alan Seeger was an Elizabethan. He had a consuming passion for beauty—his only religion. He loved women and he loved war, like the gallant, picturesque old soldiers of fortune. There was no pose in all this; his was a brave, uncalculating, forthright nature, that gave everything he had and was, without a shade of fear or a shade of regret. He is one of the most fiery spirits of our time, and like Rupert Brooke, he will be thought of as immortally young.

CHAPTER XI

A GROUP OF YALE POETS

Henry A. Beers—the fine quality of his literary style in prose and verse—force and grace—finished art—his humour—C. M. Lewis—his war poem—E. B. Reed—*Lyra Yalensis*—F. E. Pierce—his farm lyrics—Brian Hooker—his strong sonnets—his *Turns*—R. C. Rogers—*The Rosary*—Rupert Hughes—novelist, playwright, musician, poet—Robert Munger—his singing—R. B. Glaenzer—his fancies—Benjamin R. C. Low—his growth—William R. Benét—his vitality and optimism—Arthur Colton—his Chaucer poem—Allan Updegraff—*The Time and the Place*—Lee Wilson Dodd—his development—a list of other Yale Poets—Stephen V. Benét.

During the twentieth century there has been flowing a fountain of verse from the faculty, young alumni, and undergraduates of Yale University; and I reserve this space at the end of my book for a consideration of the Yale group of poets, some of whom are already widely known and some of whom seem destined to be. I am not thinking of magazine verse or of fugitive pieces, but only of independent volumes of original poems. Yale has always been close to the national life of America; and the recent outburst of poetry from her sons is simply additional evidence of the renaissance all over the United States. Anyhow, the fact is worth recording.

Professor Henry A. Beers was born at Buffalo on the second of July, 1847. He was admitted to

the New York Bar in 1870, but in 1871 became an
Instructor in English Literature at Yale, teaching continuously for forty-five years, when he
retired. He has written—at too rare intervals—
all his life. His book of short stories, containing
A Suburban Pastoral and *Split Zephyr,* the last-
named being, according to Meredith Nicholson,
the best story of college life ever printed, would
possibly have attracted more general attention
were it not for its prevailing tone of quiet, unob-
trusive pessimism, an unwelcome note in America.
I am as sure of the high quality of *A Suburban
Pastoral* as I am sure of anything; and have never
found a critic who, after reading the tale, dis-
agreed with me. In 1885 Professor Beers published a little volume of poems, *The Thankless
Muse;* and in 1917 he collected in a thin book *The
Two Twilights,* the best of his youthful and mature poetic production. The variety of expression is so great that no two poems are in the same
mood. In *Love, Death, and Life* we have one of
the most passionate love-poems in American literature; in *The Pasture Bars* the valediction has
the soft, pure tone of a silver bell.

Professor Beers has both vigour and grace.
His fastidious taste permits him to write little,
and to print only a small part of what he writes.
But the force of his poetic language is so extraordinary that it has sometimes led to a complete and
unfortunate misinterpretation of his work. In
The Dying Pantheist to the Priest, he wrote a

poem as purely dramatic, as non-personal, as the
monologues of Browning; he quite successfully
represented the attitude of an (imaginary) defiant, unrepentant pagan to an (imaginary) priest
who wished to save him in his last moments. The
speeches put into the mouth of the pantheist no
more represent Mr. Beers's own sentiments
than Browning's poem *Confessions* represented
Browning's attitude toward death and religion;
yet it is perhaps a tribute to the fervour of the
lyric that many readers have taken it as a violent
attack on Christian theology.

Just as I am certain of the finished art of *A
Suburban Pastoral*, I am equally certain of the
beauty and nobility of the poetry in *The Two Twilights*. This volume gives its author an earned
place in the front rank of living American poets.

To me one of the most original and charming of
the songs is the valediction to New York—and the
homage to New Haven.

NUNC DIMITTIS

Highlands of Navesink,
By the blue ocean's brink,
Let your grey bases drink
    Deep of the sea.
Tide that comes flooding up,
Fill me a stirrup cup,
Pledge me a parting sup,
    Now I go free.

Wall of the Palisades,
I know where greener glades,
Deeper glens, darker shades,

Hemlock and pine,
Far toward the morning lie
Under a bluer sky,
Lifted by cliffs as high,
    Haunts that are mine.

Marshes of Hackensack,
See, I am going back
Where the Quinnipiac
    Winds to the bay,
Down its long meadow track,
Piled in the myriad stack,
Where in wide bivouac
    Camps the salt hay.

Spire of old Trinity,
Never again to be
Seamark and goal to me
    As I walk down;
Chimes on the upper air,
Calling in vain to prayer,
Squandering your music where
    Roars the black town:

Bless me once ere I ride
Off to God's countryside,
Where in the treetops hide
    Belfry and bell;
Tongues of the steeple towers,
Telling the slow-paced hours—
Hail, thou still town of ours—
    Bedlam, farewell!

Those who are familiar with Professor Beers's humour, as expressed in *The Ways of Yale*, will wish that he had preserved also in this later book some of his whimsicalities, as in the poem *A Fish Story*, which begins:

A whale of great porosity,
  And small specific gravity,
Dived down with much velocity
  Beneath the sea's concavity.

But soon the weight of water
  Squeezed in his fat immensity,
Which varied—as it ought to—
  Inversely as his density.

Professor Charlton M. Lewis was born at Brooklyn on the fourth of March, 1866. He took his B.A. at Yale in 1886, and an LL.B at Columbia in 1889. For some years he was a practising lawyer in New York; in 1895 he became a member of the Yale Faculty. In 1903 he published *Gawayne and the Green Knight,* a long poem, in which humour and imagination are delightfully mingled. His lyric *Pro Patria* (1917) is a good illustration of his poetic powers; it is indeed one of America's finest literary contributions to the war.

PRO PATRIA

Remember, as the flaming car
  Of ruin nearer rolls,
That of our country's substance are
  Our bodies and our souls.

Her dust we are, and to her dust
  Our ashes shall descend:
Who craves a lineage more august
  Or a diviner end?

By blessing of her fruitful dews,
  Her suns and winds and rains,
We have her granite in our thews,
  Her iron in our veins.

And, sleeping in her sacred earth,
  The ever-living dead
On the dark miracle of birth
  Their holy influence shed. . . .

So, in the faith our fathers kept,
  We live, and long to die;
To sleep forever, as they have slept,
  Under a sunlit sky;

Close-folded to our mother's heart
  To find our souls' release—
A secret coeternal part
  Of her eternal peace;—

Where Hood, Saint Helen's and Rainier,
  In vestal raiment, keep
Inviolate through the varying year
  Their immemorial sleep;

Or where the meadow-lark, in coy
  But calm profusion, pours
The liquid fragments of his joy
  On old colonial shores.

Professor Edward B. Reed, B.A. 1894, published in 1913 a tiny volume of academic verse, called *Lyra Yalensis.* This contains happily humorous comment on college life and college customs, and as the entire edition was almost immediately sold, the book has already become something of a rarity. In 1917, he collected the best of his more ambitious work in *Sea Moods,* of which one of the most impressive is

THE DAWN

He shook his head as he turned away—
"Is it life or death?" "We shall know by day."

Out from the wards where the sick folk lie,
Out neath the black and bitter sky.
Past one o'clock and the wind is chill,
The snow-clad streets are ghostly still;
No friendly noise, no cheering light,
So calm the city sleeps to-night,
I think its soul has taken flight.

Back to the empty home—a thrill,
A shudder at its darkened sill,
For the clock chimes as on that morn,
That happy day when she was born.
And now, inexorably slow,
To life or death the hours go.
Time's wings are clipped; he scarce doth creep.
Tonight no drug could bring you sleep;
Watch at the window for the day;
'Tis all that's left—to watch and pray.
But I think the prayer of an anguished heart
Must pierce that bleak sky like a dart,
And tear that pall of clouds apart.

The poplars, edging the frozen lawn,
Shudder and whisper: "Wait till dawn."

Two spirits stand beside her bed
Softly stroking her curly head.
Death whispers, "Come"—Life whispers, "Stay."
Child, little child, go not away.
Life pleads, "Remember"—and Death, "Forget."
Little child, little child, go not yet.
By all your mother's love and pain,
Child of our heart, child of our brain,
Stay with us; go not till you see
The Fairyland that life can be.

. . . .

The poplars, edging the frozen lawn,
Are dancing and singing. "Thank God—the Dawn!"

Professor Frederick E. Pierce, B.A. 1904, has
produced three volumes of poems, of which *The*

World that God Destroyed exhibits an epic sweep
of the imagination. He imagines a world far off
in space, where every form of life has perished
save rank vegetation. One day in their wanderings over the universe, Lucifer and Michael meet
on this dead ball. A truce is declared and each
expresses some of the wisdom bought by experience.

The upas dripped its poison on the ground
Harmless; the silvery veil of fog went up
From mouldering fen and cold, malarial pool,
But brought no taint and threatened ill to none.
Far off adown the mountain's craggy side
From time to time the avalanche thundered, sounding
Like sport of giant children, and the rocks
Whereon it smote re-echoed innocently.
Then in a pause of silence Lucifer
Struck music from the harp again and sang.

"I am the shadow that the sunbeams bring,
I am the thorn from which the roses spring;
Without the thorn would be no blossoming,
Nor were there shadow if there were no gleam.
I am a leaf before a wind that blows,
I am the foam that down the current goes;
I work a work on earth that no man knows,
And God works too,—I am not what I seem.

"There comes a purer morn whose stainless glow
Shall cast no shadow on the ground below,
And fairer flowers without the thorn shall blow,
And earth at last fulfil her parent's dream.
Oh race of men who sin and know not why,
I am as you and you are even as I;
We all shall die at length and gladly die;
Yet even our deaths shall be not what they seem."

Then Michael raised the golden lyre, and struck
A note more solemn soft, and made reply.

"There dwelt a doubt within my mind of yore;
I sought to end that doubt and laboured sore;
But now I search its mystery no more,
   But leave it safe within the Eternal's hand.
The tiger hunts the lamb and yearns to kill,
Himself by famine hunted, fiercer still;
And much there is that seems unmingled ill;
   But God is wise, and God can understand.

"All things on earth in endless balance sway;
Day follows night and night succeeds the day;
And so the powers of good and evil may
   Work out the purpose that his wisdom planned.
Eternal day would parch the dewy mould,
Eternal night would freeze the lands with cold;
But wise was God who planned the world of old;
   I rest in Him for He can understand.

"Yet good and evil still their wills oppose;
And serving both, we still must serve as foes
On yon far globe that teems with human woes;
   And sin thou art, though God work through thy hand.
But here the race of man is now no more;
The task is done, the long day's work is o'er;
One hour I'll dream thee what thou wert of yore,
   Though changed thou art, too changed to understand."

All day sat Michael there with Lucifer
Talking of things unknown to men, old tales
And memories dating back beyond all time.
And all night long beneath the lonely stars,
That watched no more the sins of man, they lay,
The angel's lofty face at rest against
The dark cheek scarred with thunder.
                                    Morning came,
And each departed on his separate way;
But each looked back and lingered as he passed.

Some of his best work, however, appears in short pieces that might best be described as lyrics of the farm, or, to use a title discarded by Tennyson, *Idylls of the Hearth*. Mr. Pierce knows the lonely farm-houses of New England, both by inheritance and habitation, and is a true interpreter of the spirit of rural life.

One of the best-known of the group of Yale poets is Brian Hooker, who was graduated from Yale in 1902, and for some years was a member of the Faculty. His *Poems* (1915) are an important addition to contemporary literature. He is a master of the sonnet-form, as any one may see for himself in reading

GHOSTS

The dead return to us continually;
　　Not at the void of night, as fables feign,
　　In some lone spot where murdered bones have lain
Wailing for vengeance to the passer-by;
But in the merry clamour and full cry
　　Of the brave noon, our dead whom we have slain
　　And in forgotten graves hidden in vain,
Rise up and stand beside us terribly.

Sick with the beauty of their dear decay
　　We conjure them with laughters onerous
　　And drunkenness of labour; yet not thus
May we absolve ourselves of yesterday—
We cannot put those clinging arms away,
　　Nor those glad faces yearning over us.

Mr. Hooker also includes in this volume a number of *Turns,* which he describes as "a new fixed form: Seven lines, in any rhythm, isometric and

of not more than four feet; Rhyming AbacbcA,
the first line and the last a Refrain; the Idea (as
the name suggests) to Turn upon the recurrence
of the Refrain at the end with a different sense
from that which it bears at the beginning.'' For
example:

MISERERE

Ah, God, my strength again!—
  Not power, nor joy, but these:
The waking without pain,
  The ardour for the task,
And in the evening, peace.
  Is it so much to ask?
Ah, God, my strength again!

American literature suffered a loss in the death
of Robert Cameron Rogers, of the class of 1883.
His book of poems, called *The Rosary*, appeared in
1906, containing the song by which naturally
he is best known. Set to music by the late Ethel-
bert Nevin, it had a prodigious vogue, and inspired a sentimental British novel, whose sales ran
over a million copies. The success of this ditty
ought not to prejudice readers against the author
of it; for he was more than a sentimentalist, as
his other pieces prove.

Rupert Hughes is an all around literary athlete.
He was born in Missouri, on the thirty-first of
January, 1872, studied at Western Reserve and
later at Yale, where he took the degree of M.A. in
1899. He is of course best known as a novelist
and playwright; his novel *The Thirteenth Com-*

mandment (1916) and his play *Excuse Me* (1911) are among his most successful productions. His works in prose fiction are conscientiously realistic and the finest of them are accurate chronicles of metropolitan life; while his short stories, *In a Little Town* (1917) are, like those of William Allen White, truthful both in their representation of village manners in the West, and in their recognition of spiritual values. In view of the "up-to-dateness" of Mr. Hughes's novels, it is rather curious that his one long poem *Gyges' Ring* (1901), which was written during his student days at Yale, should be founded on Greek legend. Yet Mr. Hughes has been a student of Greek all his life, and has made many translations from the original. I do not care much for *Gyges' Ring;* it is hammered out rather than created. But some of the author's short poems, to which he has often composed his own musical accompaniment, I find full of charm. Best of all, I think, is the imaginative and delightful

WITH A FIRST READER

Dear little child, this little book
  Is less a primer than a key
To sunder gates where wonder waits
  Your "Open Sesame!"

These tiny syllables look large;
  They'll fret your wide, bewildered eyes;
But "Is the cat upon the mat?"
  Is passport to the skies.

For, yet awhile, and you shall turn
  From Mother Goose to Avon's swan;
From Mary's lamb to grim Khayyam,
  And Mancha's mad-wise Don.

You'll writhe at Jean Valjean's disgrace;
  And D'Artagnan and Ivanhoe
Shall steal your sleep; and you shall weep
  At Sidney Carton's woe.

You'll find old Chaucer young once more,
  Beaumont and Fletcher fierce with fire;
At your demand, John Milton's hand
  Shall wake his ivory lyre.

And learning other tongues, you'll learn
  All times are one; all men, one race;
Hear Homer speak, as Greek to Greek;
  See Dante, face to face.

Arma virumque shall resound;
  And Horace wreathe his rhymes afresh;
You'll rediscover Laura's lover;
  Meet Gretchen in the flesh.

Oh, could I find for the first time
  The *Churchyard Elegy* again!
Retaste the sweets of new-found Keats;
  Read Byron now as then!

Make haste to wander these old roads,
  O envied little parvenue;
For all things trite shall leap alight
  And bloom again for you!

Robert Munger, B.A., 1897, published in 1912 a
volume called *The Land of Lost Music*. He is a
lyric poet. Melody seems as natural to him as
speech.

There is a land uncharted of meadows and shimmering moun-
    tains,
Stiller than moonlight silence brooding and wan,
The land of long-wandering music and dead unmelodious
    fountains
Of singing that rose in the dreams of them that are gone.

That rose in the dreams of the dead and that rise in the dreams
    of the living,
Fleeting, bodiless songs that passed in the night,
Winging away on the moment of wonder their cadence was
    giving
Into the deeps of the valleys of stifled delight.

Richard Butler Glaenzer, B.A. 1898, whose
verses have frequently been seen in various periodicals, collected them in *Beggar and King*,
1917. His poems cover a wide range of thought
and feeling, but I like him best when he is most
whimsical, as in

COMPARISONS

Jupiter, lost to Vega's realm,
Lights his lamp from the sun-ship's helm:
Big as a thousand earths, and yet
Dimmed by the glow of a cigarette!

Mr. Glaenzer has published a number of verse
criticisms of contemporary writers, which he calls
Snapshots. These display considerable penetration; perhaps the following is fairly illustrative.

CABLE

To read your tales
Is like opening a cedar-box
Of ante-bellum days,
A box holding the crinoline and fan

> And the tortoise-shell diary
> With flowers pressed between the leaves
> Belonging to some languid *grande dame*
> Of Creole New Orleans.

Benjamin R. C. Low, B.A. 1902, a practising lawyer, has published four or five volumes of poems, including *The Sailor who has Sailed* (1911), *A Wand and Strings* (1913) and *The House that Was* (1915). He is seen at his best in *These United States,* dedicated to Alan Seeger, which appeared in the *Boston Transcript,* 7 February, 1917. This is an original, vigorous work, full of the unexpected, and yet seen to be true as soon as expressed. His verses show a constantly increasing grasp of material, and I look for finer things from his pen.

Although Mr. Low seems to be instinctively a romantic poet, he is fond of letting his imaginative sympathy play on common scenes in city streets; as in *The Sandwich Man.*

> The lights of town are pallid yet
>   With winter afternoon;
> The sullied streets are dank and wet,
> The halted motors fume and fret,
>   The world turns homeward soon.
>
> There is no kindle in the sky,
>   No cheering sunset flame;
> I have no help from passers-by,—
> They part, and give good-night; but I . . .
>   Walk with another's name.
>
> I have no kith, nor kin, nor home
>   Wherein to turn to sleep;

No star-lamp sifts me through the gloom,
I am the driven, wastrel foam
   On a subsiding deep.

I do not toil for love, or fame,
   Or hope of high reward;
My path too low for praise or blame,
I struggle on, each day the same,
   My panoply—a board.

Who gave me life I do not know,
   Nor what that life should be,
Or why I live at all; I go,
A dead leaf shivering with snow,
   Under a worn-out tree.

The lights of town are blurred with mist,
   And pale with afternoon,—
Of gold they are, and amethyst:
Dull pain is creeping at my wrist. . . .
   The world turns homeward soon.

A poet of national reputation is William Rose Benét, who was graduated in 1907. Mr. Benét came to Yale from Augusta, Georgia, and since his graduation has been connected with the editorial staff of the *Century Magazine*. At present he is away in service in France, where his adventurous spirit is at home. He may have taken some of his reputation with him, for he is sure to be a favourite over there; but the fame he left behind him is steadily growing. The very splendour of romance glows in his spacious poetry; he loves to let his imagination run riot, as might be guessed merely by reading the names on his books. To every one who has ever been touched by the love of a quest, his title-pages will appeal: *The Great White Wall,* a tale of "magic adventure, of war and death"; *Merchants from Cathay* (1913), *The Falconer of God* (1914), *The Burglar of the Zodiac* (1917). His verses surge with vitality, as in *The Boast of the Tides.* He is at his best in long, swinging, passionate rhythms. Unfortunately in the same measures he is also at his worst. His most potent temptation is the love of noise, which makes some of his less artistic verse sound like organized cheering.

But when he gets the right tune for the right words, he is irresistible. There is no space here to quote such a rattling ballad—like a frenzy of snare-drums—as *Merchants from Cathay,* but it is not mere sound and fury, it is not swollen rhetoric, it is an inspired poem. No one can read or hear it without being violently aroused. Mr. Benét is a happy-hearted poet, singing with gusto of the joy of life.

ON EDWARD WEBBE, ENGLISH GUNNER

He met the Danske pirates off Tuttee;
Saw the Chrim burn "Musko"; speaks with bated breath
Of his sale to the great Turk, when peril of death
Chained him to oar their galleys on the sea
Until, as gunner, in Persia they set him free
To fight their foes. Of Prester John he saith
Astounding things. But Queen Elizabeth
He worships, and his dear Lord on Calvary.
Quaint is the phrase, ingenuous the wit
Of this great childish seaman in Palestine,
Mocked home through Italy after his release
With threats of the Armada; and all of it

Warms me like firelight jewelling old wine
In some ghost inn hung with the golden fleece!

Arthur Colton, B.A. 1890, is as quiet and reflective as Mr. Benét is strenuous. Has any one ever better expressed the heart of Chaucer's *Troilus and Criseyde* than in these few words?

> A smile, of flowers, and fresh May, across
> The dreamy, drifting face of old Romance;
> The same reiterate tale of love and loss
> And joy that trembles in the hands of chance;
> And midst his rippling lines old Geoffrey stands,
> Saying, "Pray for me when the tale is done,
> Who see no more the flowers, nor the sun."

Mr. Colton collected many of his poems in 1907, under the title *Harps Hung Up in Babylon*. He had moved from New Haven to New York.

Allan Updegraff, who left college before taking his degree, a member of the class of 1907, recently turned from verse to prose, and wrote an admirable novel, *Second Youth*. He is, however, a true poet, and any one might be proud to be the author of

THE TIME AND THE PLACE

Will you not come? The pines are gold with evening
  And breathe their old-time fragrance by the sea;
  You loved so well their spicy exhalation,—
So smiled to smell it and old ocean's piquancy;
  And those weird tales of winds and waves' relation—
  Could you forget? Will you not come to me?

See, 'tis the time: the last long gleams are going,
  The pine-spires darken, mists rise waveringly;
  The gloaming brings the old familiar longing

To be re-crooned by twilight voices of the sea.
    And just such tinted wavelets shoreward thronging—
    Could you forget things once so dear—and me?

Whatever of the waves is ceaseless longing,
    And of the twilight immortality:
    The urge of some wild, inchoate aspiration
Akin to afterglow and stars and winds and sea:
    This hour makes full and pours out in libation,—
    Could you forget? Will you not come to me?

What golden galleons sailed into the sunset
    Not to come home unto eternity:
    What souls went outward hopeful of returning,
This time and tide might well call back across the sea.
    Did we not dream so while old Wests were burning?
    Could you forget such once-dear things—and me?

From the dimmed sky and long grey waste of waters,
    Lo, one lone sail on all the lonely sea
    A moment blooms to whiteness like a lily,
As sudden fades, is gone, yet half-seems still to be;
    And you,—though that last time so strange and stilly,—
    Though you are dead, will you not come to me?

Lee Wilson Dodd, at present in service in
France, was graduated in 1899, and for some years
was engaged in the practice of the law. This occupation he abandoned for literature in 1907. He
is the author of several successful plays, and has
published two volumes of verse, *The Modern Alchemist* (1906) and *The Middle Miles* (1915).
His growth in the intervening years will be apparent to any one who compares the two books; there
is in his best work a combination of fancy and
humour. He loves to write about New England
gardens and discovers beauty by the very simple

process of opening his eyes at home.   The following poem is characteristically sincere:

TO A NEO-PAGAN

Your praise of Nero leaves me cold:
Poems of porphyry and of gold,
Palatial poems, chill my heart.
I gaze—I wonder—I depart.
Not to Byzantium would I roam
In quest of beauty, nor Babylon;
Nor do I seek Sahara's sun
To blind me to the hills of home.
Here am I native; here the skies
Burn not, the sea I know is grey;
Wanly the winter sunset dies.
Wanly comes day.
Yet on these hills and near this sea
Beauty has lifted eyes to me,
Unlustful eyes, clear eyes and kind;
While a clear voice chanted—

"They who find

"Me not beside their doorsteps, know
"Me never, know me never, though
"Seeking, seeking me, high and low,
"Forth on the far four winds they go!"

Therefore your basalt, jade, and gems,
Your Saracenic silver, your
Nilotic gods, your diadems
To bind the brows of Queens, impure,
Perfidious, passionate, perfumed—these
Your petted, pagan stage-properties,
Seem but as toys of trifling worth.
For I have marked the naked earth
Beside my doorstep yield to the print
Of a long light foot, and flash with the glint
Of crocus-gold—
Crocus-gold!
Crocus-gold no mill may mint

Save the Mill of God —
The Mill of God!
The Mill of God with His angels in't!

Other Yale poets are W. B. Arvine, 1903, whose
book *Hang Up Philosophy* (1911), particularly excels in the interpretation of natural scenery;
Frederick M. Clapp, 1901, whose volume *On the
Overland* (since republished in America) was in
process of printing in Bruges in 1914, when the
Germans entered the old town, and smashed
among other things, the St. Catherine Press.
Just fifteen copies of Mr. Clapp's book had been
struck off, of which I own one; Donald Jacobus,
1908, whose *Poems* (1914) are richly meditative;
James H. Wallis, 1906, who has joined the ranks
of poets with *The Testament of William Windune*
and *Other Poems* (1917); Leonard Bacon, 1909,
who modestly called his book, published in the
year of his graduation, *The Scrannel Pipe;* Ken-
neth Rand, 1914, who produced two volumes of
original verse while an undergraduate; Archibald
Mac Leish, 1915, whose *Tower of Ivory,* a collection of lyrics, appeared in 1917; Elliot Griffis, a
student in the School of Music, who published in
1918 under an assumed name a volume called *Rain
in May;* and I may close this roll-call by remark-
ing that those who have seen his work have a
staunch faith in the future of Stephen Vincent
Benét.   He is a younger brother of William, and
is at present a Yale undergraduate.   Mr. Benét
was born at Bethlehem, Pennsylvania, on the

twenty-second of July, 1898. His home is at Augusta, Georgia. Before entering college, and when he was seventeen, he published his first volume of poems, *Five Men and Pompey* (1915). This was followed in 1917 by another book, *The Drug Shop*. His best single production is the Cook prize poem, *The Hemp*.

APPENDIX

I Have a Rendezvous with Death

The remarkably impressive and beautiful poem by Alan Seeger which bears the above title naturally attracted universal attention. I had supposed the idea originated with Stephen Crane, who, in his novel *The Red Badge of Courage*, Chapter IX, has the following paragraph:

> At last they saw him stop and stand motionless. Hastening up, they perceived that his face wore an expression telling that he had at last found the place for which he had struggled. His spare figure was erect; his bloody hands were quietly at his side. He was waiting with patience for something that he had come to meet. He was at the rendezvous. They paused and stood, expectant.

But I am informed both by Professor F. N. Robinson of Harvard and by Mr. Norreys Jephson O'Conor that the probable source of the title of the poem is Irish. Professor Robinson writes me, "The Irish poem that probably suggested to Seeger the title of his *Rendezvous* is the *Reicne Fothaid Canainne* (Song of Fothad Canainne), published by Kuno Meyer in his *Fianaigecht* (Dublin, 1910), pp. 1–21. Seeger read the piece at one of my Celtic Conferences, and was much impressed by it. He got from it only his title and the fundamental figure of a *rendezvous* with Death, the Irish poem being wholly different from his in general purport. Fothad Canainne makes a tryst with the wife of Ailill Flann, but is slain in battle by Ailill on the day before the night set for the meeting. Then the spirit of Fothad (or, according to one version, his severed head) sings the *reicne* to the woman and declares (st. 3): 'It is blindness for one who makes a tryst to set aside the tryst with death.' "

Miss Amy Lowell, however, thinks that Seeger got the idea from a French poet. Wherever he got it, I believe that he made it his own, for he used it supremely well, and it will always be associated with him.

At Harvard, Alan Seeger took the small and special course in Irish, and showed enthusiasm for this branch of study. Wishing to find out something about his undergraduate career, I wrote to a member of the Faculty, and received the following reply: "Many persons found him almost morbidly indifferent and unresponsive, and he seldom showed the full measure of his powers. . . . I grew to have a strong liking for him personally as well as a respect for his intellectual power. But I should never have expected him to show the robustness of either mind or body which we now know him to have possessed. He was frail and sickly in appearance, and seemed to have a temperament in keeping with his physique. It took a strong impulse to bring him out and disclose his real capacity."

There is no doubt that the war gave him this

impulse, and that the poem *I Have a Rendezvous with Death* must be classed among the literature directly produced by the great struggle. After four years, I should put at the head of all the immense number of verses inspired by the war John Masefield's *August 1914*, Alan Seeger's *I Have a Rendezvous with Death*, and Rupert Brooke's *The Soldier;* and of all the poems written by men actually fighting, I should put Alan Seeger's first.

While reading these proofs, the news comes of the death of a promising young American poet, Joyce Kilmer, a sergeant in our army, who fell in France, August, 1918. He was born 6 December, 1886, was a graduate of Rutgers and Columbia, and had published a number of poems. His supreme sacrifice nobly closed a life filled with beauty in word and deed.

INDEX

[Only important references are given; the mere mention of names is omitted.]

Abercrombie, L., 123.

Adams, F. P., 276.

"A. E." (G. W. Russell), 177–182; personality, 178; a sincere mystic, 179; assurance, 180; discovery of Stephens, 178; influence on Susan Mitchell, 187.

Aiken, C., 308.

Andrews, C. E., *From the Front*, 110.

Arnold, M., poem on Wordsworth compared to Watson's, 48.

Arvine, W. B., 332.

Aumonier, S., quotation from, 213.

Austin, A., 28.

Bacon, L., 332.

Barker, G., production of *Dynasts*, 18; remark on Shaw, 220.

Beers, H. A., 312–316.

Benét, S. V., 332, 333.

Benét, W. R., 327–329.

Bishop, J. P., 296, 297.

Blackwell, B. H., a publisher, 156.

Bradley, W. A., 297, 298.

Braithwaite, W. S., his anthology, 270, 296.

Branch, A. H., a leader, 245; poems, 256–261; education, 257; passion, 257–259; contrasted with Masters, 261.

Bridges, R., poet-laureate, 28; his verse, 29, 30.

Brooke, R., canonized, 46; Gibson on, 110; poems, 124–130; letters, 127; Howland prize, 140; compared to De La Mare, 144; *The Soldier*, 337.

Browne, T., compared to Yeats, 169.

Browning, R., concentration, 23; *Pauline*, 43; on spiritual blessings, 47; lack of experience, 72; self-consciousness, 75; *Christmas Eve*, 81; natural poetry, 96; metre of *One Word More*, 107; *The Glove*, 122; Ogniben's remark, 125; compared to Brooke, 128; temperament, 161; contrasted with Yeats, 168; Masters compared to, 265; *Confessions*, 314.

Burns, R., influence on democracy, 50.

Burton, R., 200.

Bynner, W., 303–305.

Byron, Lord, sales of his poems, 45; wit compared to Watson's, 54; common sense, 159.

Calderon, G., remark on Chekhov, 241.

Campbell, J., 189, 190.

Carlin, F., 192.

Carlyle, T., remark on Cromwell, 234.

Chaucer, G., effect on Masefield, 72, 82.

Chekhov, A., centrifugal force, 241.

Clapp, F. M., 332.

Cleghorn, S. N., 284–286.

Coleridge, S. T., remark on poetry, 249.

Colton, A., 329.

Colum, P., 185, 186.

Conrad, J., compared to Scott, 1.

Cooke, E. V., 201.

Corbin, A., 283, 284.

Crane, S., *Red Badge of Courage*, 109, 335.

Crashaw, R., his editor, 131.

Davidson, J., test of poetry, 37.

Davies, M. C., 282.

Davies, W. H., 150, 151.

Davis, F. S., 280, 281.

De La Mare, W., homage to, 46; poems, 139–145; compared to Hawthorne, 140; retirement, 140–143; *Listeners*, 141, 142; Shakespeare portraits, 142; *Old Susan*, 143; *Peacock Pie*, 144.

Dodd, L. W., 330–332.

Donne, J., reputation, 56; stimulant, 253.

Drake, F., German statue to, 61; poem by Noyes, 61.

Drinkwater, J., 148–150.

Egan, M. F., 191, 192.

Eliot, T. S., 293.

Emerson, R. W., prophecy on poetry, 142.

Erskine, J., 300.

Fisher, M. L., 295, 296

Flecker, J. E., 130–139; posthumous editor of, 130; translations, 134; aims, 135; *Oak and Olive*, 137; religion, 137; *Jerusalem*, 138.

Fletcher, J. G., 306, 307.

Foulke, W. D., 204, 205.

Frost, R., dedication by Thomas, 152; poems, 235–237; theories, 237; outdoor poet, 238; realism, 240; tragedy, 241–243; pleasure of recognition, 243, 244.

Garrison, T., 281, 282.

Gibson, W. W., homage to, 46; poems, 98–114; *Stonefolds*, 99–101; *Daily Bread*, 101–104; *Fires*, 104–106; *Thoroughfares*, 106; war poems, 107–111; *Livelihood*, 111; latest work, 112–114; his contribution, 114.

Gladstone, W. E., eulogy by Phillips, 41.

Glaenzer, R. B., 325, 326.

Goethe, J. W., Flecker's translation of, 134; poise, 159.

Grainger, P., great artist, 34; audacities, 227.

Graves, R., 155.

Gray, T., on laureateship, 28; compared to Hodgson, 115; compared to Masters, 268.

Griffis, E., 332.

Griffith, W., 298–300.

Hagedorn, H., 305.

Hardy, T., 14–28; a forerunner, 15; *Dynasts*, 16; idea of God, 19–22; pessimism, 22; thought and music, 23, 24; *Moments of Vision*, 24–28; Housman's likeness to, 66.

Hawthorne, N., compared to De La Mare, 140.

Henley, W. E., 5–9; compared to Thompson, 5; paganism, 6; lyrical power, 7.

Hodgson, R., 114–123; a recluse, 115; love of animals, 116, 119–122; humour, 118; compared to Alice Corbin, 284.

Hooker, B., 321, 322.

Housman, A. E., 65–70; modernity, 65; scholarship, 65; likeness to Hardy, 66; paganism and pessimism, 66; lyrical power, 69.

Hughes, R., 322–324.

Hyde, D., influence, 172.

Ibsen, H., student of the Bible, 261.

Jacobus, D., 332.

James, H., tribute to Brooke, 126.

Johnson, R. U., 198–200.

Keats, J., Phillips compared to, 37; influence on Amy Lowell, 246; Endymion, 251; Amy Lowell's sonnet on, 251.

Kilmer, J., 337.

Kipling, R., 28–33; imperial laureate, 28; Recessional, 29; popularity, 30, 31; influence on soldiers, 31, 32; Watson's allusion to, 45, 46; Danny Deever, 227.

Landor, W. S., his violence, 160.

Lawrence, D. H., 145–148.

Ledwidge, F., 186, 187.

Leonard, W. E., 300.

Lewis, C. M., 316, 317.

Lindsay, N. V., 213–235; Harriet Monroe's magazine, 214; Booth, 214, 220–222; development, 216; drawings, 217; "games," 217, 218; Congo, 219, 220, 226, 227; Niagara, 223; prose, 224, 225; chants, 226; geniality, 230–233; Esther, 295.

Locke, W. J., his dreams, 60.

Low, B. R. C., 326, 327.

Lowell, A. L., love of liberty, 246.

Lowell, Amy, essay on Frost, 236; poems, 245–256; training, 245–247; free verse, 248, 249; imagism, 250; Sword Blades, 252, 253; narrative skill, 253, 254; polyphonic prose, 255, 256; versatility, 256; remark on Seeger, 336.

Lowell, P., influence on Amy, 246.

MacDonagh, T., 188, 189.

Mackaye, P., 305, 306; stipend for poets, 44; poems, 305, 306.

MacLeish, A., 332.

Maeterlinck, M., compared to Yeats, 167; rhythmical prose, 255.

Markham, E., 201.

Marquis, D., 275.

Masefield, J., homage to, 46; poems, 71–97; the modern Chaucer, 72, 73, 82, 83; education, 72–74; Dauber, 75, 76; critical power, 77; relation to Wordsworth, 77–79, 84, 85; Everlasting Mercy, 80; Widow in the Bye Street, 82, 83; Daffodil Fields, 84–90; compared to Tennyson, 86–90; August, 1914, 90, 91, 337; lyrics, 92; sonnets, 93;

Rosas, 94; novels, 94; general contribution, 95; Drinkwater's dedication, 148; Aiken's relation to, 307.

Masters, E. L., 261–271; education, 261, 262; *Spoon River,* 262–270; irony, 266; love of truth, 267; analysis, 268; cynicism, 269; idealism, 269.

Meredith, G., his poems, 16.

Middleton, S., 296.

Milton, J., his invocation, 17; Piedmont sonnet, 50.

Mitchell, S., 187.

Monroe, H., her magazine, 214, 215, 283; her anthology, 283; poems, 282–284.

Moody, W. V., 195, 196.

Morley, J., remarks on Irishmen and Wordsworth, 160, 161.

Munger, R., 324, 325.

Neihardt, J. G., 293, 294.

Nichols, R., 154–156.

Nicholson, M., poems, 303; remark on college stories, 313.

Noyes, A., homage to, 46; poems, 56–65; education, 57; singing power, 58; *Tramp Transfigured,* 59, 63; his masterpiece, 59; child imagination, 60; sea poetry, 61; *Drake,* 61; *May-Tree,* 62; new effects, 63; war poems, 64; optimism, 64.

O'Conor, N. J., poems, 192; remark on Seeger, 335.

O'Sullivan, S., 190, 191.

Peabody, J. P., 206–209.

Percy, W. A., 308–310.

Phillips, S., 35–41; sudden fame, 35; education, 36; *Marpessa,* 38; realism, 40; *Gladstone,* 40, 41; protest against Masefield, 79.

Pierce, F. E., 318–321.

Quarles, F., quoted, 252.

Quiller-Couch, A., remark on the *Daffodil Fields,* 87.

Rand, K., 332.

Reedy, W. M., relation to Masters, 263.

Rice, C. Y., 205, 206.

Riley, J. W., remark on Henley, 7; "Riley Day," 46; remark on Anna Branch, 256; a conservative, 257.

Rittenhouse, J. B., 286, 287.

Robinson, C. R., 301, 302.

Robinson, E. A., 209–212.

Robinson, F. N., remark on Seeger, 335.

Rogers, R. C., 322.

Sandburg, C., 289–291.

Santayana, G., 196–198.

Sassoon, S., 155.

Scott, W., compared to Conrad, 1; sales of his poems, 45.

Seeger, A., 310, 311; Low's dedication, 326; source of his poem, 335–337.

Service, R. W., likeness to Kipling, 33.

Shakespeare, W., compared to Wordsworth, 2; compared to Masefield, 93; portraits by De La Mare, 142; poem on by Masters, 270.

Shaw, G. B., *Major Barbara,* 220.

Spingarn, J., creative criticism, 49.

Squire, J. C., introduction to Flecker, 131.

Stephens, J., 182–185; novels, 182; discovered by A. E., 178, 182; realism, 183; child-poetry, 183, 184; power of cursing, 184.

Stevenson, R. L., remark on Whitman, 146.

Stork, C. W., 294, 295.

Swinburne, A. C., critical violence, 77; Lindsay's likeness to, 217; Lindsay's use of, 232.

Synge, J. M., advice from Yeats, 164; works, 171–177; versatility, 172; bitterness, 173; theory of poetry, 175, 176; autobiographical poems, 176; thoughts on death, 177; influence on Stephens, 183.

Teasdale, S., 277–280.

Tennyson, A., continued popularity of, 10; his invocation, 17; compared to Hardy, 24; early poems on death, 67; compared to Masefield, 86–88; his memoirs, 130; his reserve, 160; quality of his poetry, 253.

Thomas, E., 152–154.

Thomas, E. M., 202.

Thompson, F., 9–14; compared to Henley, 9; religious passion, 9, 10; In No Strange Land, 12; Lilium Regis, 13; Noyes's ode to, 58; Flecker's poem on, 133.

Trench, H., 191.

Underwood, J. C., 291–293.

Untermeyer, L., 271–275.

Updegraff, A., 329–330.

VanDyke, H., 202, 203.

Vaughan, H., quoted, 308.

Vielé, H. K., 205.

Wallis, J. H., 332.

Watson, W., 41–56; poor start, 41; address in America, 43; King Alfred, 44; Wordsworth's Grave, 44, 48; epigrams, 47, 48; How Weary is Our Heart, 50; hymn of hate, 51; war poems, 52; Yellow Pansy, 53; Byronic wit, 54; Eloping Angels, 54; dislike of new poetry, 55.

Weaving, W., 155, 156.

Wells, H. G., religious position, 48.

Whitman, W., natural style, 56; Man of War Bird, 73; early conventionality, 98; Stevenson's remark on, 146; growth of reputation, 249; Sandburg's relation, 290.

Whitney, H. H., 301.

Whitsett, W. T., 300, 301.

Widdemer, M., 287–289.

Wilcox, E. W., 201.

Willcocks, M. P., remark on will, 8.

Woodberry, G. E., 203, 204.

Wordsworth, W., compared to Shakespeare, 3; Watson's poem on, 48, 49; Masefield's relations to, 77–79, 84, 85.

Yeats, W. B., 162–171; education, 162; devotion to art, 164, 165, 170, 191; his names, 165; love poetry, 166, 167; dramas, 168; prose, 168–171; mysticism, 179; relation to Lindsay, 226.

Younghusband, G., remark on Kipling, 31.